ACTING

ADVANCED TECHNIQUES

FOR THE

Actor, Director,

AND

TEACHER

TERRY SCHREIBER

with Mary Beth Barber

ALLWORTH PRESS
NEW YORK

To Katharine Elaine Schreiber
"Carry the Torch"

09 08 07 06 05   5 4 3 2 1

Published by Allworth Press
An imprint of Allworth Communications, Inc.
10 East 23rd Street, New York, NY 10010

Cover design by Derek Bacchus
Interior design by Mary Belibasakis
Typography by Integra Software Services

Images on page 8 are used by permission of James Duus, a certified Body Dynamics™ educator as well as a certified Pilates instructor in New York City. He can be reached at JDPilatesNYC@aol.com

ISBN: 1-58115-418-6

LIBRARY OF CONGRESS CATALOGING-IN-PUBLICATION DATA

Schreiber, Terry.
    Acting: advanced techniques for the actor, director, and teacher/by Terry Schreiber, with Mary Beth Barber; foreword by Edward Norton.
        p. cm.
    Includes bibliographical references and index.
1. Acting.   2. Acting–Study and teaching.   I. Barber, Mary Beth.   II. Title.

    PN2061.S356 2005
    792.02'8–dc22

                                    2005007923

Printed in Canada

CONTENTS

Private Moment, Parts One and Two • Private Moment,
Part Three • *Sidebar: The Private Moment, Years Later,
On Stage* • *Sidebar: Tipping Point of a Career* • Character
Private Moments • *Sidebar: A Gut-Wrenching Moment*
• What We've Learned

ACKNOWLEDGMENTS

My enormous gratitude and thanks to Mary Beth Barber, whose unflagging energy, skill, patience, perseverance, support, and optimism made the assembly of this book possible. I do not think you ever really know anyone until the working together gets tough and demanding. Over the last two years, we met, wrote, rewrote, cut, and assembled. While under tremendous pressure from other job demands, Mary Beth was always there with tremendous determination, energy, and tenacity. Or, in acting terms, "Mind, Heart, and Will." Whatever success this book encounters, I will always be beholden to her for her major contribution.

I would also like to acknowledge with heartfelt thanks the special contribution of Effie Johnson, who spent many hours transcribing my tapes; Mel England, who struggled through my handwriting to type up yet another draft; Margaret Dawson and J.J. Handegard, who did copyediting, Sarah Winton and Stefan Mreczko for additional copyediting and photographs, in that order, and James Duus and Jennifer McGuire for their cooperation with necessary photo demonstrations.

Lastly, and perhaps most importantly: To all the many actors who have put their trust and faith into studying with me, or enrolled with other teachers at my studio, I am deeply grateful for all you have taught me and the help you have given me to grow over the years in my teaching and the work. The joy your professional achievements have given me has made the journey together even more worthwhile.

My gratitude for working side-by-side with my gifted and extremely talented, caring, and giving teaching staff:

Carol Reynolds • Lynn Singer • Julie Garfield
• Pamela Scott • Page Clements • Diane and Peter Miner
• Sally Dunn • Peter Jensen

To Carolyn French, with deep appreciation for her belief in the book and for being my agent.

FOREWORD

There are a lot of really good actors, but very few really good acting teachers.

When I moved to New York, the path to training as an actor was about as clear as wading into the Everglades. There were MFA programs, storied studios, private academies with famous alumni, theater-affiliated repertory programs, the institutionalized legacies of famous teachers past, and innumerable well-known directors running classes on the side. Sprinkled among and around all of these were an astonishing array of charlatans and poseurs of every sort clamoring to take your money and waste your time.

Beyond that lay the bewildering swirl of training styles and even ideologies: Strasberg and sense memory versus Adler and imagination, Meisner technique, classical training, film and TV technique, scene study, and, of course, the Method, which seemed to me to be a term used to describe at least four totally divergent approaches to acting and one for sandwich-making. Everyone wanted to be a Method actor, but very few people I ever talked to seemed to have any clear idea of what it was they were aspiring to so breathlessly.

I had read more about the history and theory of actor training than most student actors I knew in New York at that time, and it still took me six months of dedicated investigation and research to be able to confidently turn away from the crap on the street before I put my foot in it.

New York was, and still is, one of the best places to train and cut your teeth as an actor . . . but the first step, finding a safe haven in which to actually explore and learn something, inevitably proves to be one of the hardest.

Terry Schreiber is one of the really good acting teachers. In 1991, the Schreiber Studio was still down on East Fourth Street, nestled in with NY Theater Workshop and La Mama. I stumbled into that little black box theater, met Terry, and found out that he needed Japanese lessons for a play he was directing in Tokyo. I had lived there and spoke the language well enough to barter equal time Japanese lessons for acting classes. I got the better end of that deal and I was lucky enough to study with Terry and perform in plays at his studio for around two years. I still count him among the two or three real theater mentors I've had in my career.

Terry was and is a great teacher for a few reasons. The first is that he has never taught as a sideline—he has dedicated himself fully to it and to building a comprehensive, first-rate training studio founded in well-refined training techniques. The second is that Terry has never tried to teach anybody "the Schreiber method." He has the humility and the wise perspective to be a true pluralist, which is to say he has explored and experienced, both as a student himself and as a teacher, most of the interesting ideas that have emerged about training actors in the last sixty years. A lot of teachers, in my experience, infantilize their students to feed their own egos, or insist on rigorous method at the expense of practical craft. Terry understands that every individual actor will best access his gifts in different ways, and also that the modern actor will inevitably be called upon to tackle a wide spectrum of texts, styles, and collaborative dynamics. No method, no theory, no dogma, or technique covers it all or works for everyone, and Terry urges students to be "multilingual actors," to develop a toolbag that gives them confidence in any situation. Whatever talents I may have brought to the table, Terry helped me become a better actor by pushing me to forge talent with craft.

That Terry has finally put the effort into organizing his ideas and approaches to actor training in this book is a real gift to actors and teachers alike. I see much in what he articulates here that is intensely familiar from my days studying with him, and also much that is new and interesting. There is practical sense and creative insight in all of it.

I recently had lunch with Terry and a terrific actor who also studied with him in those days. I'm not generally inclined to talk about acting much anymore, but we got to discussing this book and chewing over the ideas in it. Terry was still wrestling with fine points, still refining his ideas, pouncing eagerly on fresh perspectives, and as always, bursting with enthusiasm for the work of developing the best in others and himself . . . because that, of course, is what a real teacher does.

Edward Norton
September 13, 2004
New York City

PREFACE

When I started teaching many years ago, I had no idea what would eventually be the result of my efforts, aside from fulfillment of the most immediate need—training for the actors whom I would eventually cast in shows that I directed. I taught and continue to teach because I realize that, after many years of experience, I have something to share with actors.

I started on this book almost ten years ago. Before starting this endeavor, I reflected on the origins of my teaching. I had started out as an actor myself, studying with some great teachers and learning a variety of different techniques. When I moved from acting to directing, I believed that many actors could bene-fit from what I had learned, and the shows that I directed could benefit from their acting advancements. So I started with a handful of dedicated actors in a rented space and shared the exercises and techniques I had been taught. Over time, that group of actors grew . . . and grew . . . and grew.

Fast-forward several decades: The T. Schreiber Studio celebrated thirty-five years of dedicated acting training in 2004. My classes for the advanced actor reached a level I never would have expected when I started. My teach-ings have been refined over many years of experimentation, and the original exercises have grown and changed to give my students more insight and tools. Thousands of actors have passed through the doors to my acting classes. To all of them I give not only a nod of congratulations for their dedication to their craft, but also of thanks for allowing me to grow with them as a teacher as they grew as actors.

But reading a book is different from having the hands-on experience of working with an acting teacher. Reading isn't how actors learn—they learn on their feet, by interacting with other actors, directors, and instructors. When I walk through the aisles at bookstores geared toward the arts in New York City, I am sometimes shocked by how many books on acting there are in the marketplace. Why would I want to add another?

This text started out specifically for my students. I had always wanted a handbook on the work I do at the Studio. But as I wrote, and as professional actors, directors, and instructors reviewed the writing, I was told time and time again that the book should extend beyond the walls of T.S.S., that it was too important to limit its scope solely to my students.

So my goal is to put in writing what I teach in my classes for the benefit of actors currently studying with me, for future teachers who may base their instruction on the lessons they learned while at T.S.S., and as a manual to introduce those outside my Studio to what I've learned over the years. It is for this specific reason that I've structured my book as a "how to" manual rather than as a "thinking" theory book on acting or a supplement to my classes.

Many of the best exercises that I've developed require great sensitivity and bravery from the actors who participate in them. Acting requires a stripping away of the ego and emotional protections; therefore, this instruction can be a psychologically dangerous tool in the wrong hands. I disapprove of any instructor using my techniques and teachings improperly or out of context, or for her own sadistic pleasure. "Breaking down an actor" is not the purpose of these exercises, and I guarantee you that if I ever hear of someone using the basic structure of the exercises I've described in this book in a dangerous or destructive manner and associating my name with their actions, I will do all in my power to discredit that individual within the acting and teaching world.

Time and time again throughout this book, I say that the acting studio must be a place of safety, not of competition. "Breaking" an actor will not make him a better actor, but a worse one, and potentially harm him psychologically as well. If an instructor presents a safe and nurturing environment so the actors can break out of their shells and take real risks, not only will the environment be more inviting, but the acting will blossom.

One thing to make perfectly clear about this book: It is not for the novice. *Acting* is for an actor who has a strong foundation in the fundamentals of acting technique. I fear that beginning actors will not be able to embrace the exercises and techniques I've laid out, but rather fear and misuse them. There are plenty of acting books for beginners to refer to (as noted in the bibliography), as well as plenty of good instructors for the basics. New actors must utilize these resources first before venturing into the advanced exercises I have outlined in this book. All actors should keep open minds when reading this text, but—more importantly—they should become schooled and possess a strong foundation in acting by taking classes to fully understand basic concepts like Objective, Method, Beats, and the other terms outlined in the glossary.

Finally, I want to thank all my students for their requests and encouragement for *Acting*. The strongest inspiration for this book came from the many actors who have asked me for a description of my class work. Although it has taken me since 1977 to find intermittent time to finalize such a request, I deeply appreciate all the inspiration I have received.

So, here it is: my attempt to put over thirty-five years of teaching and some forty years of acting and directing on paper. Use it wisely, and enjoy!

A NOTE ON PERSONAL PRONOUNS

Every writer of instructional manuals today encounters problems with personal pronouns. How should I refer to "the actor" or "the student," since the singular pronouns include both "he" and "she"? In the past, authors had simply used the masculine pronoun, referring to every generic usage as "he." But these are more liberated times, and I have a problem with using only "he," since approximately half of my students are female.

Some authors will solve this problem by using "he or she" or "he/she," both of which I find incredibly awkward. Others change every case of the singular into the plural "they." Sometimes this works, but often a reference to the singular is needed, and a singular "actor" can never be a "they." None of these particular solutions satisfied my need to be fair, clear, and grammatically correct.

I have chosen instead to use both "he" and "she" throughout the book. One section may refer to the actor as a "he," while in the next exercise description, the actor is a "she." There is the additional question of whether to refer to all female actors as "actresses," but I chose to use the non-gendered term "actor" to refer to both female and male actors, and declined to use the term "actress" in the generic sense. However, if I am referring to a specific actor who is female, I have used "actress." So Meryl Streep is an "actress," but a generic female acting student is an "actor."

METHODOLOGY

The first question I anticipate when potential students come to an orientation for my class is, Which acting method does Terry Schreiber teach? Every teacher has his own particular methodology, the basic philosophy of acting instruction that is manifested in instruction, exercises, and scene study. The final goal of any method is acting that combines *intellect* with *instincts*, and the goal of any acting course is to produce actors who float with ease, simplicity, and spontaneity between the two. Achieving this result is not a simple task.

I usually reply, "I teach an 'American' style of acting," although for many students this doesn't clarify anything. But what I mean when I answer is, in essence, that I teach a number of methods used over time by accomplished American actors who defined the acting and training world in the twentieth century.

My own training has been from the Strasberg and Meisner point of view, as interpreted by Michael Howard, the man who learned from both and who taught me when I was a young man. This "American" style also incorporates methods from Stella Adler, Bobby Lewis, and Harold Clurman. These are the original members of the Group Theatre who went to Moscow during the first half of the twentieth century to observe the work of Constantine Stanislavski.

Stanislavski revolutionized acting in Russia (and eventually throughout the world) with his "realism" approach. Before Stanislavski, acting had been big, bold, and not necessarily grounded in real emotion. He taught his students in Russia to incorporate their own personal experiences into the work and develop a sense of realism. Actors were no longer "performing" for or trying to "entertain" the audience. Instead, they were "living." Being a member of an audience was tantamount to being a fly on the wall during a personal and private experience.

Strasberg was the first American to develop a technique, an intense "Method" approach based on observations of Stanislavski's teachings that emphasized the actor incorporating his own personal experiences into the work. Strasberg-trained actors' preparation is always steeped in the actors' own realities, lives, and behavioral experiences. My definition of the Method as taught by Strasberg is "an internalizing of everything before it can be externalized."

Meisner, Adler, and Lewis initially followed suit with this internal-to-external method, but each eventually broke with Strasberg's extreme "actor-personal" approach and developed an individual style. These three emphasized using the actor's imagination to create the reality of the character, as opposed to Strasberg's personal-experience method. Meisner, Adler, Lewis, and others work with the creative as-if. They have actors imagine themselves into the facts or "givens" of the text or exercise and encourage them to almost play the child's game of "let's pretend." A version of this as-if approach—one that also emphasizes repetition as an early learning technique—was named after its most vocal proponent and is called the "Meisner" method.

All of these initial Stanislavski observers eventually went to different parts of the United States—New York and California, mostly—and taught their own methods. Students learned from them, incorporated the teachings into their own acting, and then later taught other actors, developing unique styles along the way. I became an acting teacher in this manner. I learned from advanced acting teacher Michael Howard when I was an actor myself. From this and other learning experiences, I developed my own style and series of exercises, which I now teach.

MY EXPERIENCE

I arrived in New York City in 1960 after receiving a Bachelor of Arts in English and Speech from St. Thomas University in St. Paul, Minnesota. The majority of my acting training at that time was from college, while my experience was from the three years I spent participating in summer stock, community theater, and university productions. Up to that point, I learned "on the job," so to speak.

After college, I did what many young people who are interested in pursuing acting do—I moved to the bright lights of New York City. And, like many young people, it took me a little time to get my footing. After making a disastrous start with a teacher and studio I did not relate to, I was fortunate to find a marvelous mentor in Michael Howard.

Michael is a member of the Actor's Studio, the famous school founded in 1947 that catapulted Strasberg's teaching into the American acting world and included some members of Group Theatre. Michael has been the main source for my acting technique and appreciation of the work. Although I studied with other teachers over the twelve years that I was an actor in New York, I worked with Michael solidly for four years.

While Michael was probably my most influential instructor, I had also observed Strasberg's work, and for a short period of time studied directing with Harold Clurman, one of the Group Theatre members who worked with Stanislavski in Russia. And I have spent years studying the work and techniques of Adler, Meisner, and Lewis and their tremendous contributions to the American style of acting.

NO "ONE" TECHNIQUE

Throughout all these years of teaching, I have tested and developed various exercises. I kept some, discarded others, and assigned more basic exercises to staff members who are teaching beginning or intermediate level classes. I have taken exercises from Strasberg, Meisner, Adler, Michael Chekhov (the Russian actor and nephew of playwright Anton Chekhov), and others. I have redefined their exercises for my classes. Sometimes, I've gone my own way and developed new exercises. It has been an exciting developmental period over these decades of trial, error, experimentation, and solidification of what I think is effective for the actor.

Even with this kind of explanation, I'm still pressed by students and acting professionals to answer the question, "What technique do you teach?" To simplify matters, the style is essentially a combination of Strasberg (internal-to-external) and Meisner (as-if) approaches, but also borrows techniques and exercises from Adler and Lewis.

I strongly believe in combining these two schools of thought—the internal-to-external and as-if approaches. They both incorporate a means to an end: helping actors to open up their instruments, enlarge their imaginations, and therefore enlarge their talent. It has been my experience over the years that some actors live and work very richly from their world of reality, while others live much more fully in their fantasy or imagination. To force one system as the "be all and end all" may exclude a talent that could really blossom with a slight adjustment from the teacher to see which approach the actor relates to better.

AN ACTOR'S TOOLBOX

As Strasberg and the Group Theatre members interpreted Stanislavski's ideas, so have I reinterpreted the work of the great American acting instructors of the twentieth century and added on to their volume of work. The originals—Stanislavski, Strasberg, Meisner, Adler, and Lewis—didn't work in a complete vacuum to develop their styles. They worked with each other, and created the techniques after many years of study. It is my feeling that we must all learn from a master teacher and then go our own individual way based on his inspiration.

I believe this holds true for the actor as well as the teacher—that the actor will ultimately develop his own method of work. Instructors like me can expose actors to exercises and a system of preparation and hope the experience will be helpful in their development. As actors go on with their careers, they will develop their own method of working. Before that can happen, they need a good base to start from.

I try to give each actor I work with a "bag of good tools"—meaning an infinite variety of exercises that will help him break open a character, as well as in-depth scene interpretation. My goal is to have any actor who has committed the time and effort to this work leave my classes knowing "how to work" on his own without depending on a director to do it for him.

I do not recommend that a beginning actor dive into this manual without some experience. Nor do I recommend that any serious actor approach it as a dilettante, giving a small amount of time and effort to study and exercise. It is best, in terms of both time and finances, for beginners to put their egos aside and regain some basic techniques before plunging into this book, or onto the stage and screen, for that matter.

If beginning actors do attempt to jump forward and thrust themselves on stage without training, they will waste months just trying to understand the language and have little technique to execute what's being taught. It would be like a high-school baseball player suddenly trying to start in the majors. The kid might survive, but the odds are much more favorable if he learns more skills and attains sophistication and maturity by spending some time in the minors before advancing.

Developing good relationships with fellow actors is another reason to focus and concentrate on training. No advanced actor wants to work with a beginning actor—what would she possibly get out of the rehearsals, not to mention the performances?

And no beginning actor should be asked to compete with an experienced actor, especially since acting is by its nature such personal work, and the last thing any student wants is to be scared and intimidated. Very little learning can happen in this atmosphere, and the results will be less than satisfying. Stage work and quality film acting—acting that doesn't rely on a good editor to make raw talent look good through cutting and camera angles—demands a great deal more knowledge of craft and technique.

No Auditing in the Classroom

Because I feel the acting class should be a sanctuary of safety and trust for my students, I have a policy of "no auditing," and feel that any instructor who chooses to use this manual should do the same. Auditors violate an actor's privacy of having a place to work where she is not subjected to judgmental values. It is vital that the actor feels comfortable in the surroundings. Many times, a birth is taking place, and strangers certainly should not be allowed in the birthing room.

I also find auditing suspicious. When there are potential new students present, I believe a teacher is tempted to sell a class at the expense of the actors' process work in that class. My focus is on the actors who are my students, not on anything else. The classroom is the actors' private place. Everywhere actors go outside of class, they have to perform for others. Like an athlete, they need a private place where they can train.

Process, Not Production

All my work in class is process-oriented, not presentation-oriented. No one should feel the pressure to perform and entertain the class or the teacher while in an acting class—it's about learning, not pleasing others. Classes are about approaching a role, exploring the creative process, and taking risks in a safe environment before leaping to the stage or screen.

MIND, HEART, WILL

I attempt in my classroom, as any good instructor should, to build the three ingredients of the actor's work: *Mind, Heart, Will*. The *Mind*, in all its brightness, interprets and understands the text from the playwright and interpretation from the director. The *Heart* adds the feeling and the emotional life to create a real and honest character. The *Will* is the final component that confronts the personal protections we all have, and allows actors to put themselves—their minds and, especially, their hearts—out there in public, either on stage or in front of a camera. The *Will* is the final piece that makes a good actor available to an audience with his interpretation of a role.

Risk-taking is the key component of my instruction. I am constantly emphasizing that the actors must give themselves permission to take chances. They must open up to what can be scary emotions, to show other actors personal sides of themselves, and to give themselves permission to occasionally fall on their butts. *Sometimes failure is necessary for true learning.* Recognizing this fact is of paramount importance. A class where the actor is challenged *and* feels comfortable in taking chances is vitally important to each actor's creative growth, and is the key philosophy underlying my instruction.

PART I PROCEDURE

Acting is a presumptive art. Who would imagine that he can abandon his own personal self and become someone else, even if it is for a short period of time? To do so realistically—in front of audiences (theater) or tech crews and cameras (film/TV)—takes both a unique form of self-confidence and a complete release of self. When the actor works, he must abandon his life. The street he came from, his job, his family, conversations of the day . . . all of it must be left behind in order to be caught up in the life of the character he is creating. As I see it, there are four basic elements of the process: relaxation, concentration, imagination, and preparation.

Relaxation is the first part of the process, and the essential base to all quality acting and exploration. It opens the instrument of the actor—meaning both the body and the mind. I spend a great deal of time in this section discussing relaxation, as well as presenting a suggested warm-up that I've developed over the years.

The next step, concentration, helps create the elements of the character's life that make it real. The sensory and physical-condition exercises in Part II utilize memory and the senses to deepen concentration. Actors use it to get into the life of the character with absolute believability and truth, both to an audience and to themselves.

The third aspect, imagination, is based in the subconscious and is the key to what makes acting "real." When the body is relaxed and the mind is clear and focused, the actor can access the subconscious, where spontaneous impulses come from. The individual exercises in Part III help explore the imagination.

The final step is preparation, meaning the work necessary ahead of time to properly do a role or exercise. Preparation means everything involved in the acting process, whether it's collecting props, exploring a character, analyzing a script, or memorizing lines. Preparation is as essential as the other three elements. For example, all the initial relaxation, concentration, and imagination will not do an actor any good if he's stumped by a misplaced prop or can't remember what he's supposed to say. The minute he goes up with the words, the relaxation, concentration, and imagination will disappear as well. Scene study is where we put all the components into play.

It may seem to be magic, but in reality, there is a methodic procedure to the craft of quality acting. All four elements are essential for quality, realistic acting. By fully practicing how to utilize relaxation, concentration, imagination, and preparation, the actor can leave his own world behind and inhabit the existence of the character.

1 RELAXATION

I was casting a Broadway play a few years ago, and the producer and I saw quite a few people because the play had a large cast. At the end of the day, and without communicating about each individual audition, we had the exact same scorecard for callbacks. After three days of these preliminaries, I was curious as to what system he was using.

He told me that he ended up eliminating three-quarters of the actors not based on their audition, but based on how they walked to center stage. "There is nothing of self-image in their bodies—they are apologizing for being up there through their body language," he said. "They are uncomfortable, and their insecurity reads. They are not taking charge."

He knew even before hearing them speak that he wouldn't cast them. "I can't risk investing in them, through rehearsal and production. The tension will only get worse."

With scant opportunity to audition, no actor can afford to be eliminated because of this kind of tension. Modern plays emphasize realness, and tension interferes with rather then helps this effect. Classics require a freedom of movement to fulfill the roles. And all work—contemporary or classical—requires a body to convey a physical life.

As we grow up and deal with life, we find ways to cope with the things that life throws at us. Everyone develops defense mechanisms in both their bodies and voices. To be a well-trained actor, it is vitally necessary to spend time unlocking what years of your life have caused you to close down: your body and your voice. A well-trained instrument is an open and available one.

Relaxation is the foundation for acting. All work stems from it. There is no possible way to reach the second step of acting—concentration—without being relaxed. Concentration is total availability—to other actors, to outside stimuli such as props and sets (and the mishaps that can happen with both), and to the actor's own feelings. There is no way an actor can be open without minimizing his body tension.

Relaxation is not immediate. It requires backing off from the events of the day, releasing tension, and dropping into the full instrument—the body, the voice, and the focus of the mind—to get ready to work. An athlete would not start a game without first warming up. He would injure himself within ten minutes. How can an actor walk into a dressing room at 7:30 P.M. and possibly be ready to go for an 8:00 curtain? Every actor should have a relaxation routine to "warm up" before beginning.

TENSION—THE ENEMY OF THE ACTOR

If an actor is not relaxed in front of a camera, his work will be false and uncomfortable. The camera may focus on only the face or a portion of the body at times, but the entire body must be relaxed in order for the actor to produce honest, quality work.

Film work is essentially "eyeball acting"—the camera catches the truth of emotion in the eyes. If an actor makes love to the camera, the camera will make love back. But if there is body tension, there will inevitably be blocked emotions. The camera will see it, capture it, and reject the actor like a jilted lover who has been lied to one too many times.

Rent a quality movie with a favorite actor and watch closely. Stop and start the video or DVD and watch what the actor does with his eyes before and after a line. The camera is a truth serum, and the actor must be relaxed in order to honestly relay his thoughts.

Relaxation applies to the listener as well as the speaker in a two-person scene. So much of film work is reacting. When the camera lingers on the actor who is listening rather than speaking, watch how it picks up thoughts even when there are no lines. *An actor must be relaxed to do that well.* As Michael Caine says, film acting is like watching a duck swim—smoothly gliding along the surface, but paddling like crazy below.[1]

As an athlete limbers up and takes care of his body, the actor must get his body relaxed and ready to work. Whatever method or exercise an actor chooses to use, he must ensure that it works toward relaxation that supports vitality and expression. Unless an actor is relaxed and "into" his body first, the quality work will not follow. Tension cuts off his imagination and interferes with his concentration.

Relaxation methods serve actors in other ways as well. Our business is filled with tension—acceptances, rejections, big stakes, the promise of financial rewards that clash with the consistent gigs that pay little or no

[1] Michael Caine, *Acting in Film: An Actor's Take on Movie Making* (New York: Applause Books, 1997)

money, the constant search for work, the training, and the financial investments in headshots and other materials. While immensely rewarding, acting is one of the most stressful careers a person can choose. This stress can lead to tension that can be read in an actor's body, which will interfere with the final goal—to have a career as a successful actor. A serious actor must learn and incorporate the exercises that help him cope with the physical tension that the career choice generates, at home as well as on the set or stage.

"TO BE SEEN" BODY WORK

We each have our own muscular defense system that protects us from harm, both physical and emotional. Stress from an office job that requires smiles when screaming would feel better might lead to a tense jaw and tight shoulders. A backpack or purse slung over the shoulder might lead to tense upper-back muscles. Even the most relaxed and well-balanced people will have sections of their bodies that tense up from time to time.

Actors must have knowledge of their bodies and where the tension and locks are located. Then they have to release the tension and allow an opening up of these locked areas so the stored energy can flow.

Over the years, I've experimented with many kinds of warm-up exercises for the actor, everything from hatha yoga to Strasberg's technique of "checking in" with each section of the body. What I have found is that a proper warm-up for an actor is an individual thing. Some actors respond well to Strasberg's exercises. Others use basic stretching or more aerobic exercises like jogging or biking beforehand to release excess energy. Actors must explore different types of relaxation preparation to find what's best for them.

That said, I am not a huge fan of yoga as a warm-up routine. While I believe yoga is terrific for a personal exercise routine—it stretches muscles and instructs proper breathing techniques—I find it lacking for acting purposes. Too often, I've seen actors who are "blissed out" afterwards and not energized to work in the right manner. They are almost *too* relaxed. Yoga may serve a very hyper or tense actor, but I have found through several years of observing and doing hatha yoga that the majority of actors became too passive and laid back.

Better alternatives are methods specific to the acting world, like Strasberg's "checking in" technique or Bioenergetic exercises. They can be performed in a minimal amount of time and space, while alternatives like intense stretching, jogging, or other exercises might be difficult or impossible.

"Checking In" with Strasberg

Strasberg's basic exercise starts with an actor sitting in a chair and working through the body one section at a time. The actor explores the body, starting with checking the toes, then the calves, thighs, pelvic region, torso, neck, face, arms, and hands. As he explores each region, he flexes the muscles slightly and then releases them. The entire exercise is very thorough and includes slow neck rolls and raising limbs, then letting the limbs drop to eliminate tension and excess muscularity. This warm-up takes about forty-five minutes to do thoroughly.

I learned of a speedier version from Michael Howard that resembles a Bobby Lewis exercise routine that has a "flex and relax, flex and relax" system for each specific area of the body. Up until about sixteen years ago, I used both Strasberg's and Lewis' warm-up exercises religiously. Then I was introduced to a whole new world of acting warm-up exercises: Bioenergetics.[2]

I was first introduced to Bioenergetics when the T. Schreiber Studio hired Carol Reynolds to teach a movement class. Carol came to the studio with her Body Dynamics™ curriculum. Bioenergetics is the foundation for Body Dynamics™, but the program also includes other modalities such as Pilates[3], Feldenkrais[4], Alexander Technique[5], and CranioSacral Therapy[6], as well as Carol's extensive background in dance. My knowledge of her program is miniscule, but I do know the basics of Bioenergetics and have never known

[2] The Institute for Bioenergetic Analysis was founded by Alexander Lwen, M.D., and John Pienkos, M.D., in the 1950s. The work is based on Reichian therapy, which believes that a person's repressed emotions create muscle tension, called "body armor."

[3] Pilates is an exercise-based system developed by Joseph Pilates in the 1920s. This philosophy of exercise aims to develop the body's "center" in order to create a stable core for all types of movement.

[4] The Feldenkrais Method has been described as an unusual melding of motor development, biomechanics, psychology and martial arts developed by Dr. Moshe Feldenkrais (1904–1984). It is sometimes used in physical therapy and movement courses. Feldenkrais is taught by instructors who have been specially trained in this method.

[5] The Alexander Technique is a practice of postures that remove unnecessary tension. It takes its name from F. Matthias Alexander, who devised it in the late nineteenth century. It is often considered the precursor to other body work processes such as Feldenkrais.

[6] CranioSacral Therapy, founded by osteopathic physician John E. Upledger, is a hands-on method of evaluating and enhancing the functioning of the body, typically by using a soft touch to improve the functioning of the central nervous system.

anything more effective for defining and working with the muscular defense system in each of our bodies.

Human bodies are filled with energy. This energy is called different things by different people—an "aura" to the spiritually inclined, or millions of "biochemical electronic impulses" to the scientist. Whatever it's called, the basic idea is the same: Human bodies have energy flowing through them, from the crown of the head to the tips of the toes. And like water in a garden hose, the energy flows freely when there are no kinks of tension blocking its way.

The principle behind Bioenergetic work is to take our energy up from the floor, rather than downward from our heads, as most of us do. Frequently, when the energy is taken downward, it travels no further than our chest and back, and then sticks there. Press your thumb into the sides of your pectorals. Feel the stress? The majority of people will find two golf balls of tension living there.

Restructuring our energy source takes time and discipline. Old muscles have to be retrained to let go and release. Actors must learn to realign their spines so they are more centered in their pelvic arch.

Many people carry a great deal of tension in their feet, especially their toes. All that "holding" has to be opened up and released to feel the energy flow up from the floor. The feet must be centered so they are not turned out or turned in when standing, and the actor must be careful not to walk or stand to the inside or the outside of the feet. To be fully energized, the feet must be grounded and the calf and thigh muscle tension must be minimal.

Find Your Power Source

The most important point of the actor's body—the "power source," according to Pilates and other movement experts—is the upper thighs, pelvic, and torso areas. For many actors (and people in general), the pelvic area is the "no" area of the body. It is the sexual area of our bodies, the area that is most protected.

It is vitally important, therefore, to release the groin, anus, and buttocks. We've been trained by society to suck in our stomachs and tighten our rear ends, and certainly, a pelvic lock is necessary for some dance styles, such as ballet. But it's death for an actor and cuts him off from the energy he can pull from the floor—energy that's necessary for size and power in his acting.

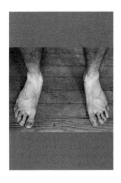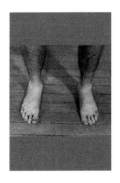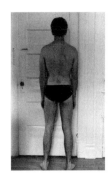

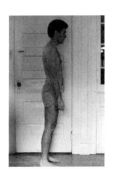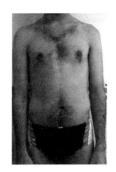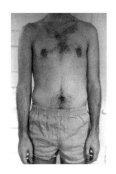

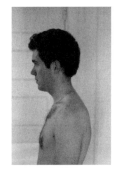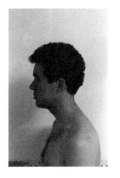

Find Your Power Source: *Pictured above are six pairs of images. The photos on the left side of each pair show the way most people carry themselves. The photos on the right side of each pair show the Bioenergetics way of standing to align the spine. The only tension in the legs is in the hamstrings. Energy must be allowed to flow up from the floor.*

These images of James Duus—a certified Body Dynamics™ educator as well as a certified Pilates instructor in New York City (JDPilatesNYC@aol.com)—are used by permission.

I emphasized the necessity for the body work because an actor's body language is being read the moment he walks into the audition space, be it a room or a stage. Equally as important is his voice, since his vocal production is also being judged the second he opens his mouth. As Lynn Singer, a vocal coach at the T. Schreiber Studio, asks, "If you sent in only your voice, would you get the role?"

No matter how well an actor can ultimately act, if he can't move well or talk well, he's gone. As a director, I've had to turn down some actors for roles because of lack of vocal production, just as I've had to turn down others because of severe body tension. I am not alone in this dilemma. Other directors have told me they've chosen not to cast actors who would otherwise be perfect for the role because of vocal problems. These actors have such a desperate need for vocal-production work that casting them is nearly impossible.

There are different types of vocal-production problems. For someone with a speech impediment or severe regionalism, very specific one-on-one work with a speech therapist may be required. But the main focus for all actors should be opening up and expanding vocal range and vocal production.

Lynn's philosophy is that actors need to return to the vocal freedom they were born with. "What baby is born with an ugly voice?" she says. An infant's voice may be loud and nerve-wracking, especially when the baby is crying, but it never has the flaws of weakness, tension, or lack of expression heard in adult voices.

Think about how easy it to hear a child laughing, crying, or even babbling from a distance or through a wall or door. This is because the young voice is free rather than protected and diffused. These protections eventually turn into vocal habits that can inhibit an actor. Many actors have spent years not knowing how to use their vocal equipment properly.

The key to using the vocal instrument is breathing. I thoroughly believe in the principle shared by Lynn Singer: "If you're not on your breath, you are not on your voice."

The first step to putting the voice on the breath is relaxation. As with movement work, Bioenergetics-based exercises can be applied to voice work. Exercises can be geared to eliminate the factors that impede good vocal production. Lynn's work, for example, starts with releasing tension from the top of an actor's head and through the body down to the feet.

Lynn then instructs how to investigate specifics like as the nasal mask. She explores vocal problems that come from a tight tongue, jaw, or neck. Students work through all the upper-torso tension that leaves them in high breath and "holding on" in the upper back and chest cavities. To counteract this tension, she teaches how to release the "holding on," as well as proper breathing techniques, how to drop this breath down into the pelvic region and the diaphragm, and then how to put the voice on the breath.

This is just the beginning of proper vocal work, of course. Once a student starts to find his voice, the next step is to explore words. While I introduce students to the concepts and importance of using language to convey the emotional life of a character in exercises like the Spoon River exercise, expert vocal instructors like Lynn emphasize this kind of training, using poetry and richly poetic prose to expand the students' background and comfort with language.

Even students who have fine vocal range and ability will often be lacking in how to properly use language to convey emotion—or even a complete thought from the text. If an actor doesn't understand what he's saying or the emotional quality behind the words, there's no way an audience will either. A beautiful voice cannot fix this problem.

While I know and understand how important this kind of training is, the work deserves more time and attention than is given in an acting class. It's why I refer so many of my students to Lynn, who not only has a significant background in vocal production, but also in literature, poetry, and drama.

Some actors make the mistake of thinking, "I just want to be in television or film, so why do I need a big voice if there is a microphone right over my head?" While there are many actors working on camera who are capable of admirable work, I believe if some of them had to put five lines together without the assistance of a good editor, they would put the viewers to sleep. Often the voice is locked or badly placed, has no support, and has no range whatsoever, or the actor can't see how to use the screenwriter's words in a deeper, more meaningful way to convey the emotional quality behind them. These actors often have no vocal colors, and the sense of rhythm—the *music* of language—is lost. Working with a vocal expert like Lynn can bring the music back.

WARM-UP PROGRAM

As I said at the beginning of this section, proper relaxation is vital to an actor—for rehearsals, for auditions, and for production. After years of experience and trial and error, I have developed a standard warm-up that I use in my classes. While it's typically easier to show someone how to do this preparation than to write about it in a book, I'm going to do my best to describe the process that I use.

Beginning Body Position

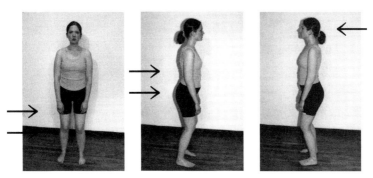

I take my students through a series of steps to achieve a centered and balanced stance.*

First, the feet are straight ahead and the actor is standing on her full foot and not to the inside or the outside of the foot. She should feel the floor up into the bottom of the foot. The feet should be planted no further apart than shoulder width.

Once she's standing correctly, and with the knees slightly bent, she tries to produce tension in the hamstrings.

The tension in the hamstrings will lead to other changes in the body stance. The butt should be dropped, and there should be a comfortable arch in the lower back. The actor shouldn't "jam" the arch down into the lower spine. The curve is not a forced arch, but rather a natural and relaxed position.

After focusing on the lower torso, I have the actor explore what's happening with his head and neck. The head shouldn't be back, down, or too far up, but rather up and straight, and in a comfortably centered position on the neck.

The body is now centered and balanced.

Relaxation "Check In"

Once the actor is centered, we move on to relaxation. I ask the actor to start by concentrating on the head and upper body, then moving his focus down the body. The effect is as if the body was a thermometer, and the relaxation body check we're going to do is the mercury going down in the thermometer.

* Images of Jennifer McGuire used by permission

Head Relaxation

- With eyes closed and in the original starting position, the actor checks out where he feels the energy in his body. Is it high or low? Does he feel his energy level is flighty and scattered, or centered and focused?

- Next he checks out his breathing. Is it high (in the upper chest) or low (in the pelvic area)? The goal is to get the breath to be lower rather than higher. He should take a deep breath so that his belly sticks out.

- While keeping his eyes closed, the actor relaxes the forehead and the temples. This is when I use a "thermometer" metaphor—the mercury starts to drop down through the body as the actor releases tension in his body from the top down.

- At this point, I bring the actor's attention to his eyes. Flickering eyelids or tightly shut eyes indicate a lot of tension behind the eyes. I tell the actor to investigate whether he can still his mind (or "stop the brain-spin," as one of my students calls it) and relax the eyes. Leave the mind behind.

- Once the eyes have released their tension, it's time to move down and relax the hinges of the jaw, and then the tongue.

- Once the mouth area is relaxed, I have the actor place his forefingers (pointer and index fingers) from each hand on the chin, with his thumbs below. The actor gently flaps the jaw up and down with the assistance of his hands. He does not do this with a lot of force, and he never works the jaw sideways. He leaves the tongue loose and makes "blah blah" sounds.

- This series of facial exercises will relax the area around what controls the tension—the brain. The relaxing of each area down the face and body is like the interior mercury dropping. After the jaw is loose, the actor drops his hands to his side.

Torso Relaxation

After the actor has focused on relaxing his head and face, it's time to move the mercury down the body.

- The actor allows the energized relaxation to move down through the neck. He lets go of the trapeziuses and deltoids, and experiences the freeing feeling of letting the shoulders drop.

- The next step is to shake some of the tension loose from the arms and shoulders. With limp wrists and using only the muscles necessary, the actor raises both arms slowly up until his arms are parallel with his ears. This produces a stretch in the upper back. After he's had his arms up for a few seconds, he then lets the arms fall to his sides. This step is repeated three times.

- He now checks in with the rest of his torso and relaxes his pectoral muscles, lats, lower back, and then abdominal muscles. He retains the original starting position, but the mercury has dropped down to the base of the pelvic area, and the actor refocuses his concentration to the floor. This is a good time for him to check and ensure he is standing firmly on planted feet, not to the inside or the outside of the foot.

Bringing Energy from the Floor

The actor started by bringing the relaxation, that "thermometer mercury," from the top down. Now he brings it from the floor up.

- The actor starts by slowly wiggling the toes, checking for tension.

- He relaxes his foot, all areas up to his ankles, and then the calf muscles. He imagines the energy or "mercury" flowing up through the base of the feet, past the ankles, and between the calves and the shins. The actor eliminates any muscle tension in the calves through focus and relaxation.

- The thermometer moves upward now, and the actor relaxes the quad muscles. For some actors, this takes extra concentration, since the quads are more tense for the athletes who do a lot of squats.

- Now he lets the energy flow up past the knees and into the thighs. The only tension in the entire leg should now be in the hamstrings.

- Now it's time for the pelvic "letting go." The actor relaxes groin muscles, anus muscles, and buttocks.

- At this point, the energy moving down the top half of the body meets up with the energy coming up from the floor and combines in the pelvic area. This area is of crucial importance. It is the body center and, along with the thighs, our power source.

Adding Movement

Once the actor has imagined the energy from the floor meeting with the energy that started from his head, it's time to add movement.

Moving the Head

- With his eyes still closed, he allows his head to drop forward with his chin to his chest. He never forces this movement, but rather allows the weight of his head to bring his chin down.

- Once done, he slowly lifts his head straight up and then lets it go back until the base of the skull is touching his back. Like the forward movement, this move is never forced, but rather allowed through the weight of the skull. He repeats this three times *slowly*, all the while checking for upper-spine tension in the trapezius and deltoids.

- Once finished with the neck forward/back stretches, he does a similar movement side to side. He leans his head toward the right shoulder as far as it will comfortably stretch. The shoulders do not move during this stretch, only the neck and head. He repeats this three times to the right and three times to the left, alternating each time.

- After he brings his head back to center, he slowly rotates his head on his neck clockwise. As with the previous movement, he does this without leaning or moving the shoulders, but rather lets the weight of the head carry the circular motion. The head is rotated three times clockwise and then three times counterclockwise *slowly*. If tension is severe, this step can be continued until reasonable relaxation in the upper spine is accomplished.

Moving the Shoulders

- After completing the head/neck rotation, the actor returns to the neutral position.

- From here, he moves his right shoulder in a slow, circular rotation, like a ball rotating in a socket. The arm muscles are slack at this point—basically, the arm just goes along for the ride. Rotation is done three times clockwise and three times counterclockwise, each time enlarging the circle of up, forward, down, and back.

Bump and Grind

- After rotating the shoulders, it's time to rotate the hips. The actor places his hands on his hips and begins a slow pelvic rotation, sort of like the old striptease "bump and grind." He should feel the rotation in the lower vertebras.

NOTE: The actor must make sure during all this body-area work that his breathing stays low and focused. He must stay on his real breath even if he is working in the upper half of his body.

Shoulder Lift

- The actor returns to his beginning stance with his shoulders relaxed and parallel.

- Once settled, he lifts his shoulders up and down quickly, touching his ears with the shoulders. He does this four or five times to release any extra tension that might still be in the upper back.

Jumping Tension Away

Aside from the neck and shoulder rolls, one of the best ways to release tension is to jump.

- The actor starts with the knees bent and then jumps straight upward, coming down on the balls of his toes and lifting his shoulders up and down in rhythm with the jumping. He should enjoy the freedom of the jumping and let out sounds.

- After a good ten to fifteen seconds of jumping, the actor returns to the beginning stance.

NOTE: Don't do this if you have foot, knee, or lower-back problems. You can also modify the jumping to protect the injury. For example, if you have one bad knee, you might try jumping on the other, but only if it's possible to do this comfortably.

Lift and Rollover

From the beginning stance, the actor lifts up and then flops over.

- First the actor straightens upward. The sensation is as if someone is lifting him up by a string at the top of his head.

- In one movement, the actor continues to lift up from the base of the spine, and then lets the weight of the head and torso carry the upper body toward the toes into a drop-over. The movement is like a puppet that is flopped forward with slack strings.

- Once over, the actor shakes out gently through the pelvis, the spine and on up. The actor should never move the legs or shake hard. It's a gentle, releasing movement—a final loosening in a rolling motion with the spine.

Good Vibrations

Now that the actor has generally loosened up, it's time to start allowing the relaxation to affect him. The goal is to have the relaxation energy move freely from the floor throughout the whole body, so much so that it vibrates just as a tuning fork will vibrate as sound moves through it. This is natural, and is exactly what is wanted with the warm-up. "Go with the vibrations," I'll tell my students.

Sometimes the vibrations will start early on in the relaxation routine. More often, it starts when the students do the Detchire and then the Bioenergetic drop-overs described below.

The Detchire

While I was in Japan, studying with experts in the Japanese theater, I was introduced to different preparation techniques used by Japanese actors. The most intriguing was called the "Detchire," which—like other energy-creating relaxation exercises—I found essential for my warm-up routine.

- The actor places his feet together with the big toes, heels, and ankles and knees touching. If the ankles don't touch, he places a sock between them.

- He then bends his knees, drops his butt, and establishes a comfortable arch in the back. He leaves his arms extended and down as if he were a construction worker with a jackhammer.

- Once in the correct position, he has the palms of the hand face the floor and then intertwines the fingers. If he is right-handed, he puts his left hand on top. If left-handed, he does the opposite. The hand position should feel a bit awkward or unnatural. (photo)

- He then breathes in through his nose and out through his mouth. As an image, he places a lit candle in front of him. As he exhales, he tries to make the flame flicker but not blow it out.

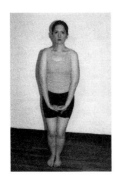 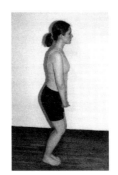 

- Once he's started the breathing pattern, it's now time to begin to bounce up and down in a rhythmic pattern, like a spring. This movement is a straight up-and-down movement that extends from the feet through the legs and knees. It should never be side-to-side or only from the knees. If the movement extends from the knees only and not the rest of the legs, the butt will swing forward and back in an awkward, uncomfortable motion. The actor must ensure that the movement is straight up and straight down, like a yo-yo.

- He keeps the steady yo-yo bouncing and candle-flicker breathing up for a good two minutes. Then he slowly comes to a halt on an interior count of five, and straightens his legs. "Feel down into the lower part of your body," I'll say at this point.

- After this brief rest period, the actor assumes the original body position of the Detchire, but this time he takes a lower starting position with the legs than he did the first time. He bounces for about a minute or two in this new position.

- Once the lower bounce is fully established, he gradually shifts his full weight to the right leg as he bounces. "Do not lean to the side, and do not lift the left foot off the floor. Make sure you are bouncing straight up and down from your right foot and not your knee."

- After a minute, he comes back through his center and shifts all his weight to his left leg.

- After a minute of bouncing on the left, he comes back to equal weight distribution in both legs and bounces for another minute. Again, he comes slowly to a stop on a count of five.

Bioenergetic Drop-Overs

- Keeping hands intertwined, he opens his feet to the original shoulder-width position, drops his butt, and resumes a slight arch in back.

- Once in the correct position, the actor releases his hands and arms to his sides and raises his arms with his fingers intertwined together, forming a steeple with his hands overhead.

- He then drops his butt, sucks in his stomach, and bends over until the hands reach or are close to the floor. Once the body is completely over, he releases the hands. The legs should be relaxed and the knees should be slightly bent—enough so he can establish tension in the hamstrings.

- Once in this position, he releases all tension in the lower half of his body except for the hamstrings. At this point, his body should start to vibrate. To accomplish this Bioenergetic release, the actor has to give up control with his mind and let his body take over. The image is as if his breath is coming from his thighs, keeping the mouth open and totally releasing the pelvic area.

- The vibrations will get stronger, especially in the legs. If the actor is very stretched out in the hamstrings, he might open his feet to the sides, or place his fingers beneath the front of his toes. If he is very limber, he should press his hands flat against the floor.

- Many times, with the vibration, emotion will come up. If it does, the actor should just let it release. Cry, laugh, scream, grunt—whatever comes, he must let it go and allow the sound release from his whole body, like it is coming from way down in the thighs with the vibration.

- After some time in this position, the actor drops his butt, sucks in the stomach, and comes to a standing position by straightening his back one vertebra at a time. He does not stop the vibration as he lifts up, nor when he is upright. "Stand and enjoy the feeling of energy throughout your body."

Back Stretch

- The actor then resumes the original position with the feet apart, knees bent, butt dropped, an arch in lower back, and the head up. He places his hands behind his back at the base of the spine. The back of one hand is pressed firmly into this spot on the spine, with the other hand over it and the thumbs locked.

- He then bends his spine backward, aiming his stomach at the ceiling. The head does not move back, however. He should focus his eyes as if he's looking at something 45 degrees in front of him.

- From this position, he creates a bow with his arms by trying to get his elbows to meet behind his back. The hands do not move from the middle of the lower back, however—they are there for support. While in this position, the actor breathes down low into his body and lets the vibrations take over.

- He stays in this position until just before it becomes uncomfortable, then drops over forward into the Bioenergetic drop-over.

- After hanging down for another minute, he raises up again by dropping the butt, sucking in his stomach, and straightening up slowly, vertebra by vertebra.

Floor Work

- After the actor has caught his breath, he lays down on the floor on his back. "Feel the difference in your body from when we started," I'll say.

- From his back, he bends his knees and raises his legs apart in the air, adjusting the position until his legs start to vibrate. The actor must release the stomach muscles and make sure his feet are not tense. "Let the position and the legs take over with the vibration." When he tires, he brings the legs down to the floor.

Floor-Stretch

- The actor then stretches out on the floor on his back, making sure his body is aligned properly. He must check that the base of the skull is against the floor, as well as the base of the spine and the back of the knees.

- His arms should be laying at his sides (three-quarters down) with his palms *up*, and he tries to open up the entire back of the hand (all five fingers and back of wrists) so it touches the floor. If he has to use a little tension to get the full hand down, that's fine. Once it is down, he relaxes it and tries to leave the full hand on the floor.

Breathe, and Release Thoughts

- Now the actor drops further into a low-centered breathing—the full kind of breath, like before dropping into a deep sleep.

- He exhales fully, and on the inhale he lets any one random thought come up. He keeps the thought as he reaches the full inhale, but then on the exhale, he lets the thought go. Then he inhales while thinking of another thought, and then releases this one. He continues to do this think-breathing slowly and rhythmically until any "brain spin" has stopped and he feels at one with his breathing and his body.

Completing the Warm-Up

After the final floor stretch, the warm-up is complete and it's time to move on to work. I ask the actors to start thinking about sitting up. "When you move, roll to your side. Use as little of your spine as possible and slowly sit up. Stay connected to your body."

They should stay connected even when they stand and begin to work with a group exercise. I have the actors check out how they feel in their body compared to when we started.

This is the kind of relaxation work I want done before you ever thinking about working on a preparation for a scene or exercise. Until the actor is as relaxed and as centered as possible, there is no way he can achieve the concentration needed for good acting.

2 CONCENTRATION

Contrary to popular belief, acting is *not* a natural process. We can only strive to make it look like it is. Once the actor is properly relaxed and prepared to fully use his body and voice, we are then ready to go to various exercises that help get to the next step—the imagination, sometimes called the "inner life" or the "organic life."

I think most people would agree that the art of acting is rather presumptive. Expecting people to feel emotional empathy for a character who has been created by a writer and then manifested through an actor is a tall order. There are myriad obligations demanded of the actor. He must fulfill a character and a text and live up to the demands of a writer and a director, not to mention the critique of critics and the audience. The stakes engender tremendous pressure and tension. Thus, I have emphasized the vital necessity and importance of the relaxation work to counter this pressure.

Stanislavski emphasizes this kind of availability in his book *An Actor Prepares*. He demonstrates concentration and availability when the character of the director in the book, Tortsov, explains the concentration needed as the "circle of light":

> In the circle of light on the stage in the midst of darkness, you have the sensation of being entirely alone. . . . This is called solitude in public. . . . During a performance, before an audience of thousands, you can always enclose yourself in this circle, like a snail in its shell . . . You can carry it wherever you go.[1]

Obviously it is not enough to just be relaxed. Nor is it enough to just speak the writer's words. There must be something beyond the script for the actors to touch the nether region of their imaginations and build real characters. Acting training helps the actor to find ways and means to trick the

[1] Constantin Stanislavski, *An Actor Prepares* (New York: Theater Arts Books, 1989).

subconscious to behave spontaneously. This isn't an easy task. The stage or the camera challenges and resists an actor's attempts to be relaxed and focused.

There is one goal I emphasize over and over: The actor must give the illusion that he is being private while in a very public place. I use the acting exercises described in this book to help the actor learn how to deepen concentration, and thereby trick the imagination or subconscious into creating an active and organic inner life.

THE SENSES—FIVE POWERFUL TOOLS

Earlier I discussed the three acting ingredients of *mind*, *heart*, and *will* to produce the ideal result of realistic and full acting. The four components of this goal are *relaxation*, *concentration*, *imagination*, and *preparation*.

A clear and perceptive mind is of major importance to interpreting a role, but our sensitivity and instincts must also be involved. Otherwise we merely create a "walking and talking head" devoid of real emotions. The acting seems "fake" to an observer. The actor must be able to return to an almost childlike experience of heightening his awareness of all five senses—*smell* (olfactory sense), *sound*, *taste*, *sight*, and *touch*—in order to fully achieve the level of concentration that appears real.

Smell (Olfactory Sense)

How easily can a random scent instantly and almost unconsciously remind someone of a loved one, a place, or an event? Why do we spend so much money and time on smelling just right? Because it's *that* important. We are constantly surrounded by odors, pleasant and otherwise. The olfactory sense—smelling—can transport us years back in our lives and bring forth vivid feelings and emotions.

Scientists affirm that the sense of smell is a key to unlocking our subconscious sense memory of past people and events. Because the nose is located so closely to the part of the brain that stores memories, these olfactory sensations register differently than the other senses like touch or even sight. The effect is that the sense of smell is directly linked to our memory bank. Heightening this awareness of smell can help an actor access a rich tool for recall preparation and onstage deepening of concentration. Many of the most experienced actors rely on their sense of smell to create their characters' inner lives.

Sound

Our ears and the cacophony of daily sounds play a vital role in our lives. We use sound to soothe us, arouse us, stimulate us, and transport us, whether the sound is music ("organized sound"), personal sounds like voices, or random noises. Closing our eyes and listening carries us to various places, people, and time periods.

Sounds alert us, warn us, and many times move us to tears and laughter. Soft and peaceful sounds like waves crashing on a beach can calm our heart rates, while violent sounds stimulate our adrenaline glands and the "fight or flight" response. All the styles of music and the daily sounds of our lives are a sum of the sensory stimulants to our ears. Consequently, these sounds are, for the actor, one of the tools used to build an inner life, feeling, and emotion.

Voices are especially important for the actor. Just as in real life, any time an actor opens his mouth, he gives away his emotional state through how he says the words. Truly hearing the emotional quality of the lines is equally important for the actor receiving the line. "Do you really hear the other actor, or are you just listening for your cue?" I'll frequently ask.

Taste

Our lips, mouth, and tongue fill us with sensual delight and cause a response ranging from pleasure and joy to distaste and unpleasantness. From the time we are babies, we learn to separate pleasurable tastes from bad ones in the most basic manner. As we grow, our taste buds grow in sophistication as well. We learn to savor and stimulate our oral response with food, drink, and other things that feel good on our lips and taste good in our mouths.

As with smell and sound, the actor can test how the recall of certain tastes calls forth a memory of a person or event. A certain unpleasant taste can bring on discomfort, sometimes to the point of nausea. Even a normally pleasant taste can create a strong reaction in the opposite manner if the actor has had a negative personal experience that incorporated that particular taste. We process the sense of taste in the same manner that we do smell. Like smell, because of the location of the tongue in relation to the brain, the sense of taste is intricately linked to memory.

Sometimes the taste doesn't even have to be real to stimulate a response. Asking students to imagine what a rainbow might taste like could elicit positive emotional responses, while the same question about motor oil (something I hope none of my students have tasted) might bring negative reactions. I watched an actor once create a vivid reality of a young woman on the verge of a nervous breakdown by endowing a sandwich with a particular shade of purple, a color that nauseated her. It was all she needed to accomplish the destined psychological and emotional state of the character. Eating that color instantly took her where she needed to go.

Sight

Our vision and ability to take in what we see is an extremely important ability to record our waking lives. How many times does something we're observing now remind us of a past place or person? How may times have you said, "He or she looks like so and so," or, "That sight reminds me of such and such"?

Actors can use their minds to see objects or sights for the character, just as they can use smells, tastes, and sounds from their memories. The more detailed the observations, the more deeply concentrated the actor. Do you really see the other actor? Are you fully aware of his responses? Do you really take in the set, props, lighting, and costumes? Most of all, do you really make direct contact?

Sight plays a significant role for the actor because of the eyes. I know it is cliché, but the eyes are the mirror to the soul—and the path to honest acting. Through the eyes, the actor not only lets the other actor in, but lets the audience gain an entrance as well. Rarely can viewers see changes in the nose, tongue, or ears as an actor is working, even in the most intimate of film close-ups. But the eyes tell everything.

Even in a large theatrical space, the audience can tell what the eyes project—as long as the actor is looking up and not hiding the eyes (and the emotion) from the rest of the world. It is sometimes frightening to open up like this—the actor can feel naked when the emotion leaks out through the eyes—but it is a major portion of sharing the work with the audience or camera.

Touch

Our tactile sensitivity is certainly the key to the sensory awareness of touch. Whether it's dealing with a prop, costume, another actor, or the actor's own body, the actor needs to be aware of what he touches. This sense can trigger both sense memories from the past and an immediate sensorial response. I've seen unprepared actors pick up props and seem to have no idea what they have in their hands. We want the sensitivity of our touch to really *feel* the object, to give the sense of touch meaning.

An actor can speak a thousand words without uttering a sound by using the sensation of touch. A fantastic example is the classic scene in *On the Waterfront* when Marlon Brando tries on Eva Marie Saint's glove. Brando puts the tiny, delicate piece of fabric over his rough and callused hands in complete silence, but the sensuality and sensitivity of that piece will be etched in my memory for all time. To hell with exploratory dialogue—Brando said it all through sensitivity to touch.

3 IMAGINATION

In advanced acting training, it's the *imagination* the actors are primarily concerned with tapping into. Imagination is the subconscious, or the "inner life," and is what makes good acting seem real. The senses help with concentration and work to stimulate the imagination and create a sense of reality. Obviously, the most direct way of working with the senses is through direct stimulation. If the actor is supposed to be sick from the smell of garbage, it would be convenient to carry a bag of rotting compost. But working in this manner isn't always practical, nor is it necessary. Every actor has a rich imagination to work from. But how to tap into it?

Accessing the imagination for acting purposes is not much different from the imaginative games played by children. When a child is playing house, there's a whole life that is a temporary part of the child's reality. Blankets and chairs become caves and houses. Play-Doh becomes sweet-potato pie. There really is a monster under the bed, and the fear and adrenaline from running from the door and diving under the covers is honest. What started in the child's imagination becomes alive. She's tricked her subconscious, and the impulses and imagination feed each other.

Children inherently possess the elements of acting—they are almost always relaxed (at least, more relaxed than adults), they have incredible powers of concentration, and they can easily suspend their disbelief and live in their imagination. As adults, we've mostly lost this ability to create such elaborate fantasies. The reasons for leaving this fantasy world behind are valid—adults must live and survive in the real world, not something made up in the mind. But the actor needs to return and exercise the imaginative muscles that she had as a child, and to intertwine this ability with a writer's words and the set.

How the adult actor gets back to opening up that child's imagination to believe in the make-believe is exactly what my exercise work in Parts II and III is for. The actor has to see what is fake and believe it is real. The other actor is her brother. The flat is a wall. The grape juice is wine. It's the imagination that propels the actor to accept and live in the alternate world of the character.

One way to tap into the creative subconscious of the imagination is through the sensory and physical-condition group exercises in Part II. They are of vital importance, which is why I typically work on a different exercise once a month. The full process of warm-up and then the group exercises not only trains *relaxation* and *concentration*, but also leads toward the third step of *imagination*. The individual exercises in Part III continue on this work.

The actor creates a make-believe world, but it is based on real observations. Stanislavski talks about his wife playing the role of a prostitute after observing working girls in the streets. She meticulously watched their actions, movements, and attitudes. She talked to them about their lives and listened to their words and speech. She used her imagination to explore in her mind what it would be like to sell her body for money. And, with all this background, she was able to live in the existence of a prostitute for the play.

Playing with the imagination is dangerous territory. I say over and over again in this book how important it is to be cognizant of the fact that an actor's tools are her subconscious and unconscious—the same stuff of psychology. They should not be experimented with lightly. There are examples of actors going so far into a role that they lose all sense of reality, or actually live as the characters they're playing. There is no need to do so. The reality can be created for the role from observation, as in the example of the prostitute character. But after the role is over, it must be left on the set or at the theater.

The best advice I have on this subject can be summed up in one word: closure. When doing the exercises in my book, the actor must come to some sort of resolution in the work. If we're exploring a sensory exercise dealing with height, I bring the actor back to safety at the end. Exploring events from the past demands resolution on two fronts—the actor needs to be comfortable with the past before even starting the exercise, and then needs to end the exercise in a place of safety and resolution. Emotional release—whether it's through crying, laughing, or any emotion in between—is the key to both quality and sanity.

* * *

FINDING EMOTIONAL RESOLUTION

Several months into Terry's class, I was in an independent film where my character is raped. I have never experienced anything like that, but by calling on certain lines from the Fallout, I was able to reach the authentic intensity level needed to get through the scene.

After the rape scene, we were supposed to film my character having a meltdown. Remembering Terry's encouragement to ask for what I needed, I told the director that I would need to have my own *personal* meltdown after filming the rape scene. I knew I had to give myself time. But I did give her and the cameraman permission to stay and film.

Immediately after the last angle of the rape scene was done, the director whisked everyone out the door except the cameraman and said that no one could enter until I opened the door. She gave me the privacy and respect to have my own personal emotional release. Needless to say, that was the take they used for the movie.

—Donna Abraham

* * *

Sometimes a role doesn't allow a release during the play or scene. Arthur Miller creates a dilemma for the actress playing Linda in *Death of a Salesman* when he has her say that she can't cry at the end of the play. The character is so emotionally wound up that it's tightly bottled—and should stay bottled until the curtain falls if she is to properly represent the character. My recommendation: Allow the tears to come during the curtain call, or take some time alone in the dressing room. "Cry your eyes out, but don't take it home with you." We have enough baggage in our own lives, there's no need to take on more from the characters we play, and certainly not from exercises done in a class setting.

Some actors who have really committed to a role have confided in me that they could see that the imagination takes over and the emotional flavor of the character seeps into the subconscious. They felt it happening, or were told by loved ones that they were someplace else or became someone different. Swoozie Kurtz once told a newspaper that, during the time playing the mother of a child murdered by a pedophile in Bryony Lavery's *Frozen*, her shoulders would rise throughout the day before the performance, only to fall during the monologue when her character confronts the killer. The play had obviously affected her life outside the theater. Her subconscious worked all day to gear up for the role in the evening, and exhibited the emotions through the physicality of her shoulders. But she also had resolution by the time the curtain fell, and I assume she could leave the theater released of the horror of the role.

Separation from this part of the imagination is not an easy task, but neither is the discovery. Sometimes actors have to explore dark parts of themselves in order to properly represent a character. Fellow T.S.S. acting teacher Peter Jensen once told me about an actor who was up for the role of a pervert. Peter asked the actor what he knew about the perversion. "Well," answered the actor with confidence, "I'm not a pervert, but I have a friend who is."

Friends won't do it. The actor must find the elements inside, or explore a parallel that can represent it. This doesn't mean that an actress has to be a murderer in order to play Lady Macbeth, but rather she must discover something within herself that gives the same reality onstage. When Stanislavski's wife played a prostitute under his direction, she built her role partly on observations and partly on the portion of her subconscious mind that imagined herself as a working girl. All actors must look deep inside and do the same—and then leave it behind when not in an acting atmosphere. They must concentrate on themselves when they are living their lives, and give the proper time and space to their characters in rehearsal and preparatory work.

I recommend that every actor take some serious thought before embarking on a difficult role or exercise. If an actor sees on paper that there's something difficult to do, she must seriously consider whether it's worth it to have to find and explore that part of herself. I don't mean to scare actors who read this book. Quite the opposite. The exercises I use are specifically designed to allow actors to explore and achieve deep inner life and imagination without sacrificing themselves. But I do want them to understand the seriousness of the journey to be undertaken. The imagination is a powerful tool, and should be treated with love and care.

4 PREPARATION

Proper preparation and training are absolutely necessary for success in the acting world. Training—be it body or vocal or both—is vital. One of the reasons why I feel the British have stolen the American stage is they can move and speak. They're comfortable in their own skin. And, with the exception of a few plays with distractingly heavy accents, they can be heard and understood. The school of naturalistic mumbling is over. The theater—as well as good television and film—is about words.

While some individuals may have a stronger inclination toward acting than others, few succeed in the acting world without working at it. The Olympic or professional athlete must train. The skilled musician must rehearse. And anyone in a skilled job such as carpentry spends hours of time learning the technique of carpentry to perfect the craft. Why should it be any less demanding and rigorous for the actor?

Preparation refers to numerous aspects of the process—from the mundane (memorization, script and text analysis, prop gathering) to the complex (sensory work, relaxation routines, vocal production, emotional work). All parts of the preparatory process are important, especially self-rehearsal and practice, whether we're talking about playing a part or preparing for one of the exercises or scenes in a class. To produce quality work, the actor must have access to the emotional reality from the imagination, but it will mean nothing if the lines aren't memorized, the voice isn't heard, the other actors or crew aren't prepared for the actor's movements, or the body is so locked up that none of the imagination work comes through.

BODY AND VOICE

It's a shame for someone to have an ability and knowledge of the acting process and then lose jobs because of body tension or poor vocal facility. As a teacher and director, I beg all actors not to overlook or be careless with these two vitally important areas, and to start honing their skills when they are beginners.

Some acting students are put off by the demand this kind of work involves. Like practice for a game, some of the body or vocal exercises will be tedious, repetitive, and monotonous. However, the successful actor must incorporate a "workout" into her daily regime. Remember, she plays the game only as well as she practices. The long way is eventually the short way.

Dedication to minimizing body tension and improving vocal production early on in an actor's development will speed up the actor's learning process for all of the work and study to come. (Taking acting classes without addressing body tensions and vocal problems is like putting the cart before the horse.) But an actor must incorporate the exercise into her daily workouts. From this attention to the body and voice—the actor's relaxation process—we then move into the next step of the work: helping the actor to explore techniques and tools to increase her depth of concentration.

THE ACTOR'S NOTEBOOK

A sensory exercise spurs wild laughter. A physical-condition exercise adds a rich inner life to an otherwise unimpressive monologue. A piece of music brings an actor's imagination into the ideal setting and mindset for a character. Wonderful! But what good is this if, in the real acting situations later on, the actor doesn't remember them?

I tell my students that it's a good idea to always have an "Actor's Notebook" so they can record their findings from class and elsewhere for future reference. As they reflect, they should note what images of events, places, and people came to mind from the sensory and physical-condition work from Part II, and what feelings or emotions these images evoked. Same goes for the individual exercises in Part III and the scene work. Actors learn so much, and should be able to apply it later on. The notebook can be a guide and a tool in the actor's future career.

MEMORIZATION

It is absolutely vital to know the words cold, whether we're talking about a monologue in the group exercises in Part II, the individual exercises in Part III, scene work explored in Part IV, or any other acting situation. An actor cannot work if she does not know what she's going to say next. Concentration is broken, imagination is lost, and no work gets done.

Equally as important to recognize are the verbal differences between characters. People speak differently from each other—they use different pauses, construct sentences in different ways, and use different words. If the actor starts to substitute her own words and sentence construction for the author's, she is no longer in touch with the character. She's replaced the character with herself, taking her further away from her intended goal: to embody the character.

*   *   *

BACKWARD WAY TO CONSTRUCT A SENTENCE

Terry gave me a difficult role to play in class—that of Lila in William Inge's *A Loss of Roses,* the story of a thirty-something actress who falls for her friend's twenty-year-old son, Kenny. Lila is sweet, vulnerable, and easily blinded by her desire to be loved by others. By nature, I'm stubborn, direct, and incredibly independent. While I do possess Lila's characteristics, they are often overshadowed by others in my real life.

I had an incredibly difficult time with Lila's dialogue. Lila never said anything directly, and I assumed that either Inge was writing a Midwestern dialect that I was unfamiliar with, or he was just a lousy writer. But Terry insisted on us being line-perfect, so I forced myself to learn the scene word for word the evening before my scene partner and I did it in class.

What a difference! During the scene, I was pulled deeper and deeper into Lila's gentleness, her mothering nature toward Kenny, and her desperate need to be loved—*through the language.* Moments of tenderness that had been awkward in rehearsal were suddenly spontaneous, natural, and painfully loving. Lila's backward way of constructing a sentence fit perfectly into the emotional quality of the character as I found myself spontaneously blushing and being overwhelmed by shyness. The language guided me and allowed me to embody a character who is very different from me.

It was a good lesson to learn: Don't paraphrase dialogue until it's truly been explored, because the writer may know something you don't.

—Mary Beth Barber

*   *   *

Some actors will come to rehearsal without having memorized the words ahead of time, explaining that they'll memorize while they're on their feet. While it may be true that the memory eventually comes, some bad habits develop. Often a line will be remembered based on a piece of blocking, and if the director changes the blocking, the actor will lose the words. The actors replace the lines with their own words in order to keep the scene going. And no work can be done in rehearsal if the actors have books in their hands—the scenes become about the books and not the acting. I've seen weeks wasted simply because the actors refused to do memorization work at home and brought the burden into the acting space. (Please see Part IV, Scene Study, for more tips on memorization.)

MONOLOGUES

For some of the exercises, I tell the students they must have a memorized monologue in their repertoire. (In my opinion, all advanced acting students should have a handful of monologues they can access at a moment's notice.) Most certainly the students in my class should always have one available for the group exercise. But if a leader chooses to use this exercise with a group of actors, it's a good idea to let them know ahead of time to memorize—but not necessarily prepare—a monologue.

Actors should always have monologues ready to go on a moment's notice anyway. If, by chance, an opportunity to see a casting director presents itself with no warning, the actor must be ready to show her work—and the only real way to do this is with a monologue.

I recommend always having two ready to go—one dramatic and one comic—and a third "classical" monologue as well. "Classical" can either mean Shakespeare or another Elizabethan playwright. Most directors who ask for classical monologues want to see whether the actor can handle language and verse, and there are alternative playwrights to Shakespeare to help demonstrate this.

For audition purposes, it is essential that the actor choose a monologue that represents her qualities most honestly. So many actors don't know how people see them, or they feel they must show something different in the monologue so they can demonstrate the acting. "No," I tell my students, "Be realistic. Show who you are, and then use the monologues to support that." If an actor doesn't hit that first beat with honesty and intensity, the agent is no longer listening.

Actors must also be careful to not pick something too dramatic or farcical. Extreme pieces will backfire and should be avoided unless they are asked for. But simple storytelling doesn't work either. I'm a great fan of Tennessee Williams, but not for audition monologues, because his monologues typically have a character telling a story rather than pursuing a strong action.

I also suggest that actors avoid movies—they are too closely related to the original actors, and often the auditioning actor will end up doing an imitation of them. Pick monologues with characters really going after something. I think that's what casting people really need to see.

Also remember that the monologue needs to be adjustable for three different atmospheres: an agent's office, on camera, and on stage. Peter Minor told me of a very talented actor who gave a theatrical monologue in an agent's office. It was an amazing piece, but the actor gave a stage audition in an agent's office. It was too much, the agent was blown away (in a negative context), and the actor was viewed as appropriate only for stage. Let it out for stage, but pull it back in an agent's office, and even more so for camera. The elements of relaxation, concentration, and imagination are the same or similar for all three scenarioss, but the intensity level must be adjusted.

These guidelines won't necessarily apply to the monologues used in the exercises in this book. The purpose of the exercises is to explore and stretch, and in these cases, the monologues may show a different side of the actor that isn't readily apparent. I recommend using the exercises and class to explore. But the outside acting world is not the place to bend and stretch—the actor will only end up misrepresenting herself. She needs to show off who she is. Next to the photo, the monologue is what she's selling. It takes tremendous thought. "Know how people see you," I'll tell my students, "and then use that information to select a monologue."

CLASS AND REHEARSAL SPACE

The space used for practice—whether it's for rehearsing or for class work—is incredibly important. The space must be a sanctuary for the actors, away from the distractions of the world. The rooms or studios used must allow the freedom for the actors to propel themselves into an alternative state of creativity, and to do that they need space, safety, and the ability to work.

The Class Space

I've never understood how some teachers can sell students on acting classes out of their home or apartment. Unless the instructor has a studio set aside that resembles a black box theater, the home is the worst place in the world to take acting classes. The distractions are countless, and the atmosphere works against the concentration needed for acting.

The ideal place for an acting class is an actual stage, with theatrical-style lights and an audience area for the other students to watch. The stage must be able to be altered to suit the project the student is working on—a pre-arranged set for another show that can't be touched will interfere with the work.

There should also be plenty of props and furniture to utilize. At the T. Schreiber Studio, we have multiple pieces of furniture and a room of props that the students can use for their sets, as well as a large box of discarded clothing that they can pull from if they need a costume in a pinch. I don't recommend that any acting teacher spend a fortune on pristine furniture or objects, since most of the stuff is going to get beat up significantly. But at a minimum, I strongly recommend—practically insist—on a simple kitchen set-up, a table and chairs, couch, side chairs, and a sturdy bed frame and mattress. All pieces should be easily movable, and the heavy items should be on wheels for easy mobility.

I also think that students need real objects to use in class—things like plates, cups, glasses (both wine and water), pitchers, silverware, pillows, blankets, bedspreads, sheets, tablecloths, cooking utensils, pots and pans, flower vases . . . anything that could be used over and over again on a set so the students can experiment with creating business. Other things like picture frames or sidepieces can add the proper décor to a temporary set. Items that are particular to a scene or exercise can be brought in by students, but expecting an overburdened actor to bring in an entire houseful of props is unreasonable and cruel—and will typically lead to fewer students.

Building a full set of furniture and a prop closet does not have to be an expensive venture. Many items can be gathered by putting out a request for donations or by visiting a local second-hand store or charity. Most of the larger pieces of furniture at T.S.S. were donated and then altered for easy mobility by students with carpentry experience.

Lighting and general set-up of an acting classroom is equally as important as props and furniture. The atmosphere should encourage the students to take their work seriously, and a proper set-up can help tremendously. There should be a set area where the exercises and scene work take place, and another set area where students sit and watch the work being done by others. Ideally, the "stage" area should be lit by some sort of simple lighting on a dimmer so students can set the tone with light levels, while the "audience" area can be dark.

Often it's impossible to create the set and lighting atmosphere that I described. The space may be rented from another facility and might not contain the materials necessary. While I recommend that a class have as much as possible—even if it means renting a space that's more expensive—if it's truly not possible, then the instructor should use some creativity and find objects and items for a basic kitchen, bedroom, and living room set. The exercises and scene work in this book will not work in an empty black box.

The Rehearsal Space

The scene work in Part IV requires rehearsal before putting the material up in a class. Rehearsals cannot take place in a highly public place or in a home. (Some of the individual exercises can and should be rehearsed in an empty home, without observers; I describe these later on.) The reasons for not having scene work rehearsal in public or at home are obvious. Just as class work cannot happen in a non-private space, neither can real rehearsal happen if there are distractions in a personal home or public space.

Actors are always short on cash, and sometimes shelling out a few bucks for a rehearsal space can be a burden. But in the long run, it's cheaper to pay for a room and seriously concentrate on rehearsal rather than attempt a partial effort in a non-ideal place. Without serious rehearsal, students will work more slowly and have to work time and time again on the same piece rather than propel quickly to a higher level of acting. Not only will it delay the student from achieving a professional level of acting, but it will cost more money in class time in the long run. A significant amount of homework is required in order to be prepared prior to stepping in the rehearsal space, of course—but this is the ideal way to work anyway. Actors will save both time and money if they approach the work this way.

The rehearsal space does not need to be as elaborate as the ideal class space that I've described. While it may be ideal to have a full set of furniture and props, a simple room with a few chairs can be used to explore the scene. I do suggest that the students bring both costumes and props with them to the rehearsal space, and utilize any furniture available to suggest real pieces. If carrying around full costumes and props isn't feasible, at a minimum, the proper footwear and any necessary props or items that can suggest those props are required to fully explore the work.

A NOTE FOR LEADERS

While many of you reading this book are actors, some may use it to teach or direct. If so, you must read this section.

As a teacher or a director who wishes to start the class with some basics tools, you have taken on a tremendous responsibility. The following exercises are extremely personal and powerful, and if you chose to utilize them, you must follow these basic guidelines.

Using your intuition, sensitivity, and good sense, you must know how far into an exercise or scene you can take an individual student or a group of actors. Do not think that encouraging, prodding, or pushing can work for an actor who seems to be rejecting an experience. Never push an actor beyond what is comfortable for her. There probably is a good reason why she is struggling, and as the leader you must adjust your method and manner according to the experience or the actor. These people trust you as they dive into some of their most sensitive areas. You are their guide. Be responsible.

The best way to keep the atmosphere safe for the actors is to first have a general awareness of each actor's past and sensitivities. Set up a one-on-one meeting before holding the class or rehearsal. Ask that she privately tell you if she has any issues or fears that should be known about beforehand. The last thing you'd want to do is take someone who almost died in a climbing accident through the Height exercise without prior preparation. A situation like this will shake your actor to the core and make her terrified of the work rather than open to it. For you, a mistake like this will plague your conscience afterward.

Sometimes you may not have been informed of a sensitive area, or the actor may not be aware of it herself. Even when I've been unaware of the specific reason or incident that causes an exercise to be hurtful rather than helpful, I've found that by trusting my instincts and listening closely to an actor, I know when to stop. I'm aware on an instinctual level of when an exercise has become dangerous and should cease. Many times, the exercise shouldn't even be attempted at a later time without some personal closure by the actor on the issue. I know this because I watch closely. You as a leader need to do the same.

When to Stop

There are always signs that indicate when an exercise has become unhealthy. If you actively watch the actor's breathing, her body language, and the words that come up within the exercise, you will get clues. Many times, I can pinpoint the clue that caused me to stop an exercise. But sometimes the reason isn't obvious—it's simply a gut feeling that "this exercise must be stopped." Trust your gut.

If you believe that an exercise should be stopped, or the actor requests that it be stopped, don't simply jolt her out of the exercise. If she is distressed, either approach the actor and slowly bring her awareness to the present while the others work, or use simple and direct verbal commands to have the actor do so herself. Honor your gut feelings or the actor's request, wind down the exercise, and allow the actor to return to a safe environment.

Therapy Is for Therapists

Remember that as a leader, you are not a therapist. Nor are you a father or mother to the actors. You are an acting instructor or leader. Confine yourself to those job descriptions. You might privately take an actor aside (never in front of other actors) and suggest therapy, but by no means should you delve into the sensitive area yourself or discuss these issues in an open classroom. Nor should you try to play parent or assume a "best friend" role outside of the acting forum. This is not your job. Taking on those responsibilities will completely nullify your role as an acting instructor for that particular individual.

I have seen acting teachers who are out to destroy the egos of their young actors, thinking that they can "rebuild" those egos in the classroom, under their auspices. This is enormously dangerous on a personal level and in most cases useless to an actor. Never try to "break down" an actor to tears by screaming at her or chastising her in front of others. And never use the exercises to exploit emotions that the actor is unwilling to share. Teachers who think that they have to be cruel in order to teach should go into therapy themselves and explore their destructive, sadistic tendencies.

It is important that you be firm in your standards about "the work." It is equally important for you to be supportive to the actors for all the times they take risks and chances. Remember, these exercises are for learning about the process, not for performance. The actor should not feel the need to entertain the class or the teacher.

Instead, she should have permission—permission from the instructor, the class, and herself—to "fail" in a supporting, nonjudgmental environment. A trusting atmosphere, created by you as the teacher, is fundamental to the growth process. Honor that trust by being supportive. Be there for your students with your complete discretion, caring, and love for the work. If you establish that trust, the actors will follow suit.

PART II GROUP EXERCISES

The following group exercises are separated into general sensory, personal sensory, and physical-condition exercises. The sensory exercises emphasize utilizing the five senses—smell, hearing, taste, sight, and touch—while the physical-condition exercises lead actors through the process of exploring their reactions when their bodies are in different states, such as pain, drunkenness, hunger, thirst, and so on. Personal sensory exercises relate specifically to experiences unique to each actor's past. All three types require a similar meditative process to initiate the work, and are vital tools in helping the actor to deepen concentration, enhance the imagination, and connect to inner life.

Before I ask my actors to dive into these sensory exercises, I lead them through the lengthy relaxation process described in Part I. I recommend that any individual attempting to do these exercises on his own or any instructor leading them do the same. After the warm-up, I have the actors either work from a comfortable position on the floor or sit on hard-back chairs, depending on the exercise.

RELAXING INTO THE FLOOR

If the floor is used, I have the actors finish the relaxation work by laying on the floor and "relaxing into it," meaning that the actors align their bodies while laying on their backs. I tell them to make sure that the base of the skull, the base of the spine, the back of the knees, and the back of the hands, fingers, and wrists (palms up) are touching the floor.

The students' breathing should be dropped down to the diaphragm by this time and should be like the deep breathing that occurs right before dropping off into a deep sleep. There should not be any shallow breathing up in the chest.

"HARD" CHAIRS

If chairs are better for the particular exercise, I ask the actors to sit comfortably, with their hands either hanging by their side or on their thighs with palms up. This is a very open body position. (The goal is to maintain a similarly relaxed state as when on the floor.) The actors should have the same deep breathing and general relaxation.

I advocate using "hard" chairs with straight backs and no arms rather than something the students can slump or relax into. A soft chair creates the wrong kind of relaxation. The actors should be ready to work, not ready to fall asleep. A hard chair will help with this, while a soft chair or couch will encourage a sleepy state.

At this point, I take the students into each exercise by utilizing their imaginations. While there are many different kinds of sensory and physical-condition exercises, I will only cover the ones I use in my advanced class. Many variations could be created from these sensory themes. Pay particular attention to the description in the first exercise demonstrated, "Height," because the details I give apply to all of the exercises. It is essential to understanding the process for the other group exercises.

5 GENERAL SENSORY EXERCISES

Our bodies are constantly sensing images, scents, sounds, tastes, and textures. These images are stored in our memories and can be utilized in an acting context. The following exercises explore some of these sensual memories in a variety of different ways that can be used later in an acting context, or simply to increase the actor's concentration ability.

HEIGHT

This particular exercise starts with the students on the floor after the relaxation warm-up. I ask the actors to lie on their backs and imagine that they've just climbed a very high mountain, one that is at least five thousand feet. They are sweaty and tired, and they have to catch their breath at this altitude. They should be working with their eyes closed. This is a must because I want them to heighten the senses other than sight first.

Touch

"Be aware of what you are laying on," I tell them. "Is it a rock slab? Gravel? Any grass? Is it perfectly hard and smooth, or are there bumps?"

While there are certain choices that the actors must make, I don't want them to *think* these choices; I want them to *experience* these choices. For example, if I ask them about the ground under their body, I don't want them to think, "This is what the ground would feel like against my body," but rather to wait and see what sensations come to them. The sensory image should come first and then the active brain responds, not the other way around. It's a subtle yet important difference. Their *imaginations* must ask the sensory questions rather than their active brains.

Sound

After having the actors explore the ground beneath them, I then instruct them to listen to the sounds at that height. This means to hear with the ears, *not think the sound*. They shouldn't think, "I might hear the wind whistle if I'm up here," but rather, "Hmm, perhaps for a second I heard the sound of the wind?" The actors must relax and just let the sounds happen, by listening with their ears.

No one is going to hear a sound for any sustained period. We're looking for brief seconds or milliseconds of something sensorial coming alive. This is the suggestibility of concentration, the tricking of the subconscious to behave spontaneously. Concentration should never be forced in any of these exercises. By forcing ideas or thoughts, the actor will unintentionally work against the exercise and his own imagination. "Just wait," I tell my actors. "The sensations will come."

Don't Use Your Brain

The subconscious will begin to feed images—events, places, and people—and the actor should treat it like a film running in her mind. Sometimes a portion of this "film" is so strong that a full memory comes alive. In this exercise, it might be images of a similar mountain or a similar hike. This full memory may be so strong that it forces the temporary abandonment of the specific task I'm leading—in this case, listening. The mind might jump immediately to a scent, a taste, or even a whole experience of an event. If this happens, the actor should go with the memory.

She must always trust the images that come. The "film" is a tool for creating an inner life or inner monologue for a character, one that is honest and real rather than "I'm making this face now because I feel a certain way." When we are angry (or sad or happy), our bodies and faces react to that emotion. It isn't the other way around. Making a face before being in the emotion appears false and unreal. An inner life consists of organic thoughts from an actor, not specific thoughts an actor gives herself to think. It is a life that is spontaneous and, in the case of this exercise, a life associated with doing the sensory tasks of feeling and listening. The actor must allow the inner life that the sensory task calls forth to be present.

Smell and Taste

We proceed from sound to smell: "What smells are on top of that mountain?" Then we move to taste, working just as thoroughly as we did with listening. Each of these senses might elicit organic thoughts from the actor.

Stand Up and See

For the next step, I ask the actors to stay connected to their bodies while they slowly sit up, using as little of their spine as possible. This means rolling to their sides much like a very pregnant woman might, and then coming to a sitting position from there.

Now it's time for the actors to open their eyes and look around. "Take in the other actors working alongside you." They are there physically in the same space. Their presence must be acknowledged. Once the actor has included them in her space, she can then exclude them, drawing her circle of concentration once more around herself and seeing the sky, the rock face, an eagle, or anything else her eyes imagine seeing from the mountaintop. Remember, concentration is total availability. Only by first recognizing that the others are there can the actor choose what to do with them next, whether it's including them on her mountaintop or continuing to look out at the view alone.

I then tell the actors to begin to feel with their hands what they are sitting on, and encourage them to explore anything else, from wildflowers to rock, from dirt to grass. They should take in and trust whatever their senses of sight and touch create in their imaginations.

When place is firmly established, I have the actors rise and—still staying connected to their bodies—walk slowly to the edge of the cliff. If anyone suffers from fear of heights, she must deal with it and respond to it spontaneously. I ask them to breathe into the fear and not put up a defense or attitude of not being scared. Some actors will walk right to their imaginary edge with smiles on their faces. Others might take a good deal of time to walk there. Some might even crawl to the edge. Once there, I ask them to look down. "It's a sheer, straight drop-off of thousands of feet. How do you feel about that?"

Leaders—Watch Closely!

As the teacher, I must make sure if someone does panic that *she keeps breathing*. If you as a leader chose to use this exercise or any exercise that evokes a strong response from an individual who has acrophobia, claustrophobia, or any other strong psychological response, make sure she consciously recognizes and deepens her breath. Lead the actor away from the shallow breathing caused by fear, which can make the fear worse and sometimes uncontrollable. Instruct her not to ignore her emotions, but rather to take on the fear with deep breaths and allow the feelings to affect her body naturally.

If there is an actor who is obviously in uncontrollable distress, gently and individually bring her out of the exercise and back to the present. This kind of work is extremely powerful, but should never evoke a response that causes the actor to fear sensory work or flee the classroom.

Scenarios for the Exercise

From here, the instructor can take the actors through a variety of sensations. I might ask them if they can imagine what it would be like to leap off and soar through the air attached by a bungee cord. Or I might have them sit down on the edge and let their legs dangle over. "Don't forget your voices," I tell them. "Do you feel like shouting? Or are you enjoying the quiet?"

Sometimes I ask them to roll onto their stomachs, slowly slide off the flat rock they're on, and then climb their way down. They must look and feel for toeholds and finger grips. I will create obstacles in the descent such as a foot or hand slipping, a loose rock, a cramp—anything that will present a problem to solve. Acting is about creating questions, not playing answers.

This is a sensory task that can be used as an offstage preparation or even in a scene. The reaction to height can range from ecstasy and exhilaration to sheer terror and anxiety. It doesn't matter whether the actor has a positive or negative response to height. What matters is whether it appears real.

If an outsider were to walk into my classroom during this exercise (which is definitely not allowed, but let's pretend), he would totally believe in the reality of fifteen to twenty actors who are using the floor as the face of the mountains, rock-climbing down the side. Their fear or exhilaration would be apparent on their faces and in their bodies. Their subconscious minds have been tricked into believing what the imagination has created, and this message is translated through the body and voice. The audience then sees reality from the actor's point of view, even if this is all taking place on the floor of a rehearsal space.

Resolution

The resolution to the Height exercise—or any of the "adventures" created in the other sensory exercises—is very important. I always end an exercise with the actors reaching safety. Ending an exercise without a safe and satisfactory resolution or sense of closure will create uneasiness and a fear of the work. Give the actor a chance for a catharsis.

FLOATING

The Floating exercise is ideal for the actor to experience the lightness of body, comfort, joy, and pleasure of "floating on a cloud." Because humans cannot fly like Superman, this particular exercise requires the actors to suspend their disbelief. The senses will still be at work during this exercise, intertwined with the imagination.

Like the Height exercise, it starts after the initial relaxation, with actors laying on the floor on their backs. I then tell them that a breeze driving a cloud picks them gently off the ground, rocks them as if in a cradle, and takes them up over cars and people. They go up past apartment floors, high up over buildings, and float in the air with birds, planes, and clouds. They can travel over forests, water, land, mountains, or any topography they want to create.

Then I chose an obstacle, such as a storm that tosses them into air pockets, tornados that spin them around—whatever I choose to invent for their adventure. Sometimes I leave this up to the students themselves. After they sink in and really enjoy the exercise, they might go off on their own adventure, with my voice as a guide in only the most minimal of ways.

While I am not detailing this exercise the way I did Height, the same guidelines apply. As in any of the sensory exercises, the floating is done with a keen awareness of sound, smell, taste, sight, and touch. I am constantly asking things like, "What do you hear in the storm? What does the cloud feel like? Does the air smell different here?" I lead them through each part slowly and watch the actors to ensure that they feel comfortable with the exercise and are breathing properly.

Finally, I bring them back to earth gently and slowly, since this exercise is about feeling light and fun, not one about fear of heights or death. The descent can be into a sensual kind of object, like a vat of whipped cream or chocolate, a hay mound, or a pile of leaves. The floating exercise induces a lot of laughter and becomes a sensuous delight.

BEACH/SUNNING/WATER

When I have a lot of new students in my class, I often introduce them to the work with the Beach sensory exercise. It has served as a good icebreaker into the work since the sense memory of sunny beaches is very strong, there is less to fear than in the Height exercise, and it doesn't require a suspending of disbelief at the beginning like the Floating exercise.

Again, this exercise begins with the same premise as the other two previously described—students on the floor, lying on their backs. "Imagine yourself on a beach by a lake, ocean, sea, or river," I tell them. "Anywhere in the world you want to be—and you have no clothes on, not even a bathing suit." While I tell them they are sunbathing in the nude, the actors are clothed for the exercise and create nudity with their imagination. "It is a perfect day.

There is a blue sky, there are enough occasional white clouds for some protection, and a gentle breeze is blowing."

One Part at a Time

The actors begin by feeling the sun's rays on just a small area of their faces or bodies, whatever comes alive through suggestion. Once they feel something in that small area coming alive, I tell them to enlarge it to other body parts. I have them take time with the first part of this exercise to really let themselves fall into the relaxed state of laying in the sun.

I also remind them to keep in mind that in being nude, they are exposing parts of the body that are not used to exposure and therefore are more tender and delicate to the sun, and tell them to deal with the slight breeze that's in the air and what it does to their skin. "And remember," I say, "be aware of what you're laying on—sand, grass, earth—and whether you have a towel or mat underneath you."

After establishing the sun, I have them keep their eyes closed and work on sounds (there are many of them on the beach), smells (also plentiful), and taste. I add details, like a rivulet of sweat running down the middle of the back, chest, or thighs. "A fly or some other bug is crawling on you," I add. When the actors have had enough sun on their fronts, I have them deal with rolling over, being sweaty, getting comfortable on their stomachs, and kneading the sand under their towels or mats and getting sand off their bodies.

Look—A Nude Beach!

Once I feel there is a fulfillment of these sensory tasks, I have them sit up and work sensorially on what they see. They should include the other actors sunbathing nude (remember the premise at the beginning of the exercise) and have their thoughts about what they're seeing, thinking, and imagining while looking at others—as well as their own self-consciousness at being nude. I tell them to test themselves by gradually uncovering their imagined nakedness. "What does that feel like?" I ask.

I also strongly encourage the actors to let the shyness or embarrassment happen. "Don't block."

In the Water

I gradually get them to their feet and have them walk down to the water's edge. "Deal with what your bare feet are stepping on," I say. "Once by water's edge, put your feet in the water. Decide whether the bottom is sandy or pebbly, or full of rocks or mud." I have them gradually ease their bodies into the water, one section at a time, adjusting to the temperature and seeing how it affects each part of the body, keeping special awareness of sensitive areas.

The actors should take this process gradually so they experience the difference in each section of their bodies, as well as dealing with the ground beneath the water and the feel of it on their feet. I tell them to feel the coolness of the water as it gets higher and higher on their bodies, section by section.

"Don't splash yourselves before submerging. Feel the temperature. And as you acclimate to the water, be aware of what you see, like the sun on the water, of what you smell from the freshwater or saltwater, and of the distortion of sounds from where you are."

Once they are submerged, I ask them to suspend belief in not being able to breathe and tell them to let themselves down to large depths. I have them explore how their limbs and bodies move underwater. Finding a lithe, rhythmic movement is great fun for the actors. "Be aware of underwater life and have an adventure of your own choosing," I tell them. "See what it's like to touch things and experience the weightlessness and flow of your own movement." As in the Height exercise, if a student has a fear of water or of being submerged, she should not block it. She should let it happen. It's all part of the exercise. (But she still needs to breathe properly, of course.)

Scenarios

As in many of these sensory exercises, I will create an "event" within the exercise that the actors must experience. Often I'll have them become confused or lost as they swim through a sunken ship, or I'll have them encounter dangerous sea life. The tension will build, but I always end it with a final moment and resolution where the actors escape from danger. The actors are welcome to create their own underwater adventures, rather than my suggesting something.

I have the students gradually emerge from the depth and work their way back to shore. "Come slowly out of the water, returning to your towel. Feel what it's like to come out of the water," I tell them. "Is it chilly? Do you have a headache? What does your breath feel like? Your skin? Deal with drying off, even the feeling of overexertion, such as dizziness, headache, heart palpitations, or exhaustion, as well as the comfort of being on shore again."

ANIMAL EXERCISES

Animal simulation is of tremendous importance, especially in its uses for character work. I include all creatures in the aviary (bird) world as well as the reptilian and mammal worlds when I speak of "animal work." I have seen many actors add rich character life by identifying their characters—their body language, postures and even personalities—with animals. Animal work is especially helpful for actors when they are really stuck in their heads and cannot connect to their bodies. It is wonderful for period plays, as it can really stimulate the imagination.

For the more in-depth animal work required for the Spoon River exercise or character work, the best resource is the zoo. Hours should be spent observing the one animal chosen for that character.

But I have used an Animal exercise for the classroom group exercise as well. For the sake of a group exercise, I ask the actors to pick animals they're familiar with. I suggest they try to get beyond dogs and cats, but to choose an animal they can picture clearly in their minds. If they choose a dog or a cat, I want them to be very specific about the breed, color, size, and temperament of that pet—to really have a sense of the animal.

The students all start out laying on the floor on their backs after the relaxation exercise as I lead them through the process, but they rapidly end up standing or sitting.

Because the actors don't have the opportunity for the kind of observation possible from a zoo trip, they have to rely on their memories and imaginations. I have them explore things slowly and deliberately—the movements, the postures, and the animal's center of gravity. I ask that they explore each part of their bodies, how the parts feel, what the posture is like, etc. Once they have found the specifics of the animal, I let them move around to smell, listen, taste, touch, and see.

Center the Animal

A key aspect of developing a character based on animal work is to decide where the animal's movement gravitates from and what defines its character— what acting coach Michael Chekhov calls the "psychological center."[1] For example, the panther's center of movement is in its pelvis, and the big cat's limbs smoothly and languidly move from this spot. An actor would mimic this center when doing this exercise.

Once the center is established, the actor can work on other movement characteristics—how it walks, swishes the tail, sits or lays down, jumps, runs, even how it stares down its prey. But the center must first be established before the other movements can be explored. When used in character work, this psychological center will define and ground a character in the actor's body.

---

[1] Michael Chekhov, *To the Actor: On the Technique of Acting* (New York: Routledge, 2002).

Once the actors have discovered their animal's psychological centers and explored some minimal movement, I then like to put all the "animals" into imaginary cages at the zoo. I'll ask them how it feels to have these boundaries—to see the bars or to feel the limitations of their cage.

It's at this point that I remind the students to add the sounds the animals make. I tell them to investigate—without straining or hurting their voices—whether they can find the same vocal placement as their animal. If they don't know the sound of their animal, I tell them to project a sound for it.

Then the adventure starts. After establishing their limited surroundings, I will create an event to cause interaction and chaos, something like someone pulling a switch to spring all the doors to the cages open. The actors, as their chosen animals, are then free to roam outside their individual cages, to explore their newly found freedom and encounter each other. They should sniff, listen, taste (with gentle bites), closely look, and touch the other animals.

For scene work, this animal sound exploration helps an actor find a character's voice. In a group exercise, it leads to a very noisy classroom! Anyone who leads this exercise is going to have quite a menagerie to deal with as a teacher, and must monitor the group carefully so that no one gets hurt if some roughhousing breaks out. And as in all the exercises, upon conclusion, I encourage the actors to reflect on their sensory experiences and inner life of images and events.

✳ ✳ ✳

THE SNOW LEOPARD

I once had to play a woman who was a child-abuse survivor. Playing to the victim side of her biography was one-dimensional and uninteresting, and as Terry says, "You can't play a negative." As I studied the character, I decided she had a strong sense of dignity and defiance in spite of her trauma.

I decided to take a trip to the Bronx Zoo and was immediately captivated by a particular snow leopard. Her mate was asleep at the back of the cage, but she approached me and looked me straight in the eye, pacing back and forth and breathing with low-pitched guttural noises. I didn't perceive aggression, but rather the need to connect and communicate, and her lonely isolation, graceful in her acceptance of imprisonment but far from a broken spirit.

Mesmerized, I took what I had observed home and worked with the snow leopard as I had in the Spoon River exercise. I moved as the leopard, motivated and propelled forward from my pelvic center. If I needed to go the opposite direction, I took a U-turn rather than backing up, and I made low, guttural sounds that almost became sighs. Using this center of movement as a psychological center shifted my perspective, and I somehow felt much more introverted.

When I applied the same psychological center to my character, I moved elegantly but deliberately from the same pelvic power-center, and spoke with a low-pitched, detached voice. When I sat, it was always sideways, with my torso leaning slightly forward and my hands straight in front on the chair, similar to how I had seen the leopard sit. The result was a surprisingly complicated woman who was described as sexual, sensitive, world-weary, aggressive, isolated, protective, and deceptively cold and calculating. It was amazing what a nuanced and layered performance was achieved through one simple animal exercise.

—Stephanie Wang

*　*　*

MEAL

The Meal sensory exercise requires hard chairs for the students. I have them sit with their feet on the floor, their palms laying on their thighs and turned up, or their arms hanging at their sides. The body should be as open as possible. I tell them to feel the chair against the back of their thighs, buttocks, and backs. "Feel your clothes against your bodies, your underwear against the skin."

Once they are properly relaxed, it's time to feast. "Now, let's have a five-course meal of your favorite foods and drinks," I say, "and someone else is paying for it!"

I start by having them, with their senses, recreate a drink—wine, beer, cocktail, or soda. "Be aware of the touch of the imaginary glass," I say. "Avoid pantomime. Look for a feel of the glass with a finger. Explore picking it up, the weight, the color of the liquid. Is there a sound from it, from ice cubes? Be aware of smell, the taste on your lips, in your mouth, the liquid going down your throat."

I then have them proceed to the first course of their choice. If it's a salad, they must deal with the dressing—the smells and the tastes. Then I work them through an appetizer prior to the main course. Although this is mainly an exercise designed for smell and taste, attention must also be paid to sight and touch. Most likely, there will be little to do with listening.

At this point, the actors' favorite meals are presented to them. I tell them that as they add each course, they should take time to explore the aroma and, especially, the tastes and textures. "Feel them on your tongue and palette, in your throat," I tell them. "Find all the succulence you can pull out of the vegetables, meat, potato, and the sauces that accompany the serving." After each course, I have the actors clear their palates with an aperitif.

Once they've taken a good deal of time with the main course, I have them top the meal with a favorite dessert. "Dive into the whipped cream, the sugar, and all the exquisite tastes." But I don't stop them there. "Top the dessert with coffee, just the way you like it . . . or maybe a brandy or cognac? Indulge yourselves!"

Their imaginary meal comes from a posh restaurant, after all, and will not cost them a cent, nor will they gain a pound. The students, if they're working well, will probably be salivating and, once it's over, have quite an appetite. I've always wondered how many of my students break out their credit cards after class and treat themselves to the meal they imagined.

CAVE

The actors, in their imaginations, start out all alone standing in front of an entrance to a cave. As in all these exercises, I have the actors be aware of what they are standing on and what surrounds the hole in front of them. I have them touch the rock, moss, or whatever objects are in front of this cave. Then I have them take a good look at the entrance. "How far does any light extend into the cave? Is there any breeze or smell emanating from within?" I tell them that they have a helmet on with a light attached, or a flashlight in their hands, and in they go for a spelunk.

"Be sensitive to touching the cave wall," I say. "Is it damp? Cold? Slimy? How narrow is it? How high is the ceiling?"

If an individual actor is claustrophobic, I tell her to allow it in her experience. But just as in the Height exercise, the teacher must watch for students who can become dangerously fearful of the sensory experience. The instructor must make sure that a claustrophobic student takes deep breaths rather than shallow ones. If the experience becomes too much and the student approaches uncontrollable distress, lead the student into the present and out of the exercise in the same manner I described earlier.

Through the Rabbit Hole

As the students journey their way in, the passage becomes narrow. I tell them that they have to crawl. Eventually the can barely get their heads and shoulders through, and they risk the chance of getting stuck. As they slowly progress through the tunnel, they move into a giant chamber filled with stalactites and stalagmites. With the helmet-mounted lamp or flashlight, they flash around to see what they can see.

"What sounds and smells are here?" I ask. "What is the taste on your lips and in your mouth?" I always add bats—thousands of them—hanging from the ceiling or darting around. I ask the students to breathe in the smell of bat dung.

Then it's time to leave the chamber, and I tell the students to pick one of several alternative routes. They must choose one, and they may have to get down onto the cave floor and crawl. "Feel the moisture or dampness on your hands and face," I say. "It's also seeping through your clothes."

In the Black, and Other Variations

"Suddenly your light goes out and you are in pitch darkness," I tell them. "You are now left to find your way out in the dark. Should you go forward, or try to find your way back?"

One of my favorite adventures is for the actors to suddenly hear water and come upon a drop-off that would have caused them to fall into a swirling underground river many feet down. They are then forced to back up, retrace their steps, and experience feeling lost and afraid for their lives as they try to find their way out. I remind them to see what tastes and feelings they have in their mouths and throats, and have them deal with getting stuck in the tunnel and banging their heads or scraping their backs.

In another variation I'll add eerie cave-crawlers. "You look up and the ceiling is covered with glowworms." I let them decide what their reaction to this will be—fascination, horror, or something in between. Sometimes I add an entire group of scurrying rats.

Finally, I tell them that they see a small light in the far distance. I create more obstacles to overcome in the journey to get to it—puddles, rocks, bones. "You hope it's a big enough hole for you to fit through," I say.

✣   ✣   ✣

ALONE IN A CAVE

I hate cramped spaces and was dreading this exercise, but once Terry started the exercise, I gritted my teeth and forged ahead. Turns out it was one of the most beneficial group exercises I did. With the Cave exercise, I explored what affect a dark, damp, confined atmosphere would have on me. In my imagination, I truly felt a sense of solitude—alone, with no light, multiple cuts and wounds, in a crevice so small that lying on my belly, I could only move an inch at a time.

The multitude of obstacles and the clearly defined goal—surviving—made all the choices I made very specific and detailed. When the exercise was over, I was physically spent but mentally charged, since I had made so many discoveries with my work.

I was quickly able to put the Cave exercise to use in a play. My character was a reclusive shut-in who stood, for the entire first act, on a pile of phone books with a noose around his neck, just waiting to jump. The experience of solitude, suffocation, and survival from the Cave transferred into the role rather well, in both the immediate circumstances of the character and the solitude in his everyday life, and I was able to give the character additional depth.

—Jason Weiss

✣   ✣   ✣

When the students reach it, the hole is rather small. "You've got to crawl up and chip your way out," I'll say. "It's not easy." Additional obstacles like rocks or tree branches will hinder their progress, but eventually the hole is big enough to crawl through.

"Once out, you find yourself high up, stranded on a cliff or knoll. Down below you is a riverbed with a very swift current." The students have gone from having to face claustrophobic circumstances to a situation that can spark a fear of heights.

But by this time, they've been though enough for the day. I tell them there's a path there that will lead them to safety. "Catch your breath and think about the sensory things that came alive in the cave." Before I have them start to head down the cliff, I have them examine themselves. "Check and see if you're all muddy, if you're cut or bruised, and what it is like to have your life safely back."

MIXED SOUND/SMELL

Now that I've explained how these sensory exercises are led, it's easy to create a number of different scenarios and settings that can stimulate the imagination. These exercises don't necessarily need to be led by someone. An actor can do this work on her own. I suggest sitting on a hard chair instead of on the floor, since it keeps the imagination more alert after the relaxation process.

Suggestions:
- A vacation place in the mountains
- A winter day in the woods
- A ski lodge around the fireplace at night
- A hike in the desert mountains
- A spring rain at night and the smell after the rain
- A garden party or wedding
- A hot, muggy, summer day in a large city like New York

The teacher can add a number of times and places for other smells and sounds to this list, but this gives an actor a good starting place. While many of my students say that the individual exercise work in Part III is the cornerstone of my advanced acting class, the sensory group exercises are a key component. I do group work once a month to bring even the most advanced actors back to the core essence of the concentrated work and the greatest tools they have as actors: their five senses.

6 PERSONAL SENSORY EXERCISES

While most of the previous exercises that explored the senses were somewhat general, it can be very useful to work on exercises that relate to our pasts and personal experiences. The following exercises emphasize our memories of places, people, and situations that were important to us.

BABY EXERCISE

This is an opportunity for the actors to explore a time when they were dependent on their senses for basic survival—and dependent on the adults who had to tend to their every need. All inhibitions are dropped when the actors return to being babies. It's amazing what happens when we are stripped of words and must communicate with sounds and tactile awareness.

The exercise is performed totally on the floor after the initial relaxation. It begins with each actor going back to a time when he was a year old or younger. "Please do not imitate a baby," I tell the actors. "Find your own baby sense memory."

I have them start to examine and explore from their toes to their heads— the smallness of toes and fingers, the feeling of their torsos, and the sense of their bodies in general. I have them touch their ears, mouth, nose, and nasal passages—even their genital area (on the outside of their clothing).

The students should stay away from making sounds at this point. Trying to add sound too soon in the exercises tends to lead the students into an "idea" of indicative behavior rather than really "living" as a baby. The initial exploration takes time. Once the actors have found truthful and organic inner lives in physical behavior, I lead them through the process of exploring their surroundings.

For this exercise, I will describe the process step by step. Having an outline is a good preparation for any leader, especially the first couple of times you are working with an exercise.

- With your eyes closed, experience being in a crib at night, asleep.

- Wake up in the night and open your eyes. Explore the shadows and filters of light in the room. Move onto your back, side, or stomach if you want.

- Hear the sounds in the room. Are you alone, or sharing a room? What kind of house or apartment sounds do you hear at night? Any outside sounds, from the street, etc.?

- Smell the scents in the room.

- See what taste is on your lips or in your mouth.

- Touch the things around you—a blanket, stuffed animal, toy attached to bed, bars of the crib, or other things.

After taking them through those sensory steps, I then instruct them to go back to sleep. Once they are settled, I tell them to come awake by wetting themselves or soiling their diapers, and instruct them in these steps:

- Now add sound to get attention. No one's coming. Turn up the decibel level. You are uncomfortable! You must get attention!

- Finally someone comes. Choose whether it's Mom or Dad. Feel them picking you up, and sense their smells, the feel of their robe, and any sense memory about them that you have.

- Have them change your diaper. Feel what it's like to be placed on a changing table and have the adult take the soiled diaper off, clean you up, put on cream and talc, and re-diaper you. Pretend it's an old-fashioned diaper and get stuck with a safety pin.

- Allow the experience of having Mom or Dad put your clothing back on, and finally pick you up and tuck you safely and snugly back into bed. What does this feel like compared to before the diaper was changed? Fade back into relaxation with this feeling.

The next step is early morning. The students should hear sounds of a household awakening, such as an alarm clock and people moving around, and be led through the steps of an early morning:

- Be aware of the room getting lighter, what you see outside the window, shadows on the wall.

- What smells are there? Of cooking? A parent comes to get you—is there a smell to Mom or Dad in the early morning? Breath, aftershave, coffee, etc.?

- Mom or Dad carries you into another room. Everything is white, and you are being undressed and put into a warm tub. Deal with the feeling of the water and being bathed with a big sponge and baby soap. He or she plays with you as you're sitting in your bassinette, sponging you, soaping you, and rinsing you off.

- Once out of the bath, Mom or Dad puts some talc on your body. As you're lying on your back, the parent puts his or her lips against your stomach and then blows, a big sound that tickles and makes noise on your belly. Maybe this parent even rolls you over on your belly, or blows "flutter kisses." Really let yourself giggle and play.

Once these babes have been dried and dressed, I have them being carried into the kitchen, and go through similar steps, encouraging them to be specific with the details. I have them recreate being fed baby food—the taste, the texture, and the smell. This is a great taste exercise for encouraging physical freedom.

I conclude the exercise by turning all the actors loose—as one-year-olds—to crawl around and explore each other in a sensorial manner. I encourage them to not just settle for sounds, but put more focus on tastes, smells, and touch.

AGE EXERCISE

We've all seen actors playing roles that are years different from their actual ages—older actors playing characters who are decades younger, or younger actors doing a fantastic job playing characters much older than themselves. Who could forget Orson Welles as Citizen Kane? Some plays progress over years of time—sometimes decades—and actors are required to make a jump from being a teenager to a middle-aged adult to a grandparent. How can actors be truthful in their choices and physicality other than through processing with their imagination how age will change them?

I have found that an important method is an Age sensory exercise. Simply thinking how a character would be at a younger or older age often leads to clichéd or unrealistic behavior. But using the imagination in a sensory exercise and observing the work closely can keep the character work for a play or movie honest and help an actor to stop indicated behavior immediately.

After concluding our physical warm-up and the final stretching out on the floor described earlier, I ask the actors to slowly get on their feet while staying in their bodies and not jumping up to their heads.

When all actors are standing, I ask them to place an imaginary full-length mirror in front of themselves. I always use an imaginary mirror because it gives the imagination much more to work from than a real mirror. In an actual mirror, the image of the actor at the current age is reflected back. In an imaginary mirror, anything is possible.

Terrible Twos

I tell them to begin by seeing themselves as two-year-olds. "Don't force an idea," I tell them. "Feel that your body is that small. Look at how your Mom or Dad dressed you. Feel the clothes. Are you skinny? Chubby? What is your hair color? Is it long or short?"

I tell them to see any other features as they touch and explore what the imaginary mirror is telling them. I don't want them to think the exercise, but to explore in their bodies what the body has retained as a sense memory.

Childhood

I have them jump from age two to five and do this age in a similar manner. Just as when they were two, the actors should look at their hair, their bodies, and their clothing. How long is their hair? Do they have pigtails? Glasses? Is there a particular way their parents combed or styled their hair? What outfit is their favorite? Which is the one they hate, but they get dressed in anyway?

Puberty

Next is the beginning of puberty. Sometimes I have the actors pretend they're naked for the puberty stage. "Look at the changes occurring in your body," I say. "Pimples, budding breasts, the beginning of pubic hair . . ." They examine the body for changes such as loss of baby fat, accumulated scars, shape of brows, type of hairstyle, etc. Then I tell them to add clothes using their sense memory to see how they were dressed as a preadolescent and what kind of clothes they picked for themselves.

Teenagers

I then work up to the teen years and ask them to observe themselves at anywhere from sixteen to eighteen. They should be observing themselves in high school, what they looked like for big events like the prom. Then I proceed to college and college graduation, using the same observation steps I described for the younger ages.

Through the Ages

Then I have the actors jump from college to a variety of different ages: thirty, forty, sixty, seventy, eighty, or perhaps ninety. Most acting students will be under these ages, but I ask them to use their creative as-if without caricaturing. I take lots of time with each decade so the students have the ability to really use their imaginations to see the clothing, the gray hair, and the wrinkles, and to feel the ages in their bodies. By the end of the exercise, the power of imagination will have given the students a much more natural idea of themselves and their bodies at different ages.

THE PLACE EXERCISE (ROOM/CLOSET/CHEST/ATTIC/BASEMENT)

Special places from childhood make for great sensory exploration. I have found that this exercise is one of the best resources for sense memory and Emotional Recall. It demonstrates very clearly how an actor's imagination is triggered by sense memory. The actor in this exercise explores a favorite bedroom closet, a chest, or a place in the basement or attic where his playthings and clothes were stored when he was a child, where he felt safe from the outside world.

I have the actors begin by sitting in chairs or on the floor after the initial relaxation, closing their eyes, and individually selecting a place from their childhood. "Start outside a door or entranceway of a favorite room or cubbyhole from your past," I say. "This could be a passageway, corridor, attic, basement, or any place that had significance to you as a child."

Sometimes there might be childhood trauma in an actor's past. The leader should emphasize that this place the actors are going is where they felt safe, not where they were frightened in a psychologically damaging way.

Once the actors have had enough time to get a few mental images, I have them approach the door to the closet, the lid of a chest, or the entry to the attic or basement—whatever opening would be most appropriate. The actors physically drop back into their spaces. "See with your mind's eye what you might be wearing at that age. Observe the smells, sounds, sights around you. What time of the day do you like to be here? Do you like this space during one season more than another?"

Then I have them try to feel the handle, knob, or whatever they are opening to get into the space. "Don't forget, you are a child," I'll say. "Check the weight of the door—is it heavy? Does it make a sound?"

Once the door or lid is open, I instruct the actors to let themselves inside their space and begin touching and exploring. They should use their other senses to help bring the sense memory moments alive. "If you're walking, do your feet make a sound on the floor? What kind of flooring is it? Look at it. Reach down and touch it."

After they've explored the floor, I ask them to see the rest of the room. "Look around. What do you see directly in front of you? What about the ceiling? Windows? Look at the furniture, the walls. And the smells—what do you smell here? Is this room cleaned often? Or is it musty and stale? Smells from an open window? Is it night or day?"

When the ambiance is established, I have the actors move around in the room or space. I have them find objects and discover items they haven't seen for years. Taste is a powerful tool and should be explored, even though they might not ever have put these objects in their mouths in real life. "Touch the objects to your cheek. Feel the texture and weight. Shake it—does it make any kind of sound?"

Variations

Once the actors feel comfortable in their private spaces, I will often do an improvisation by telling them that someone has just come into their spaces and is watching them. "Have the person cross over to you. Perhaps he has a surprise for you in one of his hands, or he wants to talk to you." Other times, I'll send in imaginary animals and let them play. In conclusion, I have the actors say goodbye to the person or pet.

The key to this exercise is for the actors to let the memories (inner life) pour forth as they continue to deepen the exploration. They should allow themselves to feel any feelings that happen to be there. This kind of work is powerful stuff, but unless their emotional response is so great that it overwhelms the actors, they should go on with the work and discover their pasts through these objects and let themselves indulge.

As with all my sensory exercises, there are different variations that can be used. One alteration is to have the actor finish the exploration and start to leave the room, but just before he leaves, he turns for one last look . . . and runs back and does something he was absolutely forbidden to do. But what began as secret glee can turn sour as I bring in someone to reprimand him for what he is doing.

A further variation is to have the actor go someplace he's not allowed to go or explore a hiding place and something he was not supposed to have hidden in that place. I'll let him get lost in the exploration of this place or object, and when he's thoroughly involved, I'll suggest that someone has just walked in and caught him.

I always tell my students not to underestimate the power of this exercise. I once did it with an actor from California who was new to New York. From his choices, I deducted that he had grown up on a beach and was a dedicated surfer. He became totally involved in recreating his California room and the sound and smells of the surf outside. The exercise was a success . . . but he never returned to class. Several sessions later I asked what had happened to him, and his roommate informed me that he had returned to California.

FACE

The Face exercise is a personalization or endowment exercise. I think it is a terrific tool to use for homework and can be projected onto an actor you are working with. For example, an actor might have a script that indicates an intense relationship with her mother, father, brother, sister, lover, or friend. In the best of all possible worlds, the actors should be able to take the time and effort to give each other exactly what they need. But often in a rehearsal period, there isn't that time. The actor enters the rehearsal not knowing his fellow actor from Adam and asks himself, "How do I get my motor running to create this?"

A resourceful actor might think of someone whom he had a similar relationship with in his life. When he meets his acting partner, he sees if there's anything of that person in the actor's face, manner, movement, or way of speaking. It can help his motor to start running and set him on the path with images and events to develop the needed intensity.

Sometimes there isn't anything familiar in the other actor, or one is playing opposite a particular actor who is like looking into a house with no one living in it. This is when the Face exercise can be used as a total substitution or endowment. To do this, the actor would find something in his non-responsive partner (feature, mannerism, etc.), that reminds him of his "substitution" and build the endowment upon that.

I encourage my students to use a face from the past, not the present. It's usually not a good idea to use people who are in an actor's daily life for exercises like this, since the work can become too personally and emotionally charged. Issues may come up, and then the acting exercise starts to resemble therapy.

After being properly warmed up, the students start by sitting in chairs with an empty chair in front of them. They allow faces from the past to flash in front of them, people with whom they had a long-term relationship but who are no longer in their daily lives.

Many different individuals may come to mind for the actors. I tell them to let those individuals be present in the empty chair in front of them. They should start this process generally. "Don't force your concentration," I say. "Let your consciousness just free-associate."

The Hair and Forehead

Typically, three or four faces will come alive for the actor. "See their hair, the cut or styling, or the lack of hair, if that's the case." Each actor can observe as many sensory details as will help to create the heads of hair on their chosen people.

I have them bring the faces in close to theirs so that there is no shoulder tension when reaching out. "Let your finger run through the hair. What do you feel? Is the hair curly or straight, dry or oily? What does it feel like against your face? What does it smell like? Can you remember a shampoo scent? Or hair oil?" I even have them try taste.

As all these sensory questions are being pursued, the actor may have zeroed in on one face, or may still be exploring several different ones. It's okay at this point if the faces change, as long as the actor is still free-associating and not trying to force his mind toward one face.

I have them move from the hair to the forehead. "Was it a low or a high forehead? A receding hairline, or a very low one?" The actors look, touch the skin, and observe frown lines, scars, freckles, or other marks to recreate the foreheads.

The Eyes

At this point, we move to the eyes. It's at this point that the actor should zero in on just one person and stay with that one person for the remainder of the exercise.

The actors move down the face to the top of the eyes and see, touch, and explore the eyebrows. "Are they slim, bushy, pointed?" Next they move to the upper eyelid, lashes, and fold of the lid. The eyes of the person are very important—probably the most important detail on the face. The actor typically experiences a lot of emotional life by looking at the eyes.

"See the eyes looking at you," I tell them. "Look at the color, the depth, and the white around the pupil." But there is more than physical features in people's eyes. "See what the eyes tell you about the person. Were they sad, happy, cold, or peaceful? What insight can you gain to the person by looking at the eyes?" I have them continue to observe the pockets beneath the eyes and see if they're dark, tired, or fresh. "Are there crow's feet?"

The Face in Total

I have them move next to the nose. "What kind of nose is it? What shape? Size?" I tell them to touch it if they like and observe specific details to define the nose and get a sense memory of it.

Once there has been enough work done on the nose, I have them move on to the rest of the face. "Are the cheeks fleshy and full, or thin and drawn? What is the shape of the upper lip? Any hair or peach fuzz? Is it thin or sensual?"

Then they move onto the mouth, starting with the teeth and observing whether they are crooked or straight, what the color is, whether they were gapped or even bucktoothed. From there, I have them see the lips and the shape of the mouth in general, seeing what the shape told the actor about the person. "Feel the mouth on yours," I say. "The person's taste, the scent of their breath. Feel their lips on your cheek."

After I have the actors proceed to the chin, I ask them to first touch the favorite part of their person's face, and then to touch the least favorite.

The Moody Face

Now the actor has really created the person, first through relaxation and then through the thorough sensory work on the face. It's time for those faces to start emoting. I ask the actors to see the faces in many moods. If they haven't ever seen the person's face in a particular mood, I tell them to imagine they have. The exercise will really catapult the actors' imaginations and subconscious.

A very important component of this exercise is the spontaneity of the moods. I tell the actors to see the following moods as if for the first time. For example, even if an actor has seen his brother's smirk a thousand times, he must react as if it's the first so he is not playing back a set attitude. It must all be first-time discovery.

We now move forward quickly through mood swings from the faces the actors have created, with me suggesting the following:

- Face is smiling, breaking into a huge grin, laughing. You are both sharing an enormous moment of joy and laughter.

- Face becomes serious, solemn, looks very grouchy and judgmental.

- Face becomes shy, bashful, really embarrassed.

- Face becomes frightened, scared, really terrified.

- Face becomes proud, beaming, bursting open with pride.

- Face becomes cold, distant, shutting you out, treating you like you don't exist, like you're an idiot.

- Face becomes soft, tender, very loving, sexual.

- Face becomes angry, yelling, really raging. The person starts to hit at you with his hands, his belt, or another object. You have never seen him this crazy or angry.

- Face has a moment of guilty realization—the person realizes what damage has been done by the rage and the face becomes mortified. He grabs you to hug you. He is crying and terribly sorry, pleading for your forgiveness.

At this point, the actor can start talking to the face, saying anything he wants to say.

Next, I have the students tell the person something they've always wanted to say but never have. Then I have them share a secret with the person. "The secret is something you've never told them," I say. "Maybe you've never told anyone. Don't just blurt it out, but work up to it."

The Monologue

I have them finish by speaking an acting monologue from their repertoires to the chosen person. The student must adjust the words to the person he is talking to as a result of the work done throughout the exercise. He must give up any previous meaning of the monologue and his former way of speaking it, and adjust to what he wants to give or get from the person in front of him.

I remind the students to stay with what they want to give or get from the person by speaking the monologue. In the Spoon River exercise in Part III, I'll go into greater detail about the importance and usage of answering the question, "What do you want to give or get from this person?" The most important aspect is that the students remember to mentally answer the "give or get" question and incorporate it.

I finish the exercise by having the students say goodbye. "You've got to get into your car, or to catch a bus, plane, or train," I say. "You've got to say goodbye." Sometimes the goodbyes are tearful; other times, they are joyful or peaceful. But they are always full of emotion.

SHOWER

While normally the shower exercise should fit in with the general sensory exercises, I categorize it with the personal sensory exercises because of the personal nature of nudity. It is an extremely important exercise for any actor, and one of a delicate nature.

Nudity—Not for Nudity's Sake

Film and stage actors are often asked to work with their bodies in various stages of undress and to do many daring and risk-taking things. A big paycheck doesn't suddenly make it easier to be nude or partly nude in front of an audience or film crew. And if asked, actors cannot try to pretend they are comfortable when they aren't. The audience will sense the discomfort; the camera will see it.

If an actor agrees to a role that requires nudity, he needs to be prepared to take some time investigating his reactions. The most important item is that he honors and validates his own personal feelings. I will go into more detail about this when I discuss the Private Moment exercise, but the Shower exercise is a good introduction to this concept. I've debated whether to include this exercise because I do not want it to be misinterpreted, so I hope the readers will please read carefully and see it as a constructive exercise and not voyeurism on the teacher's part.

The Shower exercise as I do it is a group exercise. Outside of myself, there are no onlookers. The guidelines allow the actors three choices in executing the sensory task of taking a shower. They can do it in bathing suits, in their underwear, or nude, as they choose. The important aspect, as in all the work, is that they honor their feelings. If some actors, for whatever reason, choose not to participate, they simply come to class after the exercise is completed.

After the initial relaxation, I have the actors begin by turning on the taps of the bathtub. This must be done with an awareness of touch—to the density and temperature of the water, the coolness of the tub, and even the feel of the shower knobs. Once the desired water mix is reached, the actors begin by slowly taking off their outer clothes and dealing with any feelings that are stirring about that gradual exposure.

The actors are then in their bathing suit, underwear, or naked. Those in bathing suits or underwear are to deal with the exercise as though they were naked. If an actor chooses to be naked, he must deal with taking off all underclothes. It is especially important at this point for the actors to check in with themselves and their feelings. "Don't just grit your teeth and do it," I say to them. There is no value in that, in suppressing the feelings. This exercise is about exploring and validating.

I then lead them through taking a shower. "Step into the shower, feel the water on your chest, shoulders, or back," I say. "Deal with the temperature, velocity, and the spray hitting different parts of your body. Shampoo and rinse your hair, and soap up the body either with a loofah, washcloth, sponge, or hand."

Touch isn't the only sense to be aware of when taking an imaginary shower. "Deal with smells of shampoo, soap. Be aware of the tastes, water in your mouth, even getting some soap in your eye or mouth." Nor should some parts of the body be ignored—this shower should be as realistic as possible. "Soap all over, washing private parts too." When they're done with that, I have them rinse off thoroughly, perhaps turning the water cooler if that's a natural habit.

But the exercise doesn't stop there. "Stepping out of the shower, towel down with an imagined big, warm, fluffy towel," I say. "Do you apply talc or any skin lotion? Remember to take in the smells. Enjoy and be nice to your body."

Once they're done, I have them get dressed, pretending they are putting on fresh underwear (the smell and feel) and freshly pressed clothes. Actors come out of this exercise feeling the freshness of just having taken a shower.

Note for Instructors

Make sure you are working with a mature group of actors in this exercise. They should not only feel safe and secure in your classroom and with each other, but also know and validate their own personal limits. Don't do this if you have new people to the class, no matter how advanced they might be, since bringing them in violates the trust from the established students.

And never have anyone besides you as an observer—not even fellow actors who choose not to actually do the exercise. It's not fair to the actors. Eventually they might have to get used to an audience or a camera crew, but this exercise is about *exploring* that possibility, not recreating it. My suggestion is that any instructor saves it for the end an established stretch of work—maybe a year or even more—when trust and security in the class has been established.

7 PHYSICAL-CONDITION EXERCISES

Although the following physical-condition exercises deal with sensory work, there is a key difference: Emphasis is placed on remembered body sensations and responses rather than sensory stimulations from outside the body. These exercises are extremely valuable, considering the number of plays and screenplays where the writer calls for a character to have a physical condition.

Characters are often in pain, feel cold, or are overheated, drunk, or under the influence of a narcotic. Sometimes they have a physical disability—a broken limb or a missing arm or leg—or they are affected by blindness, deafness, or a speech impediment, to name a few. The actor's job is to create the condition and then play what the character is doing about it.

A physical condition can also help define the emotional life of a character. An actor could analyze a script that doesn't call for a physical condition for her character and add one, such as, "She seems so testy all the time; it's as if she's got a migraine." I would encourage this actor to explore this, and once the migraine is established, then play what the character is doing about the migraine. This leads to a much richer character life than someone who is simply mean. "Remember, in your own life, when you experience a physical condition, it gives you a *psychological* and *emotional* state, as well as a physical one."

I will go into more detail about how to fully utilize a physical condition in the A.C.T. (Action/Condition/Telephone Call) exercise and scene work sections. For now, let's get started with how I use them in a group setting.

For all the physical-condition exercises, I have the actors sit in hard-back chairs after the required relaxation warm-up. I insist that the actors begin by acclimatizing to the chairs. Once the exploration part of the exercises starts, I have the actors begin working with the right toes and then up through the rest of the body. Both the instructor leading and the actors exploring need to be specific with body parts. For example, rather than, "I feel ill," it's, "I feel a sharp pain in my lower torso that makes me want to curl up into a ball."

Before starting, I explain to the students to not make it a "thinking" exercise, but a *feeling* and *exploring* piece of work. Their actions and responses should come from a reality that is based on how they actually feel, not from how they think they should look when feeling that way.

AN ACTOR'S SECRET

A physical condition can add a layer to a scene by having the actors pretend to have an obvious physical condition. Then I take the physical condition work a step further—I instruct them to "hide" or "internalize" the physical condition. An audience wouldn't see that the character is drunk, but rather that there was a *psychological* state that was different and interesting. The physical condition would be the actor's secret, a tool to produce the desired emotional effect.

The emotions elicited from the physical conditions can be surprising. I've seen students sob during the Heat exercise and laugh from the Cold exercise below, and vice versa. Their emotional reaction was based on their personal experiences and persona. As I will emphasize in the scene work section, if a character has a physical state or condition, the actor must work on creating it with the imagination and not skip over the prep work. That condition may be the very thing that motivates or drives the character.

Because I went into great detail with the sensory work section on how I lead the students through each part of the exercise, I will only describe each different physical-condition exercise with the necessary detail. But both the students and the leader need to remember the guidelines: Take each section slowly until a sense of reality is established, keep the breath low and centered in the body, and never continue with an exercise if it starts to become dangerous.

I also find it helpful for the actors to have memorized monologues to speak at the end of the physical-condition exercise. The students should be told ahead of time to have one memorized.

COLD

Once the students are seated comfortably, with their eyes closed, I put them in a specific place. "You are outside," I say to them. "It is well below freezing. You are wearing what you presently have on." This is an especially interesting exercise to use in the summertime, when students arrive in shorts and tank tops or light shirts. "Explore what your toes feel like inside your shoes and stockings or sandals."

Often the students will feel their feet as immediately frozen. "Move the toes slowly, keep a circulation of blood and breath getting down to the toes," I tell them. "If they are getting numb with the cold, keep them moving to avoid frostbite. Move the foot and ankle. See what it feels like when you to try to rotate the right foot." I want them to not only feel the cold, but also their footwear. "How does the sock feel against the ankle?"

Once they've explored the right foot with sensory questions, I have them move to the shin and calf. "Are your pants sticking to your leg? What is the feeling in the kneecap and going up into the right thigh? What is it like to raise the leg?"

"Now feel the cold in the cheek of your right buttock, in your private parts." I then have the cold go down the left side. "Feel the cold in the left cheek of your buttocks, and then down your left leg." I have them work with the cold going down the left side as it came up the right side—one section at a time, from the left buttock to the thigh, kneecap, calf, shin, ankle, foot, and toes.

As I lead the cold through the body, I remind the students to stay aware of inner organs, especially the heart and lungs. "Does it feel different to breathe? What does your heart feel like?" I remind them to check into the feeling in their bladders and kidneys as well.

I then have them work gradually up the torso, section by section, and down one arm to the fingers, and then down the other arm. I remind them to pay special attention to the chest area. "Is there tension in the back? Are your nipples erect from the cold? What do the tips of your fingers feel like?"

The cold is especially bad, even deadly. "The wind is howling. What does it feel like on your neck? Your lips and teeth? What is it like to breathe in this cold? Are your nostrils constricting from the cold? Feel your face—is there snot frozen on your upper lip? What about the other parts of your face—icicles on your lashes and brows? What does your forehead feel like? Your ears? Your hair and the top of your head?" But touch isn't the only sense utilized in the cold. "Be aware of the smell and taste of the cold, and the sounds."

*   *   *

ONE HUNDRED DEGREES, AND I'M FREEZING

I was working on a scene from *K2* where I had to have a broken leg while stranded in subzero weather on a ledge on one of the largest mountains in the world. So I'm there, in class, under the lights, in a full snowsuit, hat, gloves, boots . . . the whole nine yards.

Suffice to say, I was not cold.

I had done the Cold sensory exercise with Terry and was able to use that. But I've never broken my leg, so I worked with a knee injury I had when I was younger. It took some time and attention, but eventually I was able to combine the sensory and physical conditions—the knee pain, the cold, and the height of the cliff—and found that not only did the elements affect me, but they affected each other and led to some interesting results.

Before I used the sensory work, I think I played the idea of being drunk, injured, cold, hot, exhausted, etc. Now my work is much more detailed. I work from the little things, putting them together piece by piece to make the whole picture, rather than presenting a big picture and trying to show the little pieces along the way.

—Jason Weiss

* * *

Once the cold is firmly established in the actors' imaginations, I have them stand and move around. Often I tell them they have something to drink, like whisky from a flask, or a hot cup of coffee or cocoa in their hands. Sometimes I add an obstacle, such as the bottom of the cardboard coffee cup is falling out and dousing the actors with hot liquid. They must deal with both the burn of the liquid and the disappointment of losing their drinks.

The Monologue

At this point, I have the actors perform their monologues as if they're out in the cold, regardless of the initial context of the words. Once they've done this, I then have them say the monologue without letting the cold be obvious, but rather "internalized"—the "actor's secret."

The physical condition will give a rich inner life to many monologues, even if the condition works against the context of the play. Agents or casting directors won't know that the actor is working on the physical condition of cold—they'll only see a mature actor speaking a monologue with a rich inner life.

HEAT

Heat is worked on in the same manner as cold to establish a sense memory in the body. I tell my students the givens: it's at least one hundred degrees, as well as 90 percent humidity. It's the worst day of the summer. Heat is radiating off the sidewalk. There's a bad air quality warning in effect. It's sweltering.

I have them work with the same external and internal awareness as with cold, starting with the right toes and working through the body section by section. I remind them of the sweat dripping off the backs of their legs and down their spine. I bring special attention to their parched throats, and tell them they are extremely thirsty when I lead them to that part of the body.

Once heat is established, I will have the actors drink an ice-cold drink, jump in a cool lake, or take a wonderfully cold shower. As a special New York treat, I might have them play in an open fire hydrant.

Most of the time, I have the actors speak a monologue, just as with the cold exercise. Occasionally I'll do an improvisation and take them out of the city and put them in the desert or jungle without food or water, just themselves. Then the actors have to deal with not only the condition, but each other as well. It propels the actor to do something about the condition. Regardless of whether I have them finish with a monologue or with being deserted in the jungle, I always let them cool off at the end. The last thing I want is a bunch of overheated and dehydrated students.

DRUNKENNESS

Performing drunkenness well on stage is not an easy task. It requires extreme relaxation from the hips on down, especially the pelvic area into the legs. But it also requires a sense of realness, which is best achieved by exploring drunkenness through a physical-condition exercise done just as thoroughly as cold and heat.

Caution!

Students who are recovering alcoholics should be extremely careful with this exercise, or possibly not participate. Recreating the taste and smell for a recovering alcoholic can be extremely dangerous. As in all of the exercises, I encourage my students to explore and be aware of their limitations. A role is never worth a relapse, and an exercise is certainly not either.

Actors begin with the premise of having had enough to drink that they are "feeling no pain." If there are actors who have never had the experience of being drunk because of religious or other reasons, I tell them to use their imaginations and see if they can explore the as-if of the feeling. All the actors should explore their bodies one section at a time, starting once more with the right toes and proceeding as they did with heat or cold.

It's important to start simply with the toes and then move upward. Even through drunkenness doesn't affect the toes as much as cold or heat does, there still is a response in the toes. All physical-condition work requires working with one small part first and then moving the sensation throughout the rest of the body. I've found that for this exercise, it works best if the actors sit in hard-back chairs with their eyes closed and work on their toes and feet first, gradually having the physical sensation of being inebriated move up their bodies.

Once the actors have gone through their bodies section by section, I have them explore other actions. "Deal with what it is like to cross your legs. What about the other areas of your body? Your hands? Your jaw? Your arms?" I remind them of how alcohol can affect their senses. "How are sight, sound, and smell affected? Is touch different?" I encourage them to explore their individual trigger points in their bodies—sensitive stomachs, for example—and how the liquor affects these sensitive spots.

Once the physical life has been fully explored, I have them go to lifting their glass, bottle, or can. "Check for your physical feelings," I remind them, emphasizing the possible motor loss in arms and difficulty controlling the glass or can. "Be aware of the weight of the container, the click of ice cubes, or the feel of the glass." I make sure they pay close attention to the liquids they are drinking. "Raise the drink slowly, examine the smell, and listen for the sound it makes if you slosh it around. Break down the difference in taste from lips to mouth and palette, feel the liquor go down your throat and the feeling in your stomach."

Then I have the actors become aware that they may have had too much to drink. "What are the physical indications that you've reached your cutoff point? What are your internal feelings now?"

I then have the actors explore standing up and walking around. Once this has been done, I put them all in a party situation and let them socialize. The object is to create the physical condition of drunkenness, but to play sober, so no caricatures. "Try to talk normally. Experience trying to put thoughts and words together while being intoxicated." I finish the exercise by having the actors speak their monologues while attempting to hide their drunken condition.

DRUGS

Many characters in plays and screenplays are zoned out on some kind of narcotic—sometimes recreational drugs, and sometimes narcotics for medical purposes. Other times, a character will seem to be under the influence. I've also seen this exercise add a rich and colorful emotional life by an actor who uses it as a hidden physical condition. Mentally exploring how these drugs affect the actor physically can be a very useful acting tool.

No Drugs Needed

Most actors in my classes have encountered drugs in the past through experimentation, and therefore will have reference points in order to explore the effects of narcotics on the body for this physical-condition exercise. There is no need to "experiment" with a drug for the purpose of playing a role. Even someone who has never explored illegal drugs can use this sensory exercise based on other experiences. Or, go to a drug rehabilitation center and ask specific questions about various drugs and their effects. I once had a student who had never used illegal drugs. He reached back into his past, when he was given laughing gas at a dentist's office when he was twelve.

I want to make it very clear that, while actors can utilize their youthful experimentations, no one should ever experiment with dangerous or illegal substances for the sake of a group exercise—or a role, for that matter. The sensory exercises are about using the imagination to create reality. Just as I wouldn't suggest that an actor playing Hamlet actually find out what it's like to be stabbed, I wouldn't want someone to experience illegal drugs for a role.

If the actor has no reference point for something, I tell him to see what his imagination will conjure up. With enough information about the drug's effects, more than likely, his imagination will allow the experience to come to life without him ever damaging his body.

Caution!

I also want to point out that, like alcoholism, drug addiction is not something to fool around with. A recovering addict should *never* carelessly try to relive the experience of being high. I would recommend that any student who is recovering or has recovered from a drug problem first talk to a counselor about whether to do the exercise or not, and then proceed only with extreme caution.

No exercise or role is worth a potential relapse. I encourage all actors to take their health into consideration first, before undertaking the difficult and dangerous task of imaginary drug use, if they have a problem with drugs or alcohol.

Have a NICE Trip

For the students who chose to do the Drugs exercise, I have them recall a pleasant drug experience, not an unpleasant one. Some roles may require a bad trip, but for the sake of a group exercise, it's better to recall something that was fun or neutral. "Worry about bad trips when you get the role," I tell them.

I work through this exercise in the same manner as the Drunkenness exercise. The feeling of the physical condition starts with the toes and lower body, is then experienced in the upper body, and finally the head. Since each student will have her own particular narcotic experience, the students' physical reactions will be different. Those on "uppers" might be very hyper, with lots of body movements. The others on "downers" might have the urge to sit and hide. I encourage the students to do whatever would be natural on the drugs.

I will then create the same kind of party group experience that I did with the Drunkenness exercise. For some, it will be a very different atmosphere, and they will be far more into isolation and their own inner world. Others will be very talkative and social, sometimes absurdly so.

After they've had the chance to interact with each other, I have the students perform their monologues—first with the drug condition apparent, then with it hidden. Upon conclusion, I encourage them to take time to reflect and discuss the sensory aliveness that was created.

Remember, it is valueless—and sometimes dangerous—to actually get drunk or stoned to accomplish these exercises or a role, or to encourage others to do so. It is far more creative to recall and recreate the state from sense memory.

PAIN

Frequently a writer gives a character a broken limb, headache, physical beating, or impairment. These can be either temporary or permanent. Think of the work necessary to play the crippled World War I vet Moe Axelrod in *Awake and Sing!*[1] or Brick, the football star who's laid out with a broken ankle in *Cat on a Hot Tin Roof*.[2] Laura from *The Glass Menagerie*[3] doesn't suffer from simply a deformity—there's a certain amount of pain involved with her limp. These roles directly present a key physical condition of impairment and sometimes pain that is necessary for the reality of their characters. The exercise is so students can re-experience a pain they've had themselves in order to learn how to apply the work to different characters.

Start Small and Specific

This exercise starts once again with the students sitting in straight-back chairs with their eyes closed. "Select a real pain you once experienced. Start with the pain's center in an *exact* and *specific* place in your body." The key to this

---

[1] By Clifford Odets
[2] By Tennessee Williams
[3] By Tennessee Williams

exercise is to start small and get a sense of where the pain center started. "You can look for it by feeling the specific area where it was located," I will say. "Sometimes touching or flexing a muscle in the area helps. If it's an injury in the mouth like a toothache or split lip, use your tongue to find it."

Once a brief second of the sense memory of the pain comes alive, I tell the students to enlarge the center of the pain and see how surrounding areas are affected. The pain gradually radiates outwards and spreads. I will take them through these steps slowly until the pain has become large. "How does the pain affect the rest of you? What body adjustments did you have to make?"

But there's more to pain than just feeling. Our other senses react as well. "Was there any taste to the pain? A smell? A sound? How is your sight affected?" Now that the pain has been fully established, I have them move their hands to the center again. "What was it like to touch?"

Pain and injury will interfere with our ability to move and behave normally. I will tell my students to get up out of their chairs and move around. "What is it like to try to stand? To walk? To sit again? Can you lay down?"

Variations

There are various improvisations a leader can take the actors through at this point. One might be putting the actors into an emergency room of a hospital, awaiting their turn, or even creating a situation where they each have to get to a hospital by themselves. "How does the pain affect you psychologically and emotionally? How easy is it go get dressed? To catch a cab or get into a car? Can you drive? There's no one you know around to help you. How are you going to deal with this?"

✳   ✳   ✳

PAIN, SHIN SPLINTS, AND THE HIGH SCHOOL BASKETBALL BENCH

The first thing that came to mind when Terry asked us to choose a pain was the shin splints I developed in basketball practice in high school. Within minutes, I had imagined the excruciating pain, with one shin worse than the other.

When Terry instructed us to do something while experiencing the pain, I tried to dribble an imaginary basketball, but found I couldn't put any weight on the one leg. I had to stop and sit. All of a sudden it hit me—I had to be taken out of the game in high school because of the pain. I was right back there, watching the game from the sidelines.

I saw my coach, my teammates, the girls from the other team, and the time clock. I heard the ball bouncing on the court, the squeak of shoes on the court, and the general hubbub in the background.

The sensory exercise quickly became an emotional one. Being denied the right to play brought me to tears. It wasn't the pain that made me cry, but the frustration and disappointment, wanting something so badly and not being able to have it. I've used this physical condition and sense memory several times later on in various scenes. It seems to work very well for plays by Tennessee Williams, maybe because the longing of his characters is so palpable.

—Felicia Pensiero

* * *

Once they are at the hospital, I direct their attention to the other students in the room. "What do you hear?" I'll say. "Are they just making sounds? Crying? How does hearing them affect you?"

Another improvisation could be that they are victims of a natural disaster. Typically, a leader will see changes in personalities because of the pain and imperative to get help. It's helpful for both the leader and the students themselves to observe what personalities emerge when everyone's good behavior is down because of the pain.

The next step is to add words on top of the pain and emotions that have risen from it. I will lead the students into speaking one of their monologues—first with the pain readily apparent, and then again with it as the "actor's secret." The actors will see how the psychological and emotional results of pain can affect a monologue, and how the pain exercise will give a rich emotional center for some roles, even if the script does not say that the character is in pain.

BLINDNESS

The Blind group exercise is a little different than the previous group exercises that I teach, since the actors must pair off rather than working individually, and then eventually work together in a big group improvisation. But the results are twofold: It helps develop trust in an acting partner as well as ground a physical condition in the imagination.

I have the actors pair off after the initial relaxation, and each one chooses a role: "seeing" or "blind." The "blind" partners must close their eyes and keep them closed at all times, or, if this is not an easy task, be blindfolded. They are completely dependent on their partner to be their eyes. The "seeing" partner will act as their guide. "Lead them to touch things, taste, smell—in other words, use all senses but sight."

I then tell the "seeing" partners to take their blind counterparts—with the blind actor's hands on the seeing partner's arm—and lead them around the room. Then I encourage them to actually go outside. "Walk your partner down the street into a nearby deli. Have them purchase something with your assistance as needed, then lead them back."

Once the pairs return, I reverse the procedure. The formerly blind partners are now the seeing leaders, and vice versa. "For the blind partner, observe how other senses become heightened. See how the sense of touch, if left alone without sight, becomes acute." It's the same with hearing and smell as well, although touch is the first sense most "blind" actors notice.

The "seeing" partners must learn how to watch their partners closely to give them guidance and to help them. It takes much more acute observation than usual. I also always give the actors one rule at the start of the exercise. "A warning: Only do things with your blinded partner that you would want done to you. Don't play tricks." Otherwise, this exercise can obviously lead to injury, and also to mistrust between acting partners, which is exactly the opposite of what makes good acting.

DEAFNESS

Deafness as a physically condition can be worked on in a similar way to blindness. "Deaf" students can plug up their ears with something safe, like high-quality earplugs, and depend on a partner for the other four senses to communicate. The "deaf" actor should go out on the street and investigate what it's like not to hear street noise. "How well can you read lips?" I sometimes have actors try running dialogue from a scene or carrying on a conversation this way.

DON'T GO ALONE

I don't recommend that an actor attempt to do these sensory exercises in a public setting without a partner. Accidents can happen. Someone who is practicing blindness may not open his eyes to see an oncoming car until it's too late, and someone practicing deafness might not hear a siren or warning shout when needed.

Individuals who have impairments like deafness or blindness require many years to adjust and build up their other senses so they can go out into public places safely. A practicing actor has not. I would recommend that anyone trying to practice this alone stick to his own house or apartment, where things are familiar and the chance of injury is lessened.

The feeling or sensation of being blind or deaf will stay in the sense memory after the exercise is finished. It's especially important for the student to take notes in his acting notebook. Students should also observe real individuals who are sight- or hearing-impaired for character development. I will go into further detail in the scene work section, but remember this: For character development, it's important to know how long the character has been impaired. Adjustments will have to be made based on the length of time, since a newly blind person will be more clumsy than someone who's been blind since birth.

OTHER IMPAIRMENT

There are a number of acting situations where some kind of impairment work is necessary. There are often roles that require a loss of the sense of smell, for example. I often will encourage my students to test being without smell by pretending to be extremely congested in the nasal mask and nose. This can either be practiced by plugging up the nose with some cotton, or by working from the memory of an awful cold in the same manner as the Pain exercise.

Smell isn't the only sense lost in those situations. Taste is also affected by a cold or other illness, or by smoking. Both can be used as a hidden "actor's secret" too. Remembering the taste in the mouth from a horrible bout with the flu can take an actor right back to the psychological state necessary for a character.

While I rarely use this as a group exercise, individual actors will often need to work on the absence of a limb or serious speech impairment for a role. I will suggest that they do an initial relaxation warm-up on their own and then see what it's like to do tasks minus an arm or a hand. "Try it with making the injured or missing limb be the one your normally use. It creates much more of an obstacle than having the limb you are most comfortable with."

I will often suggest to an actor playing a character like Moe Axelrod, with his wooden leg, that he bring in a leg brace to rehearsal, as well as practicing at home. Significant research and practice is vital for John Merrick's speech and other impediments in *The Elephant Man.*[4] not only must the impediments seem real, but the actor still has to be understood by the audience.

[4] By Bernard Pomerance

The physical aspects of a disability or impediment are only part of the whole characterization. The actor must always remember to deal with his emotional response to the impediment as well. A costume that binds an arm, using a crutch, or being in a wheelchair will give an actor a lot to work with, but it's important to explore beyond simply missing a limb to find out how it affects the emotions and, eventually, the interaction with other characters.

All this body work has to be done without tension. "There is no reason to hurt yourself," I will tell my students. "The warm-up may need to go beyond what you normally need. You may need to stretch out very well before and after. Care of your body is of utmost importance. There's no excuse for risking permanent injury. In many cases, you are the one who has to look out for yourself."

INSANITY

The first rule for playing insane people is this: The characters do not see themselves as strange, mad, or insane. They think they are completely sane, and that the world around them is out of focus. For them, it's everyone else who's crazy. This rule must be kept in mind when doing a play like *Marat Sade*,[5] *One Flew Over the Cuckoo's Nest*,[6] or *The Boys Next Door*.[7]

The Tic

In the Insanity group exercise, I typically start with the actors sitting on the floor. I ask them to search their minds for a specific eccentricity of theirs. It could be a slight facial tick, the biting of a lip, tugging of an ear, cracking of knuckles, pulling or sweeping back of hair—something that is unique to each individual actor. I have them each start to do this behavior normally, but constantly. Then I tell them to build it, then more, and more, until it totally controls them.

"Let it build into a compulsive disorder," I tell them. "See how you are affected physically and how the senses operate if this eccentricity, this disorder, totally controls you. Remember, you don't see yourself as being the slightest bid odd. It's the world around that's out of joint."

When these eccentricities are fully externalized, I see how the actors relate to each other. "What have you picked up on from other people's

[5] By Peter Weiss

[6] I'm speaking of the play by Dale Wasserman, from Ken Kesey's novel that was adapted in the 1970s into the award-winning movie.

[7] By Tom Griffin

mannerisms? Is there an emotional or psychological effect that you notice from the eccentricity?"

* * *

INSANITY, ANGER, AND MY HAIR

When Terry said to find a personal habit of ours at the start of the group exercise, my hand immediately went to my hair. It's always in my face, and I'm always shoving it out of the way. As the slight "hair flip" got larger and larger during the exercise, so did a rising anger. Eventually I was using both hands to pull back the locks, shoving my palms across my scalp. But my hair wouldn't stay in place, and I could feel rage searing through my body.

Fifteen minutes into the exercise, I could see that everyone in the room looked pretty nuts. But what I noticed more was that they stayed out of my way. They avoided me, wouldn't make eye contact, bowed their heads . . . one guy actually ran in the other direction when I changed my path abruptly. I could feel my eyes shooting darts, and had some fun with scaring everyone else.

Learning that I could find such rage from a simple tic was a wonderful discovery, and I noted it in my actor's notebook for future use. "You could definitely play Lady Macbeth or Medea," said a fellow actor. "What were you so angry at?" asked another. I'm not sure they believed me when I shrugged and said I wasn't angry at anything monumental, but simply my hair.

—Mary Beth Barber

* * *

Physical tics aren't the only things students might use in this exercise, or in preparation for a character. "Do you talk to yourself?" I'll ask my students as they are wandering around interacting with each other, and as their mannerisms take over their bodies. "What if you went public with that?" At this point, the room will be filled with what appears to be complete raving lunatics.

These tics will often bring emotions that can be hidden otherwise. Anger, frustration, tears, and laughter are a few examples that come from these tics—emotions that can be used to create a psychological base for scene work and monologues. I will often have the students pair off and say the monologues to each other—once with the tics fully present, and then again with them hidden as an "actor's secret," that gives the words a deep subtext.

CONCLUSION

The exercises I have talked about in this chapter and the other chapters in Part II, produce wonderful and unique individual behavior, not clichéd choices, provided they are done correctly. The cliché can be valid, but often ends up being obvious and usually not very interesting. Other directors or teachers reading this book may have many valid and terrific sensory and physical-condition exercises they that do or that they could add. I have only dealt with the ones I use to create interesting, organic behavior in a group setting.

That doesn't mean these exercises are limited to a group setting. I will often take and alter them for individual actors when I'm directing. Many of my students will use these group exercises as a base to explore on their own. I encourage directors, teachers, and actors to do so—always keeping in mind the safety guidelines I have included throughout.

PART III INDIVIDUAL EXERCISE

Students have told me of the great benefits they have gotten from the exercises that I teach—from the group exercises that I have already explained, but especially from the individual exercises in this section. Over the years, I've worked with a number of different techniques that I've been exposed to—borrowing from this or that teacher, book, altering an exercise, and creating exercises of my own. From this, I've developed a series of "tools"—work for my students that provide them with a solid background they can rely on for their own acting. The core components are the five individual exercises. They teach these five basic concepts:

- *Creating a character* (Spoon River exercise)
- *Creating a scene* (Action/Condition/Telephone Call, or A.C.T. exercise)
- *Freeing the instrument* (Song Exercise and/or the Fallout)
- *Exploring the subconscious* (Emotional Recall exercise)
- *Validating the self* (Private Moment)

The individual exercises do much more than their simple subtitles indicate, however. A physical condition is the key component to the A.C.T., for example. The Fallout uses short phrases to get to the core of an emotional response and trigger sense memories from our past. The Emotional Recall triggers sense memories in a different way and incorporates them into a "scene." Part Two of the Spoon River exercise emphasizes the "psychological center," the techniques I've learned from Michael Chekhov's work that I introduced in the Animal group exercise description. The Private Moment—while having the "validation of the self" as the most important learning component—also requires the actor to plan out a scene that tells a story in twenty to twenty-five minutes, often without words.

These exercises are unlike the spontaneous group exercises, however, in that all of them require a great deal of preparation before the students do them in class. The Fallout and Song Exercise appear to be the exception to this rule, but I've been told that students think about the Fallout for weeks before having to do it, so much so that it feels like preparation. And most of the exercises have two or sometimes three parts that are explored in different sessions and take weeks to properly execute.

A NOTE FOR LEADERS

Leaders who wish to use these exercises must remember the deeply personal nature of this work, and students must remember never to violate their own sense of trust. Some students will take great risks immediately with these exercises. That does not mean everyone should. An instructor should never push an actor who is reluctant, and an actor should never cross her own personal bounds, whether it's nudity, disclosing sensitive and personal information, or tackling events from the past that are unresolved or too difficult to be useful as tools. Remember, the purpose of these exercises is to open up actors, not shut them down so they're afraid of the work.

The other key to any student or leader is to remember that these exercises are for learning, not for performance. The minute a student worries about how she appears doing these exercises or a leader tries to elicit a particular response or look, the exercises fail in their primary goal: to explore technique.

So, that said . . . let's begin!

8 CREATING A CHARACTER— THE SPOON RIVER EXERCISE

At last—actual written dialogue! The Spoon River is the first of the six advanced individual exercises in my classes, and a perfect introduction to character development based on the playwright's words—or, in this case, Edgar Lee Masters' poetry from the *Spoon River Anthology*. It's also the first that requires a significant amount of homework—preparation before class. As the first solo exercise in my class, the Spoon River work is a great introduction for what's to come and for the actor trusting herself as her true creative source.

SPOON RIVER, PART ONE—INTRODUCTION TO THE CHARACTER

The exercise starts with the purchase of a copy of the *Spoon River Anthology*, a collection of poetry first published in 1915 by Masters, a novelist and poet. The book was eventually turned into a play of the same name, with the characters based on the poems. I insist that the actors in my class buy the book, not the play, as the book gives an actor a wider selection of characters.

Each poem in the book is the epitaph for the deceased fictional members of the town of Spoon River, Illinois. The epitaphs tell the stories of the townspeople of Spoon River quickly and succinctly, in just a few poetic lines. From these words, the actors must discover the "givens" of the characters—the information that is known or assumed based on these lines. Masters himself gives the actors one of the first "givens" in the introduction: He writes in the first few pages that all the characters are dead and reside in the Spoon River main cemetery.

Homework: Create a Character

I ask my actors to spend some time at home reading through the different poems and selecting one that resonates personally with them. If something strikes the actor right away, she should read it through a few times and then start working with it. Even if the reasons why the poem has personal meaning are elusive on the first read, the significance will become apparent during the homework process.

The actors can cross gender, but only if the poem would still make sense. For example, George Trimble speaks of how his political downfall "was due to my wife," who pushed him to support Prohibition, leading to the distrust of his supporters. A gay woman in the modern era may refer to her partner as a wife, but it wouldn't work for the time period we're dealing with. George Trimble is always male.

Other characters, though, can transfer to the other gender. For example, Sam Hookey, who ran away with the circus after falling in love with Mademoiselle Estralada, *can* be female. The actress must accept the poem's assumption that Sam joined the circus because of a woman—"Mademoiselle Estralada" cannot be changed to a male name, because those are the words of the poem. (The actor will also have to deal with Sam Hookey's final fate—being eaten alive by lions!) But there's nothing else in the poem that denotes gender, and therefore both men and women can play the role.

Create a Biography

The next step is to work up a character biography based on how the character, her parents, and maybe even her grandparents arrived in Spoon River, Illinois. The actor could use her own personal family history if it's appropriate for the character, or she could make one up completely from scratch. I want the actor to know:

- What the father did for a living
- If the mother worked in addition to tending the home
- Number of brothers and sisters
- Where the family lived—in town, or, say, on a farm
- Level of education
- If the character married and had a family
- How old the character was at time of death
- How the character died
- How long the character has been dead
- Any other details the actor thinks are necessary or important

I ask that the actors write out their biographies in order to keep these details fresh for the classroom portion of this exercise. The key is to include real and credible details based on the historical time period. The characters must have been born sometime after 1825 and died before 1914. The timeframe is especially important, since the cutoff date is definitely 1914. For example, if an actor says her character arrived in Spoon River in a Pink Thunderbird, she'd be historically incorrect and immediately lose all foundation of her character's biography.

"Read about the time period and the territory," I tell my students. "Be creative, but be historically correct." Education level and career are two areas where the actors must be especially careful. There were some college-educated men and a handful of women at that time, but they were the exception and not the rule. "Justify your conclusions based on the text of the poem," I tell them.

"Don't go overboard with the details, especially long explanations of the family history," I'll tell my students. "Describe the general characteristics of your character's ancestry—your grandparents were Irish potato farmers escaping the famine, your parents were Pennsylvanian freemen who were part of the Freedom Train, or whatever history you want."

As I said, this can be the actor's own family's history or one made up, as long as it is historically accurate. "Find the defining moments in your character's life, the slices of memory that define who you are." Sometimes actors can get bogged down in the minutiae of life and ignore the main events and key characteristics. "I don't want random details. I want the important stuff, the details that evoke pictures and memories."

Students must not only know where their characters were from, but also where they ended up when they died. "You must know what brought you to Spoon River."

The other moment that must be defined is the character's death. This must be known before entering the classroom. How he or she lived and finally died is what the *Spoon River Anthology* is all about.

I'll often have to remind students that this isn't an American history class, but an acting class. "Create a life that stimulates your imagination and helps you to find the character's psychological and emotional base." Remember, the words of the poem must be adhered to when building the biography. "Create clear givens for your character to work from, based on the text of the poem and your own imagination."

Parallel Dialogue

Once the student has finished the biography, she follows with "parallel dialogue." There are two main ways to work with parallel dialogue: 1) The actor keeps the bulk of the poem intact but plugs in replacement or fill-in words or names from her own personal experience, or 2) the actor completely rewrites the poem in her own words, keeping with the main gist and conclusion but using words that have a deeper meaning for her.

Fill-in Words

The example I usually give to demonstrate the "fill-in words" technique is Margaret Fuller Slack's character. Her first line is, "I would have been as great as George Elliot." To a reader from the nineteenth and early twentieth century, the meaning of this line would have been obvious—everyone knew of the famous writer Mary Anne Evans, who broke into the male-dominated writing world by using the pen name George Elliot. But the reference would probably be lost on a modern reader or actor, and without personal meaning, the words might fall flat. But fill in the name with someone else—"I would have been as great as Meryl Streep"—and suddenly the line comes to life.

If a student chooses to take the fill-in words method, she must be careful to keep with the context of the poem. Meryl Streep is a perfect substitution for George Elliot, since both are names of admirable artists. Using an odd choice might elicit an interesting response, but distracts from the meaning of the words. "As great as Monica Lewinsky" would be completely inappropriate for the context of the poem.

Rewritten in Own Words

An actor can completely rewrite the poem with her own words, but like the fill-in words method, she must stay within the confines of the actual poem. Spoon River's Margaret Fuller Slack is a woman who considers herself a great talent, but who spent the bulk of her life caring for a large family without ever getting the chance to pursue her writing. An actor wishing to rewrite the poem in her own words might see parallels in her own life of having to pay her own way through school or supporting loved ones and never getting the chance to focus on acting. Taking the Margaret Fuller Slack epitaph line by line and rewriting it with the parallels in your own life works beautifully—as long as the meaning and overall intent are still the same.

Both methods are highly effective, even with the most philosophical or barest of the *Spoon River* poetry. Some students can use a few new words here and there for the words to come to life. Others will see direct parallels to their own lives and use current examples. "The most important part is to make the words *yours*," I remind them. "And remember that parallel dialogue, like the biography, should be written out before the actor arrives to the class."

Name the Emotion

Before a student comes in to class to do the Spoon River exercise, I want her to know the compelling emotion behind the character. There is always an emotional quality to each and every one of these poems, clearly defined in the last two lines. The last two lines are the payoff of the poem and will tell you very clearly what the characters felt about their lives.

For me, there are five prime, or base, emotions to choose from:

Anger

Sadness

Fear

Love

Joy

The actor must make sure she names one of these visceral emotions. Many actors tend to name a feeling. I want the *core* from which that feeling arose. For example, an actor may say that a character feels cynicism, sarcasm, contempt, feistiness, snideness, self-loathing, or sardonicism. All these feeling are manifestations of *anger*. Anger is the core emotion, and the rest are the results of that anger. The emotion should be clear in these short poems, as it drives the characters.

✻ ✻ ✻

MRS. SIBLEY SAID NOTHING, AND EVERYTHING

When I scanned the *Spoon River Anthology* for a character, the one that resonated with me was Mrs. Sibley, a mysterious character with an illusive poem of seven simple lines that gave little information about her life. I thought I might have been on the wrong path—most of the other poems gave a lot of detail, and Terry had told us to choose a character who resonated with us. How could Mrs. Sibley resonate with anyone? She didn't even have a first name.

The secret of the stars,—gravitation.

I started with the first line and allowed my mind to create a picture. What came was a family of four—father, mother, and two daughters— sitting on a beach at night. My character was the older sister.

The secret of the earth,—layers of rock.

While the beach image sprang up as if from a dream, the "where" and "when" came from detailed research. In the late 1800s to the early 1900s, women couldn't vote yet and few had an education, but many who did were involved in the Progressive political movement. I chose my hometown to be Galveston, Texas, a booming port town—until a hurricane killed almost everyone in 1900.

The secret of the soil,—to receive seed.

Suddenly things started to fit into place. I gave myself a name—Maggie. I drew from personal histories of Galveston hurricane survivors. I wrote page after page in my actor's notebook—the hurricane, my father's untimely death, the marriage to Reverend Sibley, and the move to Spoon River.

The secret of the seed,—the germ.

My pen wouldn't stop. "My husband's psychosis became apparent when we moved to Spoon River. For weeks he would leave me with simply my books for company, only to come back in drunken jealous rages and beat me for infidelity when I hadn't seen a soul for days."

The secret of man,—the sower.

None of this parallels my own life. Nor are the details anywhere in the poem. But because of my research, imagination, and concentration, Maggie's life felt real even if it was nothing like my own. "It was one of these beatings that caused me to miscarry at six months. I buried the child under an oak tree. He never even knew I was pregnant," I wrote, as Maggie Sibley.

The secret of woman,—the soil.

In class, when I had to read the poem out loud, my voice lilted into a hard Southern twang—not because I tried to, but naturally, as my own accent. When I quietly explained my biography and burying the child, I was surprised by the tears on my face because I hadn't tried to cry. If anything, I had tried to fight them.

My secret: Under a mount that you shall never find.

When I, as Maggie, started to get bogged down in the sorrow of the dead baby, Terry wouldn't let me. "You survived a hurricane, you survived a terrible marriage. You are a survivor. Don't act a negative. What did you, Maggie Sibley, do about all this?"

Fortunately, I had written these details as well—how Maggie moved to Chicago and became a suffragist, lived an independent life, and became so politically strong that her husband didn't dare touch her again. Terry reminded me to focus on the strength, not the sorrow—and it was Maggie Sibley's strength in the words when I finally "gave" my little sister the story of the miscarried baby under the oak tree in Spoon River.

—Mary Beth Barber

*　*　*

It can be easier to initially name the prime emotion in a poem that has lots of descriptive words about feelings, but the emotion is also there in the philosophical speeches from some of the characters. If an actor does choose a seemingly unemotional poem, she must find out what the character is trying to hide by masking deep feelings with intellectual words.

Sometimes, selecting an emotion opposite the seemingly obvious choice is important. As an example, there are some poems where the character committed suicide. Normally, to hear of a suicide is sad and depressing. However, from the character's point of view, it may have been a gift, a release, joyously "shuffling off this mortal coil." Therefore, without violating the intention of the poem, the actor is seeing and justifying such an action from the character's positive viewpoint.

Memorization

The final step of the homework is memorization. *It is imperative that the actor can recite the poem in her sleep if necessary.* She won't get the full effect of the exercise if the poem is not completely memorized before she comes into the classroom. These are short poems, not lengthy Shakespearean monologues. No experienced actor should find this memorization cumbersome or attempt to do this exercise without having the words down cold.

In the Class

As I said before, all the characters in the poems are dead, and, like Emily in *Our Town*[1] this is the one day they get a chance to come back to Earth and talk about how they felt about their lives and the circumstances of their death. The stakes are high. These few words must convey a full lifetime.

But we don't start off by immediately tackling the emotional quality of the poem. Some proper grounding of the poem as spoken words is necessary, as is the actor simply getting used to being in front of the class.

[1] By Thornton Wilder

Initial Reading

After a proper warm-up, I'll seat the actor in a hard-back chair in front of the class and ask her to read the poem—not to recite it, but to look at the paper and read it. The actor starts with the name of the character and then reads each complete thought, one at a time. (Typically, each line contains one complete thought.) She must take time to look up between lines and reflect on the words, to let the words in and to receive them. This first reading should be as if it's the first time she has ever read the poem, with each thought perhaps taking on a new image.

"Let us in to your inner life through your eyes. Break the fourth wall. Share your connection with us." Many actors find new, fresh, and sometimes wonderfully surprising images during this first step.

Name the Emotion

Upon conclusion of the reading, the actor should be able to tell the class the prime emotion of the character based on the last two lines of the poem. Some actors may change their mind from what they had initially planned because of what the class reading evoked. That's okay—it's better to change an initially planned emotional quality for an honest one than to try to pursue one that's not grounded.

Don't Act a Negative!

I always tell the actors to be aware that they cannot "act a negative." For instance, an actor tells me, "My character is depressed." At which point I will say, "When you're depressed, how does the depression manifest itself?" An actor can't play depression. It would lead to acting that would be as interesting to watch as the daily habits of a sloth. I've seen actors almost fall into the same trap when the primary emotion is the hopelessness that comes from sadness—the character just gives up. No audience would sit to watch someone give up and not care about his own life. These are examples of "acting a negative."

I tell my students to instead turn that emotion into a positive action, a "doing" action. "Okay, you're depressed," I'll say. "What are you doing about the depression?" Or, "Fine, you're sad. This situation sucks. What are you doing about the sadness?" The actor must fight for the character throughout, whether it's a nine-line poem or a three-act play.

One actor in my class who said, "My character is depressed," informed me that when she's depressed she gets angry. "Yes!" I replied. "Now we have an active emotion—a positive choice—to play and drive the character."

Sometimes an actor will say to me, "But this poem isn't emotional." Not true. All of the poems, be they straightforward or philosophical, have a driving source of emotion. Many times the emotion doesn't "ring out" until the end—the last two lines. But it's there from the top and it motivates the poem. As I said earlier, if the words themselves don't say the emotion, find out what the character is *not* saying by using these words to mask it.

This work can apply to real acting situations as well. Many times a director will give an actor the emotional result he wants to see, and it is up to the actor to produce it. As I detail the rest of the exercise, I'll show that if the actor does the work thoroughly, she will learn a process to achieve the desired emotional result.

Once the emotional choice has been named by the actor, I then want the actor verbalizing in the first person, "I," as we proceed to the next step.

Telling the Biography

At this point, I have the actor keep her papers on her lap and talk directly to her fellow students as the character. She tells us the story of her life from what's she's created in her biography.

I will allow students to refer back to their notes during the biography part of this exercise if a reference, date, name, or detail is needed to be referred to. But I've seen too many students try to read their biography without grounding themselves in the character they've created and without making contact with the class. I've had to ask them to put their papers down and simply tell us about themselves. The Spoon River exercise breaks the fourth wall—it takes courage to look fellow students in the eye and tell them who you are. That's why this exercise is so important.

I Am Always "I"

I also insist with any character discussion in scene study or the Spoon River exercise that the actor always stays with "I" rather than "he" or "she." Using the third person distances the actor and separates her from the character immersion we are attempting to create. The final result in performance is that we will see what the actor has created from her mind, heart, and will. Hopefully, it will be a creation she has birthed, not some abstraction known as "he" or "she," devoid of anything to do with the actor as a person. "We need your involvement and your commitment," I'll tell my students.

Reading the Parallel Dialogue

Once the actor has told her life story with the biography, it's time to refer back to the poem and the parallel dialogue that she prepared. She reads or recites her parallel dialogue the same way she read the poem at the beginning of the class portion of the exercise, taking in each full thought one at a time and allowing these words to have an emotional impact.

Of special importance, of course, are the last two lines.

Who Are You Talking To?

Lastly, the actor must pick a figure from her own life to talk to. This is the only part of the Spoon River exercise where a student must use a real person from her actual life. For the other parts like the biography or parallel dialogue, she had the option to create a realistic fiction or use her own life and history. For this part, it must be someone in the actor's life.

"Do not be general with this selection," I remind them. "Pick a person who really motivates you and is a 'live wire' to your imagination. It could be your father, mother, brother, sister, lover, best friend—someone who has played a significant and emotional role in your life."

As the actor names her person and prepares to speak the poem, I'll clear out an empty space in the back row of seats for her focus so she won't be distracted by having to look at a fellow student. In this empty space, I'll have her place her person.

The actor must also decide whether she wants *to give* or *to get* something from this person she is talking to in the empty space. It is vital not only to be speaking to someone, but for the stakes to be as high as possible. Remember, all characters want to *give* or *get* something at all times. This is important for all actors to remember, for long scenes as well as short speeches, as in the Spoon River exercise. When auditioning with a monologue, the actor must place a person out there over the auditioner's head, and know what she wants to give or get from that person.

"Keep in mind, this is your one and only time to come back from the dead and talk about your life. The person you pick to speak to is an integral part of your immersion process," I'll say. Typically, "getting" something from the person is the stronger option, although I've seen some wonderful pieces done with "give" as a choice.

The Poem

Now it's time for the actor to put the process together and do the selected piece. If she hasn't arrived at the desired psychological and emotional state for the character by this time, there is no point in going on.

The actor, still sitting in a chair, does the poem, allowing images from the biography and parallel dialogue to infuse the words. Because it is a poem and she is speaking verse, she must drive through the poem uninterrupted without taking long, thinking pauses. The payoff comes in the last two lines, when she can let out the emotional result.

Some Thoughts about Language

If the actor has done her homework, the bulk of what is needed to act the poem will be there. What may be lacking now is the special work necessary to raise and savor the words. Poetry presents a heightened reality, and when the actor is connected, she must use the words as an added extension.

Our American, casual way of speaking has not only reduced our vocabulary, but also brutalized our speech habits. Many of us have lost our use of language colors, and therefore our range in ability to convey meaning. There are more than a few occasions when after doing all this work, the final effect and realization of the poem is sabotaged by speech or vocal problems.

Other times, however, the actors just need to will themselves further to "get out there" with what they are saying. The Spoon River text is poetry, and the very fact of that will carry the vocal embellishment. The same advantage applies to many plays as well. Think, as an example, of rising to the beautiful poetry in the language of Tennessee Williams, or the words of Shakespeare, Chekhov, Henrik Ibsen, George Bernard Shaw, Oscar Wilde, Noel Coward, or Edward Albee, to name a few.

I constantly tell my actors not to be afraid of the words. "Savor them, open them up, and taste them." As in Shakespeare, when Masters uses a metaphor, it must be driven through to its completion in order to make sense. It cannot be broken up with pauses, or we as listeners will be lost in understanding it.

Many actors have a tendency to do all the work required for ultimately performing the poem very well. Then, they will come to the last two lines and throw them away. But the last two lines are the *point* of the entire poem! "Actors—it's your point. Don't be shy about letting it ring out loud and clear."

What We've Learned

I use this as an opening solo exercise for new actors in class. It provides a wonderful get-acquainted session and helps me to get a grasp on the imagination of the actors and what stimuli they respond to. It is also very helpful for breaking through the fourth wall, getting their personalities and qualities out in front of a group. A primary focus of all the work is to provide a safe atmosphere where the actors can trust themselves.

There are also a tremendous number of resources learned in this exercise, especially homework tools. Creating parallel dialogue is a great exercise when working on any speech in a script. It's a way of getting under and supporting the playwright's words. It is especially helpful with Shakespeare, once you have mastered speaking the verse and have a full understanding of Shakespeare's words.

One of the many other reasons I like this exercise is that with more abstract plays, very little, if anything, is "given" by the playwright as far as character background. The actor, as a character, is often not given many details and must on her own create a previous life prior to her entrance.

A Note on Parallel Dialogue

At no time am I advocating an actor substituting her own words in a performance or run-through. I am a tyrant on behalf of the text and upholding every word the writer wrote. Parallel dialogue is a homework and early-rehearsal tool only.

A Quick Review

Here's a quick recap of what is learned from Part One of the Spoon River exercise.

At Home:
- Name the emotion—anger, sadness, fear, love, or joy
- Memorization before coming to class
- Biography
  - *Correct historical details*
  - *Overall background*
  - *Defining moments*
- Parallel dialogue
  - *Fill-in words*
  - *Rewritten in own words*

In Class:
- Initial reading—let the words in and receive them
- Don't act a negative!
- I am always "I"
- Who are you talking to?
- To give or to get?
- Heightened language

SPOON RIVER, PART TWO—ANIMAL WORK AND "PSYCHOLOGICAL CENTER"

Now that the actor has done Spoon River, Part One, she not only knows the poem backward and forward, but also has a keen insight into the character through the biography and other work. It's time to add on external life, the specific idiosyncrasies of a character—in this case, through animal work that establishes a character's "psychological center."

Homework—A Field Trip

The first step to Spoon River, Part Two, isn't actually homework; it's a field trip. Each actor goes to a zoo and selects an animal to use for the exercise. The key point is to observe closely. While at the zoo, the actor must find an animal with the general characteristics that resonate with her image of her Spoon River character.[1] I don't want the animal to be chosen randomly or too quickly. "Take your time, walk around, and observe. Find one that really fits or suits your character."

Once the actor has decided on an animal, she sits and observes it closely. I encourage this observation period to be around an hour or so, maybe more. "Observe its movements, sounds, attitudes, and actions. See how it walks and sits. Does it move rapidly or slowly? Does it make a sound?"

Interaction between other animals is very important as well. "Are there other animals in the cage or open pen with your animal? How does your animal react to these others? Is it in charge—an alpha male or alpha female? Or does it retreat and hide? Does it prefer to exist in its own world, or does it interact with the other creatures and things? Is it an observer, like a bird on a high branch? Or does it interact with everything in its environment, like a curious monkey?"

Center of Movement

Once the actor has gotten a good idea about the animal and its behavior, it's time to observe the most important part—the "center" from which all the animal's movement originates. A crocodile's center of movement would be in its underbelly, for example. A stork's would be up high in its chest. Each animal has a different center of movement.

During the observation, the actor should try to subtly simulate the animal's center of movement and sound—at least, as best as possible without bringing attention to herself or scaring the animal, of course. If it never makes a sound, the actor should project one, ensuring that the sound can be comfortably reproduced without vocal strain.

---

[1] The "animal" doesn't have to be a mammal—it can be a fish, reptile, bird, insect—any creature at the zoo other than a human. For the sake of this exercise, when I refer to "animal," I mean any nonhuman creature at the zoo that's larger than a protozoan.

The most important observation is the center of movement. "How are the limbs affected by this center? How about the neck? The head? What about the eyes and how it observes and interacts?" The center could affect the sound too.

Before leaving the zoo, the actor should know some key elements about the animal:

- The name and habitat of the animal
- The animal's main food source—is it an herbivore, carnivore, or omnivore? Hunter? Scavenger?
- The sound the animal makes
- How the animal walks
- Its center of movement

The Psychological Center—An Explanation

Finding and observing the animal's center of movement is the key to this exercise, and an extremely useful method to finding and defining the psychological center of a character. People have psychological centers that define their movements in the same way that an animal's center will define its movement.

Michael Chekhov was one of the first acting coaches to explore the concept of finding an imaginary body and center of movement for a character. In his book *To the Actor : On the Technique of Acting*, he encourages actors to picture physical characteristics and apply them to a character's psychology. He uses an example of a character who is lazy, sluggish, and awkward, and asks the reader to picture the body of such a person. Perhaps such a person would have a short, plump body with a thick neck, hanging arms, and an oversized head, he says. The actor should then use the imagination and pretend that he has that kind of body, even if he doesn't resemble that in the least. The result? The psychological characteristics come from the movements he makes as if he had a fat, drooping body.

Chekhov then instructs the actors reading his text to explore the *imaginary center* of these movements. The center can be anywhere—in the torso area for a character who likes a good meal, or in the forehead for a big thinker. The placement of this imaginary center—the *psychological center*—will significantly affect the movements and personality of a character. I like to expand on Chekhov's technique and use animals and their psychological centers for character work.

At Home

A day or two after the zoo trip, the actor reviews her notes on her animal and practices "being" the animal while at home. "Find in your body the psychological center of the animal. This center is very important. It's the key to the animal's movement. Remember, do not just imitate the animal." Once the actor is grounded in this movement, she should try moving her body with the animal's psychological center. "Make sure you move without muscle tension," I remind the actors preparing this exercise. "Remember, the animal is not tense." It naturally moves the way it moves.

* * *

ROSE RITZ, FANCY PEACOCK

I was struggling with one of the many characters I was playing in a production of *I Love You, You're Perfect, Now Change*. The other characters were close in age and experience to myself, but "Rose Ritz" was a middle-aged divorcee. How would the audience possibly buy me in this role?

Then I remembered the second part of the Spoon River exercise, and it all came together. I went to the zoo and decided to make Rose a peacock. The new center of gravity aged me, and by speaking in the register of the bird's sound, I found a whole new voice. I became this incredibly interesting and neurotic woman who I never knew was there, and the character I thought would be my weakest became an audience favorite. Critics said, "Rose Ritz stole the show!" It was quite a shock, and a true learning experience.

—Hillary Parker

* * *

"Do some activities around the house as the animal. Once the movement is well grounded, bring back the biography and parallel dialogue to the rehearsal. See how the physicality can affect the homework portion of this exercise." The point is to review the notes and mentally prepare the characteristics of the animal before coming into class. "Now, you not only have your character's inner life from the biography and the parallel dialogue, but also the outer life with physical behavior."

In Class

The first step—as with all acting—is proper relaxation before the exercise starts. When doing the Spoon River exercise, Part Two, I prefer to have two or three actors at once so they can interact with each other. The actors start by sitting in hard-back chairs with their eyes closed, dropping into the preparation based on work in Part One—biography and parallel dialogue, whichever will get them to the desired psychological and emotional state. As they are doing this, they begin to physically take on the animals.

"Find the 'center' for the animal," I tell them first. Once they're secure in their selection of physicality while sitting, I'll have them open their eyes, get up, and move around. "Retain your animal's center—let the center dictate how you move, how you use your arms, how you position your head."

As the actors start to move around as their animals, I'll remind them to take in their surroundings. "Look at the other animals. What is your reaction? What about these people out here looking at you? Take them in. Who do you feel safe with? Not safe with?"

The actors can't forget about their voices. "What kind of sound does your animal make? What about when it's interacting with other animals—does the sound change? How about with the humans?" The vocal production will be determined not only by the rehearsals and the actors' memories, but also by how they stand, sit, walk, and move—in essence, from their center.

Poem and Physicality

I'll typically let the animals meander around for about five minutes so that the actors become grounded in the movement and sounds of their animals. Then I'll bring them one by one to the center of the room while the others continue working with the animal movement and behavior.

I'll ask the actor to stand in an upright position—to get grounded while keeping the animal's center. "See how that center affects your arms, legs, head, and torso as you stand. Now focus on the empty space, as you did in Spoon River, Part One. Put your person—the person you wanted to give or get something from—on the back wall, in that space. Keep the physicality from your animal, keep that psychological center. When you're ready, speak your poem."

The effect the animal work and the psychological center have on the speaking of the poem can be enormous. The body language is completely different from how the actor is in normal life, but if she's relaxed, the new way she's moving and holding herself looks natural. She's doing a character piece of work, and the words of the poem will often have new layers of meaning, as well as character vocal quality.

After doing the poem standing, the actor will then sit and do it in the chair to explore the two choices and see which one feels best.

After the first actor has gone, I'll bring each of the other actors to the center and have them repeat the process. Once done, I'll often have them face each other in chairs—keeping the emotional quality built by the psychological center and animal work—and have them speak the poems to each other. It's as if they've gotten the night out in the cemetery and are making small talk at a social—a ghoulish thought!

"Before speaking, decide if you had a relationship with the other person. Do you know her? Or is she a stranger?" I'll remind the speaker to want to either *give* or *get* something from this fellow Spoon River resident, and that this is the only chance she'll have to say what she wants.

I'll also remind the other actor to keep her concentration. "Really hear what she's saying to you and let yourself react." The effect of all this work—the individual preparation and the interaction—is highly, but naturally, emotional.

What We've Learned

Understanding and using the psychological center is very helpful, as is the animal work. They are of enormous value for performing the classics, as well as many contemporary roles. But the psychological center isn't limited only to animal work. Actors can choose psychological centers for their characters without going through all the steps of the animal exercise.

One of the best examples I've ever seen of using the psychological center work was from a stage actor playing the lead in *In the Matter of J. Robert Oppenheimer* by Heinar Kipphardt. The actor was playing Oppenheimer, the head scientist in developing the U.S. atomic bomb. Oppenheimer was a man of science and advanced intellect, and the actor used this characteristic to determine the psychological center of movement: the center of the forehead, the pineal gland. Every movement was led by the spot in the center of his forehead, and he would not answer another character until he had physically moved his face toward the other actor and centered his pineal gland on that actor, as if he were talking with the gland and not his mouth. It was as if he couldn't communicate until that center was focused on whomever he was talking to. The external effect was fascinating.

These two techniques are extremely useful for multiple roles, especially the animal work. This tool can be especially helpful in not only creating the behavior of one character, but helping to define the difference between characters when doing two or three different roles in the same play. Often, the multiple characters played by one actor will be two-dimensional characters from the writing, and the actor has to go to unrealistic extremes to define the differences. But I guarantee that by trusting this work and having each character be a different animal with a very different psychological center, the actor can have clear delineation between roles and not have to rely on a wig, moustache, limp, or some other obvious external trick.

Let's go through the process of doing Spoon River, Part Two, and exploring the psychological center and animal work:

- A field trip to the zoo and taking time to choose an appropriate animal for the character
- Close observation of movement, attitude, actions, interactions, and center of movement
- Information on animal before leaving the zoo
  - *The name and habitat of the animal*
  - *The animal's main food source—is it an herbivore, carnivore, or omnivore? Hunter? Scavenger?*
  - *The sound the animal makes*
  - *How the animal walks*
  - *Its center of movement*
- Psychological Center—Applying the animal's center of movement to a character's psychology (Michael Chekhov)
- Rehearsal—Moving as the animal without tension
- Rehearsal—Moving with the animal's center while doing chores around the house
- In Class—Interaction with environment and people as animals, and the psychological effect
- Effect of animal and psychological center work on the words of the poem
- Emotional effect of interacting with other Spoon River residents

9 MAKING A SCENE: THE A.C.T. (ACTION/CONDITION/TELEPHONE CALL)

The A.C.T. is the first exercise that my students do that emphasizes action and the creation of a scene, with the secondary benefit of using sensory details and a physical condition to enhance the emotional reality for the actor.

As noted in the title, the initials of this exercise stand for *Action*, *physical Condition*, and *Telephone call*. All three elements must be planned and rehearsed in advance by the actor.

The activity and physical condition must be explored and rehearsed ahead of time. While the actor should recollect the details of the telephone call before the day of the exercise, the call should not be rehearsed or planned. It should be a real phone conversation the actor had at least two or more years ago, the most difficult one he has ever had to make that he'd be willing to share with the class.

This exercise has all the elements needed for actors to produce in full scene work, which are 1) answers to who, where, when, what, why, how; and 2) the givens, objectives, actions, and obstacles in the scene.

That said, the best way to further explain this exercise is simply to describe the process.

ACTIVITY

First the actor—as himself (the "who")—decides where the scene should take place (the "where") and at what point in his life this scene took place (the "when"). He then chooses an overall event or activity (the "what") that has some importance (the "why"), filled with five or six tasks that must be done to complete the activity (the "how"). For example:

Sample Overall Activity: "I'm in my apartment and must get ready to leave for the airport."

Sample Tasks: Shaving, brushing teeth, selecting what to pack and what not to, checking tickets, finding passport, final luggage check.

The *givens* in this scenario are well known to the actor—he's living his own life, after all. The *objective* is to get out the door and to the airport, and the *overall activity* is comprised of the tasks described above that must be accomplished to leave for the airport.

Finally, when choosing the overall activity, the actor should be sure to create *obstacles* in accomplishing the tasks. For example, the passport might not be where it's expected to be, there might not be enough toothpaste, a favorite shirt might be dirty, or one shoe might be missing. The obstacles chosen should be difficult to handle, but not so devastating as to take the actor in a different direction other than accomplishing the tasks and fulfilling the objective—getting to the airport, in this case.

The actor isn't limited to setting the scene in his apartment. He may set the scene anywhere he wants, ranging from a childhood place to current living quarters. He could be in a college dorm, a locker room, a gymnasium, a room at school, his bedroom as a teenager, or his apartment, as long as he is alone. Perhaps the selection of his A.C.T. scene setting is related to the physical condition he chooses, or maybe dictated by when and where he made the phone call he chooses for the exercise.

PHYSICAL CONDITION

The next step is to choose a physical condition that the actor has experienced at some point in his life. The most common choice is a pain he's experienced in a specific part of his body. The physical condition and the activity are not necessarily related in any way, but often an actor can have the activity come out of the physical condition, or the physical condition may be a result of the activity.

For example: The actor has been out jogging and really turned his ankle. That night he has a big date to go to a dance club. He comes back to his apartment, gets his shoes and socks off (task 1), and examines the swelling. He attempts to walk on it (obstacle 1) as he looks for some ice (task 2), and discovers he's out of ice (obstacle 2). He grabs a bag of frozen vegetables instead and ices it with that (task 3).

Then he decides to wrap the ankle, and he searches for the ace bandages (task 4) as the bag of vegetables keeps sliding off (obstacle 3), only to find he doesn't have enough bandage to properly wrap it (obstacle 4). He wraps it anyway and improvises using masking tape (task 5), and tries to get dressed in a suit (task 6), but has trouble because of his foot (obstacle 5). Once dressed, he puts on his dress shoes (task 7), but they won't fit (obstacle 6), and he opts for wearing his sneakers instead.

The scene in this case (minus the phone call) is about a young man attempting to do all he can to prepare to go on a date that evening. Simply watching him getting dressed isn't interesting. But watching him struggle with the problems is fascinating. How will he walk on that ankle? How will he wrap it? Does he dare wear the sneakers with a nice suit? In other words, an actor should try to create all the acting obstacles he can for this exercise.

✣　✳　✣

SISTERLY LOVE

I chose to reenact getting ready for a good friend's wedding for my A.C.T. I was a bridesmaid, so I had tasks like ironing the shawl, stuffing my purse, writing a card, wrapping a present. Before tackling the other tasks, I painted my nails, which I did purposely. This created an obstacle that heightened my concentration—everything was much more difficult—and according to observers, pretty interesting.

I also had a "female condition" as my physical condition, and every move was excruciating. But my concentration was fully on completing the tasks (despite the pain), and I never gave one thought about how I looked or what my classmates saw. I was able to achieve a sense of heightened concentration that was new to me.

As for the phone call, I decided to confront my sister. We're not close and she intimidates the hell out of me. It wasn't a phone call I ever would actually make—I fear that if I tried, she'd hang up on me. But for the exercise, I said what I really thought—that I was worried about her and cared about her. I encouraged her to take care of herself.

Terry encouraged me to open up to the fourth wall—not to break it and make eye contact with the audience, but rather to leave myself in full view even if my instinct was to look down and hide. He told me to pick a spot on the fourth wall for focus as we had in the Spoon River exercise, and that the exposure would open up my vulnerability without my being conscious of it.

He was right. I ended up calling my sister twice in the exercise, since I hadn't told her everything I had wanted to the first time. After his words of encouragement—combined with the focus from my tasks and the physical-condition work—I trusted myself through the fear of exposure, took a risk, and found a vulnerable and honest state that I never thought was possible.

—Debbie Jaffe

*   *   *

The physical condition shouldn't ever just be mimed, but rather grounded in a reality based on the actor's real-life experience of the condition. For example, if the actor chooses to have a sprained wrist, he shouldn't simply hold his wrist or pretend to wince. Rather, he should recreate the sensation of a sprained wrist through physical-condition and sensory work. If the actor is properly relaxed and concentrated in his imagination, the expressions and limitation of movements from the injury will be natural and honest because they are based on his own reality.[1]

If the actor chooses to enter the scene with a physical condition (rather than have it happen in the moment), it is important that the injury or condition has recently happened. For example, a long-term knee injury won't work for this exercise because a person in this condition will have very different behavior and coping methods for obstacles from someone who has just started suffering from the injury. I don't want the actor in the scene to have made previous adjustments for coping with the injury over a period of time.

Injuries aren't the only physical conditions that can be used. There are many others, such as a violent headache or toothache, stomach or menstrual cramps, bad back, horrible sunburn, massive hangover, and many others. The key is that the actor should have experienced the physical condition at some point in his past.

If it's an injury that is chosen as the physical condition, sometimes it can come from the activity. An example scenario might be that the actor is alone preparing dinner for a very important event. The overall activity is making dinner, while the individual tasks are the various food preparation tasks, such as cleaning, chopping, mixing, etc. Near the beginning of the exercise, he slices his hand open with a knife. The actor must stop, bandage the cut, and then do his best to continue doing the tasks of chopping vegetables and other food preparation, but now deal with the new element of the injury. Things that were relatively simple prior to the injury suddenly become very difficult. But he can't stop making the dinner—it's too important.

[1] See the Pain sensory exercise in Part II

Sometimes the physical condition can have nothing to do with the activities. For example, an actor once used a soccer injury while having to get a drink for her mother in the next room and then change clothes for bed. The two incidents happened at completely different times and were completely unrelated. They worked because of the grounding in her imagination of the pain from the injury and the sensory detail recollected from doing a simple task for her mother and changing clothes for bed.

PREPARATION AND REHEARSAL

Before I describe the telephone call, I want to discuss the Activity and Condition preparation. The rehearsal and preparation for the A.C.T. in class is very similar to the Pain or other physical-condition exercises I described earlier, only that the actor must do the work on his own rather than being led by me. Before starting to rehearse, the actor should sit and, with his imagination, start the pain in one small spot.

Once his imagination is firmly rooted in the memory of the physical condition during rehearsal, he then tries to complete his chosen activity. Through the rehearsal, he explores how that physical condition impedes the tasks of his overall activity. The physical condition should add more obstacles to an overall activity that is hard enough to do when feeling well.

I insist that the actor rehearses the condition and activity at least twice on his own before attempting the A.C.T. exercise in class.

TELEPHONE CALL

For this part, the actor should go back through his memory track and select an actual phone call that was very difficult to make, but one that he'd be willing to recreate in front of the class. I always suggest going back at least two years for the selection, since something recent is going to sound scripted. The actor may also say things he wanted to say but that were suppressed when the actual phone call was made.

And, as I said before, in rehearsal at home, the actor does not rehearse the phone call, only the activity and condition. Prior to doing the exercise in class, he only needs to remember whom the phone call was to and why he was making it (objective).

A.C.T. IN CLASS

The actor sets the stage himself and tries to recreate the chosen setting as much as possible using available furniture and props. I always encourage the use of personal items to help give the space the sensory details that the actor can use. For example, if the scene takes place in the actor's apartment, he might want to bring in the knickknacks that sit on his coffee table. The more things that can trigger a sensory response, the better.

Before doing the A.C.T. in class—or any scene or exercise, for that matter—the actor must do a relaxation and concentration warm-up, as well as working on sensory and physical-condition details. If the condition is present at the top of the exercise, he should explore the center of the injury or condition as he did in rehearsal. If the condition is the result of an activity during the A.C.T—like the cutting of the hand example—the actor should simply focus on relaxation and concentration so he doesn't project the injury at the top of the scene. The rehearsal at home should give him the grounding he needs to live in the reality of the injury as it "happens" (relaxation and physical condition) on stage.

Often, a student will prepare for the scene and then have to come out and set up the stage for the exercise. If he's done a great deal of physical-condition work and is firmly rooted in the sensation, I'd rather have him ask a few fellow students for help in setting up the set than blow all the prep work by moving furniture around and working against the limitations of the injury. A high level of concentration is necessary for this exercise, and the actor should never do anything that would take him out of that concentrated state until after the exercise has begun.

The exercise itself starts simply with the actor entering, or starting on stage performing the tasks involved with the overall activity and living in the physical condition, with all the obstacles that arise. The exercise should take twenty minutes maximum, and should have been thoroughly rehearsed at home. A student should never come into the exercise and "wing it," since the results will be less than satisfactory and a real injury might occur if the scene has not been planned and practiced.

NOTE: The phone call is pending from the beginning of the scene and helps to heighten the stakes, along with activity and physical condition. The actor enters the stage thinking in the back of his mind, "I must make this phone call after I get x, y, and z accomplished and before my exit."

After about fifteen minutes of mostly nonverbal moments establishing the activity and condition, the actor must "will" himself to the telephone. This is the end of the rehearsed portion of the exercise. For the final portion, the actor initiates the conversation with the person on the other end and says whatever words spring from the remembered call.

During the call, the actor must establish a focal point on the fourth wall. We want to see the eyes and what's going on, and not be shut out by the actor looking down into the phone's mouthpiece. Most importantly, the actor must sustain the physical condition throughout this phone call. The call itself should last between five and ten minutes, until everything that needs to be said has been said. "Remember, you can say things that you wanted to say but didn't. Will yourself to go out on the edge. Make the call dangerous."

✦　✦　✦

CLEANING UP, THE HANGOVER, AND THE CONFESSION

Playing the role of Peter in a production of *Eastern Standard* by Richard Greenberg at T.S.S., I had to reach my emotional apex at the end of the scene by professing my doomed love for another character. As I prepared and analyzed, I saw that there were parallels to the A.C.T. exercise. The scene took place the day after a bacchanal at a beach house. The mundane yet necessary activity was cleaning up the mess. All the characters were suffering from hangovers, including my character. And then, of course, at the end of the scene was my emotional explosion, which was on the level of the emotional phone call from the exercise.

In rehearsal, I focused specifically on each sound, word, and movement—and the impact it had on my pounding head and sickened stomach. Peter was somewhat of a clean freak, so there was plenty to clean up. But he wasn't an emotionally explosive character, so the final outburst needed some impetus to appear natural. Supplementing the emotional flow of the scene by staying true to the pain and sickness of a hangover, I was able to build on my character's inherent frustration and annoyance in order to compel that final emotionally vulnerable confession at the end of the scene.

—Jason Salmon

✳　✳　✳

The exercise demonstrates that having to do tasks while experiencing a physical condition leads to a heightened psychological and emotional state. This state adds to what's at stake when the actor finally picks up the phone. The physical condition and activity propels the actor to the emotional stakes of the phone call.

Keeping the physical condition throughout the call is the key element to this exercise. A pain leads us to a psychological and emotional state. The actor working on tasks with a physical condition creates high stakes for himself as well as a heightened inner life—an inner life that counteracts the very static action of talking on a dead phone. Hopefully the actor will begin to learn the technique of creating the same heightened inner life of a character.

WHAT WE'VE LEARNED

There's a lot of value in this exercise for scene work. If nothing else, it helps the actor with the technique of making a phone call. Plays, especially ones by beginning playwrights, are filled with phone calls. The actor finds in this exercise that he may only briefly get a sound of the person he is calling, but other images like the person's face, clothing, or expression will come alive. The phone call also nails the importance of personalization: personalizing whom the actor is talking to and what he needs to give or get from that individual. The essentials of acting a scene are in this call: who, what, where, why, how, and objective.

The value of the added physical condition and the activity is to heighten the stakes for an actor in a scene. Acting is about doing, and with the A.C.T. exercise, the actor experiences the creation of obstacles to solve. All plays need behavior, props, objects, tasks, and activities. I feel that even the most abstract plays need these things, possibly more than the naturalistic ones do. No character is just standing there reciting lines, not even in Shakespeare. If so, an audience member might as well purchase the record and save on a high-priced theater ticket.

Here's a recap on the steps involved in prepping for and presenting this exercise.

At Home:
- First individual exercise with elements of a scene
- Putting together three elements: *Action*, physical *Condition*, and *Telephone* call
- Activity elements:
  - *Who—the actor*
  - *Where—location of the activity*
  - *When—time period in actor's life*
  - *What—overall event or activity*
  - *Why—the importance of the activity*
  - *How—the tasks to fulfill the activity*
- Recreate the sensation of the condition—don't pretend!
- Plan out the activity—the tasks and obstacles

- Rehearse Activity and Physical Condition at least two times before class
- Choose a real, difficult (and emotionally resolved) phone call from past, but do not plan or rehearse it

In Class:
- Recreate setting with props
- Extensive warm-up
- Extensive sensory work before beginning exercise if coming into exercise with physical condition
- Importance of concentration throughout exercise
- "Willing" oneself toward the phone call
- "Hearing" the person on the other side of the line
- "Seeing" images concerning the person (facial features, details of previous events and places, etc.) out of the objective
- Sustaining physical condition throughout call
- Emotional and psychological effect of condition on conversation
- Making the call "dangerous"
- Physical condition and tasks create the emotional stakes for phone call

10 FREEING THE INSTRUMENT— THE FALLOUT AND THE SONG EXERCISE

Frequently there are moments called for in a play or film script that will be very personal. The actors come to rehearsal knowing where they will have to go to find the inner truth. Some actors can jump right into the scene without fear. As I've said throughout this book, acting that seems spontaneous—what an observer may call "real" versus "staged"—requires relaxation and concentration. Once these two steps are achieved, it's time to put the entire instrument of the brain, body, and emotions to work.

There are certain types of scenes that are more difficult than others. Some actors have trouble expressing anger honestly on stage or for a camera. Others may experience difficulties with sentimental scenes. Love scenes that involve nudity are extremely personal, and therefore extremely problematic to perform in front of an audience or in front of a group of strangers and technical crewmembers. It's only human nature to protect ourselves by putting up emotional blocks that we can hide behind.

But for the actor, the blocks must be broken through. These types of situations are bound to cause great fear and trepidation, and they need a large amount of understanding and support from the director. It would only be human nature for the actors to "want to put the brakes on." The resistance has to be carefully worked through in the rehearsal process.

But what if the actor is on his own? Perhaps the director is more concerned with structure and technical details, as often happens in film work. Or what if it's an audition, or a second, third, or fourth callback? Talk about pressure! A job is at stake. Perhaps it's a career-making role. No one but a fool would get up the morning of such an audition and feel not just excited and anxious, but also that he has to downplay the anger and resentment at what he is being put through. Even before arriving at the audition or on set, the actor often has thoughts like, "I hate those people (the director, producer, or casting person)." The anger is rather primal, almost like a little kid saying, "I hate you, Mommy," or, "I hate you, Daddy." The actor doesn't really mean *hate*, but it comes from a legitimate place of not being in control, and the result can be like a temper tantrum in the mind—an "acting out."

The actor has an analogous feeling when he is under pressure to show his most personal side and innermost feelings, and be judged on them. "Oh God, I'm going to be tested and tested again!" he thinks. "What do they want? What are they looking for? Haven't they seen what I can do and offer them? Crap! After all, this work, time, and energy, I still may be rejected!"

It's vitally important for the actor—while away from the audition, stage, or set—to acknowledge these emotions, not to stifle them, thinking, "I'm an actor and I shouldn't have these feelings." Not acknowledging these feelings of anger means the body is stuck with them, and the actor becomes tense and blocked. The situation makes it difficult, if not impossible, to access acting choices.

The next two exercises, the Fallout and the Song Exercise, are excellent examples of work that helps an actor to open up and feel comfortable expressing a full range of emotions. While they both seem simple—actors use short phrases in the Fallout and song lyrics in the Song Exercise to express emotions—they achieve the complex task that I call "mind-to-heart-to-will," which is an important component in good acting.

First, the *mind* of the actor hears and repeats lyrics or words—"I love you," for example. The actor has an emotional response to the words—in his *heart*. He must then find the gumption or *will* to push forward and express the emotion and present it for others to see. Hence, "mind-to-heart-to-will."

The process of mind-to-heart-to-will is so fast, it's practically immediate, just as it is in real life. Which emotions are difficult for the actor to express instantaneously depends upon the individual. Someone may decide that expressing excessive anger isn't good, for example, and after years of suppressing it in life, may have trouble doing so as an actor. An overly romantic teenager who's had his heart broken may be tentative about expressing tenderness as an adult. The walls are a natural part of life, but a block to good acting. These two exercises work toward breaking down these walls and giving the actor a choice—keeping some of the protections up as necessary in life, but opening up the protections that are necessary for acting.

A NOTE FOR LEADERS

The Song Exercise or the Fallout should only be done when an actor is at an advanced stage of growth in his work. This is very important for a leader to remember. *Don't do these exercises when an actor is in the early stages of learning his craft.* If he's not ready for it, he's not going to get anything out of it. It will be terrifying, and that is not the way to work. Even an advanced actor will find these exercises difficult. I have never had anybody come out of the Song Exercise or the Fallout saying, "This was the worst experience of my life." I've had nothing but positive results with these exercises—*but* I make sure that the actor is ready to attempt the exercise.

For the teacher, this is one of the most difficult exercises to lead. An instructor works his butt off because he's not only leading, but also closely monitoring the student. The leader has got to know the person he's working with—to know what areas of emotion to bring out of the actor.

For instance, if the actor is someone who is already very aggressive and easy to anger, there's little point in dwelling on the bombastic side of this exercise, and attention should be paid to the tender, sensitive parts. If you're working with a big, macho man, nine times out of ten he's going to have a lot of problems with the sensitive areas. But if the actor is a calm romantic who has no trepidation with tenderness, the anger sections may need more exploration. The more you know about the actor, the more you can tailor some of the phrases for him to connect with his reality or the as-if. It's important that you've had somebody in class long enough prior to doing either exercise that you know him well.

FALLOUT

I have put this exercise together from my many years of teaching by combining sections from exercises that I did in the past, ending up with this all-encompassing workout called the "Fallout." It includes principles of Bioenergetic work and has served as a magic release for a number of actors. It is a very long exercise, taking a good hour, but during the work, the entire class remains riveted and working with the actor.

I call this exercise the Fallout because the actor "gets out" or "falls out" by expressing feelings and emotions in their most simplistic form. One of the most important aspects of the Fallout is for the actor to affirm how many sides of himself (how many different feelings) he has at his disposal. It is an extremely freeing and exhilarating exercise.

The Fallout is basically a verbal exercise. The actor stands in one place and occasionally moves his feet, but always returns to a standing, open position. I will say phrases that the actor will repeat back, allowing any emotion to come up that the words elicit. The exercise is about the actor giving up control of his impulses and letting himself "happen" in the moment. It is not about calculated line readings, but about leaving himself open and vulnerable to wherever the phrase may take him.

Memorize a Monologue

The Fallout does not require the type of homework or planning necessary in the other exercises, with the exception of the memorization of a monologue. "Choose something you've never worked on before, and only memorize the words. Do not work the monologue in an acting sense." The monologue will be used at the end of the exercise, and it is important that the actor has not already imposed a way of performing the monologue, but rather is open to the availability discovered throughout the Fallout.

While an intense preparation is not needed for the Fallout, an actor must be mentally prepared for this exercise by acknowledging its difficulty. Some students compare it to jumping into a pool from a high diving board. The shock is lessened if you're prepared and open to doing the work. This kind of acknowledgment is also important for helping the actor to get grounded in his body and his breath.

In-Class Preparation

The actor *must* spend at least thirty minutes relaxing and warming up before starting this exercise, preferably alone in a quiet space like a dressing room. Once he is fully relaxed, I have the actor begin the work by standing in an open position as in the Bioenergetic work—facing forward, feet centered and shoulder-width apart, with the knees slightly bent. I always check and correct turn-out or turn-in of the feet and make sure the actor is standing on his full foot, and not to the inside or outside of it. The bend in the knees should be slight. "Relax the calf muscles and the leg so that the only tension is in the hamstring area," I'll say. "Drop the buttocks, find a comfortable arch in the back, relax groin muscles, anus muscles, and buttocks, and breathe down into the pelvic area."

For Leaders—Danger Signs

As we get into the exercise, many actors find that their fingers or toes will start to tingle or their lips start to go numb. The leader will see signs of this if they start to shake out their hands, or their hands start turning white. Ask the actor if his fingers are tingling. It's a sign that he is not breathing correctly and neither air nor blood is getting to the extremities. *It is vitally important to stop this exercise until the actor is breathing correctly again.*

Get the actor to first let his breath drop down, and then have him work on exhaling. If he is wearing tight pants, ask him to open the top button. The tingling sensation can happen at various times early in the exercise out of fear, anxiety, or emotions that the actor is uncomfortable with expressing. It's a natural tendency for all of us to jump up into chest breathing when we are uncomfortable, but that state is one step from panic.

Make the Emotion Work For the Actor, Not Against Him

Sometimes, honest reactions to real emotion work against good acting. For example, the first emotion I work on in the Fallout is fear. The actor surely knows fear—fear of the work, fear of the audience, fear of success, fear of actually getting the job, fear of not being able to move an audience to tears or laughter, or fear that he won't be the slightest bit interesting, for that matter. Why *wouldn't* an actor in touch with his real self have these fears?

But these fears cannot lead to immobility or stagnation. While freezing may be an honest response to fear, it does not serve the actor. The difference between life and stage is that the actor must always attempt to work from an open instrument. And fear does not need to have that particular reaction. There are many heroes who *took action* because they were terrified—the point being that fear did not freeze them, but caused them "to do." As the actor works through the phrases, from "I'm scared" to "I'm really frightened" to "I'm terrified," the images that are elicited become stronger. This is where the leader really has to make the actor aware of being on the breath, and putting the feeling into the whole body rather than just getting stuck in the chest, where fear usually lodges itself. Playing a moment like this, on stage or on film, requires the actor's full instrument—body and voice. The actor's tension must be separated from the character's tension.

Loaded Action Verbs

As you will see from the sample of phrases I will throw out on the following pages, I use very loaded action verbs. This is analogous to the actor selecting heightened action verbs to play in a scene. When an actor is not playing with heightened action verbs, the work can be credible and honest, but usually not very stimulating, and sometimes downright dull. By making the stakes high with action verb selection, the actor will stimulate his mind, heart, and will.

As you, the teacher, progress along, you will easily see what phrases mean something to the actor, as opposed to the ones that don't. Ask the actor to not just dismiss a phrase because he's never "had that experience," but to go to an as-if to see what might happen. Make sure the actor is not playing a response to the phrase, but having the initial, basic response instead. If the actor is going back into his head and killing the impulse instead of staying in the feeling of the moment, make him aware of it.

Pre-Exercise Conference

If you are a teacher and choose to explore using this exercise, please keep in mind that I stay with the same general format with both male and female actors. Be careful, never violate a trust, and use your awareness and judgment. Often it's a good idea to have a conference with the actor before the exercise to see if there are any vulnerable points you as the leader should be aware of.

Also remember that if somebody has confided in you and it's private and personal, do not use that either in a scene or in an exercise like this. Make sure that the actor can handle anything you're giving him and respect his privacy, and it will be a positive and valuable experience.

The Exercise Format

The following lines are what I use during different parts of the exercise. The words that I say are in plain text, and the answers the actor gives are in italics. For the exercise, I throw out a phrase and the actor will repeat it back—often three or more times—until I instruct him with a different phrase. "Simply repeat the line after me," I'll say. "Keep saying it, letting the feelings the words evoke come up. Don't pause or think about it—just say the words."

I always begin with a little warm-up to deal with the actor's anxiety.

Warm-Up Phrases

TERRY: I don't want to do this.
ACTOR: I don't want to do this.

T: I hate this exercise.
A: *I hate this exercise.*

T: This is a stupid exercise.
A: *This is a stupid exercise.*

T: Goddamn it, Terry.
A: *Goddamn it, Terry.*

T: You're picking on me, Terry.
A: *You're picking on me, Terry.*

T: You're a big bully, Terry.
A: *You're a big bully, Terry.*

T: There are new people here.
A: *There are new people here.*

T: I don't have to do this shit.
A: *I don't have to do this shit.*

T: I want to go home.
A: *I want to go home.*

T: I want my blanket.
A: *I want my blanket.*

T: What color is your blanket?[1]
A: *Blue.*

T: I want my blue blanket.
A: *I want my blue blanket.*

T: I want my mommy.
A: *I want my mommy.*

T: I want my daddy.
A: *I want my daddy.*

While the first series of lines will typically be aggressive ("Goddamn it, Terry") or defensive ("I want my blanket"), the actor usually accesses some feelings of need with the latter two lines—"I want my mommy" and "I want my daddy." Leaders, remember: Keep the actor repeating the line three or more times until he starts to make a connection.

---

[1] Often I will toss out a question if there is information that I need for certain parts of this exercise, such as the color of the actor's blanket. When the actor is asked a question, he should answer it as simply as possible—preferably with one word or name—and then the exercise proceeds as before.

We then launch into the main portion of the exercise, beginning with fear.

> T: I'm scared.
> A: *I'm scared.*
>
> T: I'm really frightened.
> A: *I'm really frightened.*
>
> T: I'm terrified.
> A: *I'm terrified.*

The actor may be expressing fear about the work, or these phrases may trigger other images in his life when he felt fear about something else. As the actor builds these phrases and allows the body to release the feeling behind these words, I want him to be aware of the breath and to stay grounded. Fear naturally takes us into hyper-energies, and the actor's job when connecting with any of these phrases is to keep the instrument open and breathing from deep down in the body.

Moving on from the "fear" phrases, I counter with other emotions.

> T: I'm shy.
> A: *I'm shy.*
>
> T: I'm very bashful.
> A: *I'm very bashful.*
>
> T: I'm really embarrassed.
> A: *I'm really embarrassed.*
>
> T: I'm all red.
> A: *I'm all red.*
>
> T: I'm all naked.
> A: *I'm all naked.*

Wonderful vulnerability typically occurs with these phrases, and the actor really connects to his emotions. One of the hardest moments to play on stage is when a character is embarrassed or humiliated. We all live in personal dread of this kind of moment in our own life. These little sentences are so very important for an actor to give over to, and to open up this kind of vulnerability.

When the actor gets to "I'm all naked," I add, "There you are. You're standing in front of the class and they are all looking at and sizing up your body." I have the actor look around at the class as he says, "I'm all naked." Then I have the actor look down at his nakedness. I will allow any physical response the actor might have, such as covering genitals with hands, and then ask him to gradually open. Even though he is obviously fully clothed, I have never seen an actor not connect to the as-if of saying, "I'm all naked," and experiencing emotionally what it would be like to be naked in front of the class.

At this point, the actor is deep into the exercise, and I take him through different eras in his life with the phrases I choose. To save space here (as well as make this section more interesting), throughout most of the rest of this I will simply write the phrases as I say them and not include the actor's response, since he simply repeats the phrase. As in the beginning, the actor will repeat the phrases back three or more times.

Childhood

We segue from the "I'm all naked" section into:

> T: I'm a little boy (*or girl*), Daddy.
> T: I'm a little boy (*or girl*), Mommy.

I want the actor to let the child in him out and deal with himself as a little kid. I ask him if he had a nickname.

> T: Did you have a nickname?
> A: *Yes. Tootsie.*
> T: I'm little Tootsie, Daddy.

Again, very lively feeling impulses arise out of these phrases, kicking off a sense memory.

> T: I'm too little, Daddy.
> T: I'm a little lard-butt, Daddy.
> T: I'm a little lard-butt, Mommy.

Most kids weren't called "lard-butt" by their parents, but the students almost always go to the as-if with this pet name from their parents.

> T: Kids pick on me, Daddy.
> T: Kids pick on me, Mommy.
> T: They call me names.

T: What were you called?
A: *(let the actor fill in the blank)*
T: They call me _____.
T: Go beat them up, Daddy!
T: That ride is too big, Mommy.
T: I'm going to fall out.
T: I'm gonna get hurt, Mommy.
T: It's too deep, Daddy.
T: It's too deep.
T: It's over my head.
T: I can't touch, Daddy.
T: I can't touch.
T: I'm sinking.

Have the actor keep in mind the repetition of the phrases. While my statements are spoken in a calm, simple manner, the actor will place a different emotion on the words. The response from the actor will often be something like this:

A: *I'm drowning! I'm drowning! I'm drowning! I'm drowning!*
T: Don't swim away, Daddy.
A: *Don't swim away, Daddy! Don't swim away! Don't swim away!*

I always observe closely what opens up for the actor out of this kind of remembering experience. But just as importantly, I am very aware of the actor's breath during this section, ensuring that he stays grounded.

I will follow the water experience with a temper tantrum.

T: I won't do it, Mommy.
T: I'm not going.
T: I'm not going, Mommy.
T: I hate them.
T: They break my toys.

Here it helps to substitute names.

T: Who did what?
A: *Billy broke my bike.*

I encourage the actor to stamp the floor, one foot after another, like he is stamping a person with his feet. This is great for opening up thigh and pelvic energy. That space is a big holding area, and the actor should feel it open up after stamping his feet.

From the temper tantrum, I have the actor center himself once more and give him a moment to catch his breath. Then I launch into other aspects of the parent/child relationship. Most of us had one parent who was more difficult to approach after a failure of some sort. The leader can work back and forth, taking some phrases to Mommy and some to Daddy, such as:

T: I can't do it, Mommy.
T: I can't do it, Daddy.
T: I give up, Daddy.
T: I'm not good enough, Mommy.
T: Don't make me, Daddy.
T: I don't know how, Daddy.
T: I give up, Mommy.
T: I quit, Daddy.
T: Show me how, Mommy.
T: Don't yell at me, Daddy.
T: Leave me alone, Mommy.
T: Help me, Daddy.
T: I flunked the class, Mommy.
T: The principal wants to see you.
T: The teacher doesn't like me.
T: I hate that school.
T: I'm not going back.
T: I'm going to run away.
T: I'm going to go live with (*actor fills in*).
T: I'm in trouble, Mom.
T: Don't tell Dad—he's going to be mad.
T: I'm going to get a lickin'.
T: I need your help, Dad.
T: I didn't make the team, Dad. (*name the sport*)
T: Coach said I was a sissy (*or too fat, too skinny, etc.*).
T: All the kids laughed.
T: I'm not good enough.
T: I'm not pretty (*handsome*), Mommy.

A lot of this is negative bombardment, but it's designed to open up vulnerability.

Early Teen Through Teenage Years

Now I go to the preteen and teenage years.

> T: I asked her/him out, Mom. (*name the girl or boy*)
> T: She/He is really cute, Mom.
> T: She/He is really sexy, Mom.
> T: She/He is really sexy, Dad.

Tell the actor to see his mother or father's face when saying these phrases. For an adolescent, saying that someone is sexy to a parent will almost always get an emotional result.

> T: I made the team, Dad.
> T: I won the game, Dad.
> T: You should have seen me.
> T: You should have been there.
> T: I'm the Homecoming Queen/King, Mom.
> T: The Queen/King kissed me.
> T: Right on the mouth.
> T: In front of the whole school.
> T: All the girls/boys were so jealous.
> T: I got to ride with the float.
> T: I totaled the car, Dad.
> T: The police want to see you.
> T: They found drugs.
> T: I need your help, Mom.
> T: I need your support, Dad.

To both parents:

> T: Stand by me.
> T: Believe in me.

Early Adult

Now we move ahead to the years after high school.

> T: I'm in love, Mom.
> T: I'm in love, Dad.
> T: I'm moving in with her/him. (*to both parents*)
> T: I'm old enough.
> T: I'm a young woman/man.

T: I'm not a little girl/boy, Mom.
T: I'm not a little girl/boy, Dad.
T: It's my choice.

This is a suggestion of a format. A leader can certainly add or insert new phrases. I do suggest that any leader mix the negative and the positive. Keep them short, but make them highly charged.

From here I go to having the actor telling off his parents. There is some movement involved with these phrases, but the actor must keep the feet grounded and push with the arms while staying very loose in the shoulders. The "come here" movement is as if the actor is flinging a beach ball from the front of him up and over and behind his head. The "get away" movement is the opposite—taking the beach ball from behind the head with both hands and flinging it forward.

I have the actor tell both parents to:

T: Come here. (*Arms pull them forward.*)
T: Get away. (*Arms push them away.*)

Egg this on by saying, "What? What? What?" as the actor goes back and forth, rapid-fire, between "Come here" and "Get away," like this:

T: What?
A: *Come here!*
T: What?
A: *Get away!*

I continue the repetition and get the actor to work physically. Once that has been worked through, I continue with:

T: Get out of my life.

Just as in the previous section, I'll have the actor repeat this phrase many times, using "both of you" to answer the question of "who," and "right now" to answer "when."

T: What?
A: *Get out of my life.*
T: Who?
A: *Both of you.*

This is repeated until we get a chant going. Then I'll add:

T: When?
A: *Right now.*

Once I've got the actor saying these statements, I add in the releasing of some four-letter words.

T: Fuck off.
A: *Fuck off.*
T: Who?
A: *Both of you.*
T: Do what?
A: *Fuck off.*
T: Who?
A: *Both of you.*
T: You're assholes.
A: *You're assholes.*
T: Who?
A: *Both of you. You're assholes. Both of you.*

This kind of scenario may be strange for some, since many actors may never have said these expletives to their parents. I encourage them to go to the imaginary as-if. "Let yourself have the words," I'll tell a tentative actor. "You're going to be saying much worse than that in scripts."

Then we move on to some even more difficult name-calling of parents.

T: You're a big prick, Dad.

I'll have the actor repeat that, and actually see his dad's face. This can produce an incredible side of anger, shock, and other emotions that are perhaps kept under wraps by the actor. Then we move on to Mom, making sure the actor sees his mom's face as he says the words.

T: You're a big cunt, Mother.

I'm not trying to be needlessly vulgar here. Many times, we get dialogue in a play script or movie that is filled with four-letter words, often said to characters who don't deserve them. An actor can't just say the words because the character's saying them, without acknowledging his own feelings about the words.

For example, I detest the word "cunt," which I just used. It's an ugly word, and I have almost never used it. But I may have to say it in a play at some point. I want to have the *real* response behind saying it, not just to say it because the character uses it. I want to acknowledge and explore my "I don't like this word" feeling behind the word. The real emotion might give me a whole other impetus in saying a line like that.

"Many times, you're going to get lines to say or actions to play that you hate," I'll tell my students after the Fallout is over. "Don't deny your feelings. Acknowledge that it is very difficult for you to play somebody who thinks or acts that way. Tell yourself, 'I hate this, but the person I'm playing thinks this way and I have to get behind it.' Start by acknowledging your feelings about it, not just being a good soldier and going on and doing it."

Out of this bombast, I get into expressing the need for comfort.

> T: I need a hug, Dad.
> T: I need a hug, Mom.
> T: Touch me, Dad.
> T: Touch me, Mom.
> T: Hold me, Dad.
> T: Hold me, Mom.
> T: Kiss me, Dad.
> T: Kiss me, Mom.
> T: Love me, Dad.
> T: Love me, Mom.
> T: I hurt. I hurt.

Again, back to the vulnerability and need, beginning with:

> T: I want. I want.

I usually have the actor start stamping his feet again. I want him to get into his current age through this part of the exercise.

> T: I want.
> T: I need.
> T: Gimme. Right now.

I'll start the "what" chant, as with the telling off of the parents.

> T: What?
> A: *Gimme.*
> T: When?
> A: *Right now.*
> T: It's mine.

A: *It's mine.*
T: You can't have it.
A: *You can't have it.*

Adult Relationships

Next I take the actor through the process of breaking up with someone and getting the person out of his life. I tell the actor to picture someone from the past—perhaps an old boyfriend, girlfriend, ex-husband, or ex-wife—but not say names. With that impetus, I have the actor then say these phrases.

T: Get out of my life.
T: Get your shit outta here.
T: You're an asshole.
T: You're a lousy fuck.
T: You're a big fucking baby.
T: Go back to your mother.
T: Go back to your mommy.
T: Go back to your daddy.
T: Go live off somebody else.
T: Get off your ass.
T: Get a job.
T: You cheated on me.
T: You lied to me.
T: Don't ever come back.

These phrases get the actor into adulthood—and as an adult, he puts a mixture of hurt and rage out front.

From this rage and hurt, I have the actor calm down by dealing with somebody in his life who is a lover. The first thing the actor does is choose a first name to use. The person could be a past love, a current lover, or someone who could potentially be a lover.

T: Pick someone from your life—opposite sex or romantic possibility.
A: *Marcia.*

From here we dive into the romantic, sensitive side.

T: I really need you, Marcia.
T: Hold me, Marcia.
T: I'm very fragile.
T: Touch me.

T: Touch me all over.
T: The way I like.
T: Kiss me.
T: Kiss me all over.
T: Put your mouth there.
T: Use your tongue.
T: I really like that.
T: I want you inside me (*to be inside you*).
T: You feel so good.
T: I love you, Marcia.
T: Marry me, Marcia.
T: Let's have a baby, Marcia.

Finale—The Award

At this point, I have taken the actor from childhood to present—and through a whirlwind of emotions. To conclude the exercise, I have the actor begin by saying the following very slowly. I have them use their first name, middle name, and last name.

T: I . . .
A: *I* . . .
T: Michael . . . Lee . . . Jones . . .
A: *Michael . . . Lee . . . Jones* . . .
T: am . . .
A: *am* . . .
T: very . . .
A: *very* . . .
T: handsome (*beautiful*).
A: *handsome* (beautiful).

After two or three repeats of handsome/beautiful, I change the word to "sexy." I have the actor say the words one at a time, so that any feelings that are there can occur.

T: I . . .
A: *I* . . .
T: Michael . . . Lee . . . Jones . . .
A: *Michael . . . Lee . . . Jones* . . .
T: am . . .
A: *am* . . .

T: very . . .
A: *very* . . .
T: sexy.
A: *sexy.*

After the actor's done saying he's sexy, I have him finish with an award.

T: I, . . .
A: *I,* . . .
T: Michael . . . Lee . . . Jones . . .
A: *Michael . . . Lee . . . Jones . . .*
T: thank . . . you . . .
A: *thank . . . you*
T: for . . .
A: *for* . . .
T: my . . .
A: *my* . . .
T: Oscar.[1]
A: *Oscar.*

I have him repeat this phrase a few times to see how it feels.

A: *I, Michael Lee Jones, thank you for my Oscar.*

The Monologue

The last step of the exercise is to do the monologue. The actor doing this exercise must remember to bring in something that's fresh, new, fully memorized, and not "prepared" in terms of the emotion behind the words. It's at this point that he speaks the words.

"Don't act the monologue. Stay connected to the center and presence in your body. Do the monologue to all of us and allow the words to connect to any images from the exercise." It's interesting for the actor to experience speaking the words from his present "center"—how easy it is to hook up the words from the monologue with images.

I find the monologue at the end of the Fallout to be a wonderful way of showing students how this tool can work to open up different emotional centers. Rarely have I had a situation where an actor doesn't add color and emotion to a monologue in a way he never would have thought to

[1] Replace with "Tony" if it's more appropriate for the actor.

before. The relaxation, the breathing, and everything else that's gone on in the exercise leads to the open state he's in, and leaves him absolutely ready to work.

✳ ✳ ✳

THE FALLOUT—A WAY TO WARM UP

I was midway through Terry's program when I left to do *Talley's Folly* by Lanford Wilson, in South Carolina. I was playing Sally. I had to enter the stage in quite a state of passion. Having just done the Fallout before taking the role, I used it as a means to get me where I needed to go at the top of the show. I had a quiet dressing room all to myself, and was able to relax and concentrate specifically on the short phrases and questions from the exercise. Using it as a warm-up took me to feelings of anger, love, vulnerability, happiness, exhaustion, passion, and more . . . and with an honest sense that served as a perfect emotional catapult to enter the stage.

—Kimilee Bryant

✳ ✳ ✳

Application of the Fallout

Many actors who have trained with me have found this exercise to be enormously helpful with film work. When an actor is doing take after take, it can be difficult to drop back into the same emotional area. A former student once told me, "I relied on the Fallout for this one day where we did the same take over and over again. The director finally said to me, 'How can you do that? You've done it eighteen times and it's been just as full every time.' It's because of experience with the Fallout."

SONG EXERCISE

While I usually do the Fallout for most of my students, there are always a few who don't take to the exercise. For these students, the Song Exercise achieves some of the same results—the full expression of mind-to-heart-to-will—but through a slightly different method that incorporates singing. I will often suggest the Song Exercise for an actor based on my observation of his body, tensions, lack of physical freedom, or will to "get out there" with himself. This has far more movement than the Fallout, and sometimes, through the strenuous movement, the actor will connect to the "will to let himself happen."

Background Needed

Like the Fallout, I require that the actor has been in class with me for at least six months, feels comfortable in the class, trusts me and the class atmosphere, and has the will to tackle this exercise. Any actor in my classes can do the Song Exercise, even if he doesn't consider himself a singer. In fact, it's often the non-singers who have the best results. The main drawback of the Song Exercise is the amount of time it takes—about ninety minutes or more—but the benefits outweigh the extraordinary class time commitment.

Actors gain freedom from doing this exercise and, in most cases, take another step toward freeing the instrument and letting their individual qualities and talent appear. An amazing aspect of the Song Exercise is that as the actor progresses, his singing typically gets better and better. Even already trained singers will open up to the words with new and exciting images. Most of all, both singers and non-singers get on their full breath, and thus their full voices.

Name That Tune

For the Song Exercise, the actor selects a slow romantic ballad with lyrics that have strong meaning for him. The exercise works much better when not using an "up-tempo" melody. Actors should also avoid songs with a lot of lyrics. One with a simple refrain is perfect.

It is of vital importance that the actor gives himself a good deal of time to do relaxation work before starting the Song Exercise. I also recommend bringing bottled water for occasional throat dryness.

The actor begins by aligning his body in the standard Bioenergetic standing position that I've described earlier in the book. The head should be straight on, the knees should be slightly bent but relaxed, the butt should be dropped a bit, and there should be a comfortable arch in the back. The chest should be straight and solid, not caved in, and the head should be centered and supported well on the neck, without tension.

Sing a Song to Start

Step one of the exercise is to sing the song through for the class without any direction or instruction from me. "Allow all the anxiety and nerves to be there."

Sing It Ugly

The next step is to ensure that the student is relaxed. I'll have him drop over from the waist (with a slight bend in the knees) and shake out the torso by rotating from side to side. The neck should be loose as well. I then have him sing the refrain from this position, with the jaw and tongue hanging loosely and the song sung with big, full, ugly sounds, almost as if his entire mouth is numb from Novocaine. "Make sure you are using the words," I'll say. "Hang on to the vowel sounds, but relax the jaw and tongue and use the mouth as one big flap."

The instructor will typically need to help the actor achieve this kind of body relaxation, especially since the students who do this exercise typically have problems with the Fallout specifically because of body tension. I normally kneel down in front of the actor and place my hands on his shoulders to help him to rotate from side to side. I also manipulate the neck, move the head from side to side, and massage the back, especially the trapeziuses and deltoids. I then brace myself behind the actor with my right leg up against the back of his left side and do more kneading of the upper back muscles.

After I stop the massage and relaxation assistance, the actor continues singing in the same big, ugly sounds. I tell him to drop his butt and suck in the stomach, making a slow arch up through the spine as if someone was climbing up his back, vertebrae by vertebrae.

Sing It High

Once he is standing erect, the actor raises his arms parallel to his ears, elongating the fingers and stretching as high as he can stretch while remaining flat-footed. This stretch should be done without tension. I'll then have him take the song up an octave and keep going up until he is completely in his nasal mask and singing the vowels with an "open" sound. The actor achieves this by sending the voice into the nasal sinuses, and the result sounds like someone speaking underwater. By the end of this good vocal warm-up, the actor's vocal instrument should be open, full, and ready to work.

One . . . Word . . . At . . . A . . . Time

Now, I want the actor to sing the song one word at a time and explore what images the words conjure up. Not only is this a wonderful way to explore a song without obligation to a specific rhythm, but it's also an equally interesting way to explore words. If the actor is available to his imagination and open to feeling as a result of the extensive warm-up, a great deal of inner life will begin at this point.

Whole Body Singing

Next the actor moves in a large rectangle in the open stage space, incorporating the song into his entire body. "You can hop, skip, jump, cartwheel, somersault—anything you want," I'll tell him. "The important thing is to use all your limbs and really get loose."

Sing a March

After a sufficient amount of this general movement, I start to direct different styles. The first one I typically choose is a march, where the actor sings the song as if he's in a procession and begins to march in his best military manner, with precise left and right turns, while singing the song in cadence.

While he's doing this marching movement, I like to heckle the actor by having him repeat certain meaningful phrases and encourage him to get louder and louder, especially when he connects with a strong image from a phrase. I encourage the actor to release some anger and ask him to put some people under his feet whom he would like to stomp on as he marches. After he narrows his choices down to one person, I tell him to stomp the person into the ground, then to continue stomping on the person's body just where he would most like to stomp on the person. The actor can really cut loose with a temper tantrum for a minute or so.

By the time all this stamping is finished, the actor is really down into the lower part of his body and should experience feeling much wider in the pelvic area as well as the thighs.

Different Styles

I then have the actor move into other musical styles. He continues the movements of walking in the rectangle, but changes the song into a big ballroom waltz. After the waltz comes a cha-cha, a rumba, a tango, the Macarena, and any kind of rhythmic dance like that with a Latin beat. At some point, I like to throw in the polka. If the actor doesn't know the style of the dance, I'll have him guess and jump into some form of movement. As these different dance ideas are thrown out, the actor lets go more and more.

We start to conclude with a disco dance, a rock, a punk rock, and doing the song as a rap number. As I said before, the actor does not need working knowledge of these dances or musical styles. What is necessary is that the actor leaps in and commits to whatever gut reactions or images come to mind.

Burlesque

This first section of the Song Exercise concludes with the actor pretending he is the headliner act in a burlesque show. He does not have to actually take his clothes off, but I want the actor to deal with what it would be like to be a headline stripper. The class is asked to cheer and catcall as the actor's name is announced. Applause follows the exchanges, and the actor gets into his "bump and grind" using the song and miming stripping.

Many of the actors doing this exercise—as fed by class response—really cut loose. Others feel awkward and shy. Both responses are valid—the key is that they must stay in their feelings. The shy actors must allow themselves to be shy, and the ones who start to thrive on the energy should allow themselves to have fun.

Make It Mean Something

The next step is to add personalization. The second half of the exercise is done with the actor singing the song to his mother and then his father—all the while allowing new images to come as he expresses the words of the song to each one of the parents. Many times, I put a chair on stage and have the actor sing the song while pretending to sit on a parent's lap. This step in the exercise usually triggers something—with one of the parents in particular—and gets quite emotional. The entire exercise is about encouraging students to drop the defenses, the covers, and the guards and become emotionally naked in front of others.

This exercise, like the Fallout, is about the actor giving himself permission to be free, spontaneous, and open. It epitomizes the term mind-to-heart-to-will. The actor only uses the lyrics of the song during the exercise, and allows the rhythm to change according to images and feelings as they arise. The Song Exercise is not to be confused with psychodrama or the pushing out of emotions. It is about allowing the actor's subconscious to behave spontaneously and concurrently with the actions the actor is doing. Others in class watch the results of the actor connecting to his emotions as he allows himself to open up, but they have no idea what the emotions directly relate to. The actor's sense memory is still the actor's private thoughts.

Kid Singing

After singing the song to Mom and Dad, I'll take the actor back to grade school. "It's your school recital, and you're singing to the full student body," I'll say. Almost everyone had to sing at some point growing up, whether it was in grade school or later on in junior high or high school. "Try to remember your music teacher or teachers. See them at the piano, or in front of you, directing and conducting."

I ask the actor where the recital is taking place, and whether he is in an auditorium or on a stage. "Examine how your mother or father dressed you, or whether you dressed yourself. What is the style of your hair? The clothes? What is the time of year?" I continue with other similar details. Then I up the stakes. "Place your parents out there in the auditorium. Your whole family has come, including grandparents, aunts, and uncles. Make it a big day."

Then I have the actor start singing. "Hear the music teacher give you your note, and then sing to us, using the other actors in class as your former schoolmates. Remember a child who was your first big crush, and then make an actor in class that person and sing to her. Then sing at the kid who always bullied you. Conclude the 'recital' section by singing to your parents and grandparents."

Love Songs

I follow the recital by having the actor sing to somebody who was his first real big love. I'll ask the actor to name the person, which causes a very organic, youthful response. I start the section with the actor imagining touching the hand of his crush, then entwining fingers. I emphasize that the actor should recall sensory detail and try to feel the other person's hand—the size of the palm and length of the fingers, whether the hands are sweaty, and other details.

This line of coaching continues with me telling him to put his arm around her and angle in for a kiss. I start the potential kiss with the actor breathing in the girl's ear, then advancing to the cheeks, and finally to a full-blown kiss. "Make it a big soul-kiss, if you want." The actor continues singing through most of this, unless quiet when acting out the kiss. It always amazes me, no matter the age of the person I'm working with, that he becomes that innocent kid again. We see it happening right in front of us.

The next transition in the exercise is to sing the song to the first person the student ever made love to. I want the actor to drop into the remembered feelings that surrounded him in the moments right after "that first time." No one doing this exercise has to give details about such a private moment, since the only words used are from the song. For instance, in the above example of losing your virginity, it will have been a great first time for some and quite the opposite for others, but the actor does not divulge details about his experience. The way the song is sung will give us the picture. The actor does not need anything else to delineate his feeling about the event.

Next I progress to the actor singing the song about something he wants more than anything else in the world. The actor is asked to put that goal out in front of him. "Give it a size, a shape, a color. Now, physically reach out for it as you sing. Get your hands on it, pull it in, and hold it against your heart. Now share your victory with someone. See how proud that person is of you."

The next step in the exercise is very difficult and takes a lot of courage on the actor's part. As he continues to sing the song, I ask the actor to imagine making love to somebody. I want him to use his body and the floor as necessary. I give the actor the image that "this person really loves you and trusts you and has really given herself totally up to you." So, in the first part of this section of the exercise, the actor is the aggressor and touching what he likes to touch, and touching the person the way she likes to be touched. "You, the actor, are the lover."

Then I reverse roles and have the actor be subject of the sexual affection. "Somebody is making love to you," I'll say. "Explore what it's like to accept this, the feel of someone else's hands and mouth." This section of the Song Exercise gets into wonderful body freedom, abandonment to images, and a very sensual side. And, as I said before, it takes great courage, risk, and will.

Again, I don't want the actor to do anything that would violate him. The exercise is not about taking off clothes or doing anything lewd, but about dealing with sensual images, the body, and sexuality. An actor's physical freedom with his sexuality is a very important part of the actor. Ultimately, it is part of his talent and what he's presenting on the screen or on the stage. I usually reverse the lovemaking from aggressive to passive two or three times to allow the actor to give himself more physical permission.

A Lullaby

The last step of the exercise is for the actor to pretend he has his child, a newborn baby, in his arms. I ask the actor to give us a name for the child and then to sing the song to that baby. He then proceeds to sing the song to the spouse or lover, and then show the baby to his parents, the baby's grandparents, while singing the song all the while. Lastly, I have him sing the song while showing the baby to the class.

Sing It Loud!

To wrap up the exercise after all these different emotional events, I ask the actor to imagine his favorite fantasy of where he might be singing the song. Accordingly, he can pick a nightclub, a cabaret, a Broadway stage, the Metropolitan Opera House . . . wherever. "Now," I'll say before the final wrap-up, "live out the fantasy of performing the song."

The Song Exercise is a wonderful exercise in finding a physical freedom, of "getting off the words," creating images, and—most of all—exploring a way to find more freedom of expression. The more the actor is willing to open up and get rid of defenses and guards, the more access he has to himself that can be tapped when playing a character. It is about finding range and not just playing the "same old, same old." The work should always be about taking chances, and the Song Exercise is a huge first step to really taking those risks.

A NOTE ON LEADING THE FALLOUT AND SONG EXERCISE

It takes a lot of work on my part—or any leader's part—to do exercises like these. Not only does it take an extremely long period of time (typically an hour for the Fallout and ninety minutes for the Song Exercise, as I said before), but it requires staying ahead of the actor and being sensitive to what the actor can or cannot handle. If you intend to lead these exercises, be sensitive to whom you're working with. Do not push too far in the same directions, but mix it up. For instance, the singing to the parents at the beginning of the Song Exercise can get very emotional. Once the actor gets to express the emotion, get off of it and move on. Do not push the person to totally come apart.

You the leader must use your own reason, sensitivity, awareness, and judgment with each individual actor you're working with. You should know by the time you do either of these exercises what some of the specific actor's blocks are. Therefore, you can encourage and support the actor, and loosen up some of those blocks. But don't force. The blocks can be like a thick brick wall. You can't run through it; you must find a way around or over it.

Never point out an actor's blocks in front of the class. This can be very intimidating to the actor. If need be, have a private discussion about what you've discovered. Don't embarrass an actor in front of his peers. As the teacher, you are responsible for that actor, who has entrusted himself to you. Do not take advantage of that individual's trust. You can have a system of work, but you must be acutely aware of what the actor is ready to do and what the actor is not ready to do.

And make sure that the actor is advanced enough to handle these exercises. I think it can be terribly damaging for a young actor to get into a class that is just too advanced for him. I don't just mean the actor who is young in years, but also the one who has started on a career later in life. Chances are, the older the actor is when he starts his training, the more tight and locked up he's going to be. So you've got to be careful with these tools.

Acting, Not Therapy

Remember, you might be tapping areas you don't know everything about or are not qualified to deal with. *I am absolutely, categorically, and completely opposed to any acting teacher trying to be a therapist.* I know I've explained this in other sections, but it's especially important to remember when dealing with these two exercises because of their sensitive nature. Therapy is not what the work is about, nor is it a means to explore the latest psychological fad, whether it's Scientology, or experiential or transformational workshops, or whatever the latest "ism" is. The work is not another means of personal growth, but about exploring acting tools and acting growth. If it helps the personal growth, fine, but stay focused on the acting instrument.

It must always come back to the craft of acting—how to help the actor open up the imagination and find full freedom of expression. The explanation of the work does get personal, but a leader has got to know where to draw the line. It's a delicate line between what belongs in work with a therapist and what belongs in an acting class.

Anyone teaching acting is going to touch many diversified backgrounds that can include alcoholism, drugs, incest, abuse, and other pretty traumatic experiences. Be very, very sensitive and aware. You'll get the signs. And if you do surmise that these traumas are the cause of an actor's blocks, you have no business as an acting teacher digging into these problems. That's something for therapy, and you should make the actor aware—*privately*—that therapy would be a good idea. Exploring neuroses has nothing to do with acting. Be very strong with that rule as your guideline.

WHAT WE'VE LEARNED

The Fallout and the Song Exercise are two of the most powerful tools in the actor's toolbox. Taking the risks involved with these exercises leads directly to an ultimate acting goal: freedom of the acting instrument. Let's go through the lessons we've learned.

- Permission to let yourself open up and happen without the fear of judgment

- Importance of breathing

- Taking energy from the floor

- Effects of working on personal emotional areas

- Importance of keeping high energy centered in the thighs, pelvic area grounding.

- Using the voice properly by keeping it on the breath

- Self-affirmation of all the feelings expressed and those capable of being expressed

- Realization of which emotions are blocked and need to be worked to be a versatile actor

- Monologue—once dropped into the body and open, the immediate accessibility to the written word

11 EXPLORING THE SUBCONSCIOUS— EMOTIONAL RECALL

The Emotional Recall, or E.R., is a three-step exercise that I have used for the past thirty-four years of teaching. It can also be called "Effective Memory." To give credit where credit is due, Lee Strasberg developed this exercise, garnered from his work with Stanislavski's exercises. It's one that Lee used to great effect with the Group Theatre and later in his teaching at the Actor's Studio. I was introduced to it by Michael Howard and considered it to be an invaluable training and process tool. It is an exercise meant to incorporate three elements of acting—*life*, *behavior*, and *words*.

LIFE—Inner life, or the inner monologue. This is the thinking and emotional state behind the eyes that leads to honest facial expressions and body language. A character's thought process.

BEHAVIOR—Physical tasks that are being done by a character in completing an overall activity.

WORDS—A writer's words.

These three elements aren't just part of acting—they're part of our natural state as human beings. Many times in real life, we have these three different levels of concentration at the same time and actually live this exercise.

Example: You are in your kitchen, washing the dishes. A CD is playing on your stereo unit. (1) You are aware of the lyrics and melody of the song. (2) You are aware of the details necessary to getting the dishes cleaned—how much soap to use, where to scrub, etc. (3) Suddenly, while both listening to the song and cleaning the dishes, a memory is recalled from your subconscious.

Sometimes the memory is of a recent event, but often it is from the distant past. Regardless of how long ago the event occurred, your imagination takes you to a place where you relive the event in the back of your mind. You begin to smile, laugh, get sad, or get angry. There are probably words running through your head, even if you're not speaking out loud.

You've just been doing all three components of the E.R.

This particular exercise as I use it in my classes has all three parts and must be done in three separate class sessions. The first requires no preparation other than choosing an event from the past to recall. The second and third both incorporate behavior—in this case, an overall activity with various tasks. Like the A.C.T., the second part of the E.R. requires rehearsal. The third part also requires rehearsal, as well as the memorization of a monologue that suits or parallels the moment of the recall.

The Emotional Recall is more than an exercise used to teach a process in the classroom. It is a valuable tool that can be used over and over again in scene work and for monologues, both on stage and for audition purposes. The application of the E.R. is especially useful for very complex monologues and emotionally difficult roles. I'll describe how to use the exercise after the explanation of the process in my classroom.

EMOTIONAL RECALL, PART ONE

For step one of the Emotional Recall, I ask the actor to chose an event from her past that had a strong impact. I encourage my students to choose an event from childhood. The event should, at a minimum, be something that occurred at least seven years ago. A recent event is too fresh, and the actor will try and "think" the event rather than "find" it through sense memory.

Another qualification of the event for this exercise is that it has to be something that ended in a large moment—a "traumatic moment," so to speak. "Traumatic" does not necessarily mean something unhappy and awful. It can be a great moment of joy or a great moment of surprise. But it must be an event that ended in a large emotional response.

In addition, I'll ask my students to pick something that deals with an emotion that is difficult for them to perform when called for in a script. Common suggestions are events dealing with embarrassment, humiliation, or loss of control, since I think these emotions are the hardest to play on stage. Other possibilities are great anger, fear, surprise, joy, silliness, or vulnerability. The actors know themselves best, and I encourage them to select what will help them to free an area otherwise blocked in their work. If they can open up their own emotional life through the recall, then actors have another piece of emotional equipment to add to their availability and skills. "Make this exercise worthwhile by exploring something new and difficult, whatever that means to you," I'll say.

While the event should be one that had an impact, it should also be one that does not have unresolved emotional weight in the present. I want the actor to pick an event that she is now emotionally and intellectually resolved about. No student should ever choose anything that is unresolved. Using an unresolved event won't lead to good acting—it leads to acting from neurosis. Neurosis is never a healthy acting tool. Neurosis needs to be worked on with a therapist.

I ask the actor to tell me in advance what event she'll be working with. If I feel it is something that belongs in therapy rather than in an acting class, I'll ask her to look for something more suitable to the exercise. Again, *the event must be a past, preferably childhood experience that the actor is now intellectually and emotionally resolved about.*

There are certain elements that make some events better than others for Emotional Recalls. For example, the better ones don't have a lot of dialogue during the event. There's not a lot of "he said" and "she said." The less dialogue and the more sensory detail in the event, the better for the exercise.

It's also good to decide where to start before coming to class, and to start the recall shortly before the event. We do not need to work on the entire day and night leading up the situation. There will be plenty of sensory detail to fill twenty minutes before the actor must will herself toward the event.

In Class

Prior to working in front of the class, the actor goes to a private space and gets relaxed, centered, and ready to work. Proper relaxation is essential for this exercise.

Starting the exercise, the actor sits on a hard-back chair, as with the sensory exercises from Part I. As an additional warm-up, she does three or four "drop-overs" from a sitting position in the chair. A sitting drop-over is done by lifting up from the lower back and letting the weight of the head and torso carry the actor into a drop-over between the legs.

In this position, I have the actor shake out her upper torso and rotate the neck in a hanging, relaxed position. I encourage her to relax the jaw and the tongue, and to allow for sounds. With the mouth properly relaxed, the noises should sound as if the student has a mouth full of Novocain (like the Song warm-up) and can't get his lips around the words. After a half a minute or so, I have her "roll" back up slowly through the spine. We then repeat the drop-over until the actor has released excess tension.

Once she is relaxed, I have the actor sit in the chair with her eyes closed. Her hands should be resting on her thighs with open palms or hanging at her side. The legs should be about shoulder-width apart.

Advice for the Actor

I will then give the actor some advice before beginning the recall. "Once we start, I don't need well-constructed sentences. Stay away from descriptive narrative. Although it's a verbal exercise, the fewer words, the better."

I remind the actor that she is not writing a novel. "Stay away from commentary and naming feelings such as, 'I hate that, it's so pretty, it smells good,' or others. Don't worry—likes or dislikes will be conveyed. We'll get the message about how you feel by the way you do the sensory work."

I also ask the actor to push away from "the moment" of the recall before beginning. We want to establish the place and the time with all the sensory details, and if the actor is too focused on the event, we'll never get there. The actual event should be treated as the "second act" of a play. The actor has to play the first act to get to the second. "Push away from the moment as if it's the second act—work on the first before getting to the second."

Location

Once I feel the actor is in a relaxed state, I'll start the exercise. "Now, slowly open your eyes, focus on the back wall over our heads, and start with where you are." The actor then responds with short answers.

> *Terry: Where are you?*
> Actor: My backyard.
> *T: Where is that?*
> A: St. Paul, Minnesota.
> *T: Time of day or night?*
> A: Late afternoon, around three thirty, four o'clock.
> *T: Time of year?*
> A: Spring.
> *T: What month?*
> A: Late May.
> *T: Are you standing or sitting?*
> A: Sitting.
> *T: What do you see directly in front of you?*

After establishing the location and the season, I always lead with, "Are you sitting or standing?" Even if the actor says she's standing in the recall, I want her to remain in the chair for the exercise.

I always remind the actor to give details about what she sees, feels, hears, and smells—not "feeling" descriptions, but rather colors, shapes, sizes, and other descriptive detail. I will help the actor to be specific by directing her to describe what is all around her. "What is to your left?" I'll ask. "What is to the right?"

I also include what's overhead and what's beneath her feet. Grass, concrete floors, institutional florescent lights, and party balloons . . . these are all details that have caused sensory memories to flood back to students of mine.

Clothing

   T: What are you wearing?

I start with the feet and have her give details about the shoes (color, old or new, the style), socks, pants, shorts, dress, feel of the clothing material, shape of legs (thin, pudgy), feel of the skin, whether there are any cuts or bruises on legs. I'll remind the actor that during this sensory/sight exploration, she can use touch to explore the feelings of her clothes and body. I've seen a grown woman rub a scab on her pubescent legs and be transformed back to eight years old again!

I'll then have the actor move to the torso and describe the clothing. Again, detail is important. I'll have her describe her arms (thin? chubby?), fingers (rings? clean fingers? dirt under the nails? chew your nails?), wrists (watch? bracelet?), neck (pendant?), hair and ears (long hair? short? cap or hatless? color of hair? earrings?), and face and mouth (freckles? braces? glasses?).

When working with a woman, I'll often ask, "Are you wearing a bra?" Because so many E.R.s deal with adolescent memories, this question will often bring back a flood of honest shyness and place the student emotionally back in that time period.

The actor should not second-guess the details she describes. It is not helpful for her to think, "I was wearing jeans . . . no . . . was I wearing shorts? Maybe sweatpants?" The actor must trust and go with what comes to her immediately.

Atmosphere and Senses

Next I'll move to the sounds. "The people to your right, can you hear them? What are they saying? Any other noises in the background?" The actor describes what her ears remember hearing. I want to make sure the actor is really listening with her ears—not thinking about what sounds she should hear, but really listening for a sound. If she was indoors, what are the sounds in the house? A refrigerator buzzing? Air conditioner? If she was outdoors, what can she hear in the distance?

We'll then move to smells, the most important sensory aspect for this work. It has been proven scientifically that smells are the key to our memory bank, that scent memories are stored in the brain differently from sight or touch. The more I work in acting class with smells, the more I see that scent is more powerful than the other senses. So instead of just naming a smell, I'll tell the actor to breathe in the scent, to find it in her nostrils, way back into his sinuses. When she does, the memories will spring to life.

Lastly, I'll have her explore taste. Like smell, taste can enhance the sense memories immensely. I'll let the actor run her tongue on her lips to see if there's any remembered taste on the lips, inside her mouth, on the palate, or in the throat.

By this time, if the actor has not dropped into being in the place of the event, she's not going to during this session. As a leader, I will see this very clearly and stop the exercise. There's nothing wrong with delaying an exercise for a later time, but continuing one that isn't working can destroy a student's confidence and belief in concentration.

No Comment

A key to this exercise is to keep the actor from commenting on what she sees, hears, feels, smells, or tastes. Comments like, "Oh, that's really pretty," or, "That's really cute," or, "That's ugly," are not helpful to this exercise. I will pull my students away immediately from these "result words." We don't want result words. We want exploratory sense words. An observer can tell if the actor thought something was ugly or pretty by the way he describes it on a sensory level.

Move to the Moment

At this point, I have the actor move forward. "Will yourself forward toward your event," I'll say. Remember, the actor must stay in the present. The event is happening now. As a leader, I must be careful that the actor doesn't get into "then" and "I was," as it will completely distance her from the exercise. She'll be "reporting" the event rather than living it. As a leader, I will still guide the exercise, but I'll let the actor take over more when she is willing herself forward.

As the actor heads steadily toward her moment, a leader must make sure she continues to work with sensory details. There is a tendency to rush as the moment approaches. I do my best to help the actor to stay in the moment. If you ever choose to lead this exercise, the leader's reminders to stay with sensory details will not throw the actor, but will serve to deepen the moment when it actually occurs.

As the actor relives the event, she'll often either freeze or cease talking about what's happening as she's reliving it. "Keep going, keep going," and, "Words, words, words," are helpful phrases I use for guidance. And when the actor hits the moment, I will encourage her with, "Let it happen. Let yourself go."

Re-Experience

If the actor is working well, she will re-experience the exact same moment of the original event. The actor will be amazed by what has been stored in her mind and body. Sometimes the actor releases feeling and emotions that were there at the time but perhaps not expressed until this exercise. *It is vitally important for the actor to express all the emotions she feels during this exercise and not keep them in.*

At this point the actor, in most cases, will still be in the chair. Every once in a while, something so strong—a memory or an emotion—will come back and propel the actor to her feet. I've seen actors push chairs back in a retreat and jump forward in shock—all the while reliving the experience.

Finishing the E.R.

Once the moment has subsided, I will help the actor to find a catharsis. If the event was traumatic, maybe a parent or a friend held them and comforted them. Perhaps the actor solved the situation herself and escaped from something frightening on her own. The exercise should always end at a calm moment. It is very important that the leader help the actor to leave the exercise during a time of safety.

If there was someone else there after the event, it is very important that the actor experiences the feeling of being with that person again. I will continue to ask questions as I did in the beginning. "Describe what the person hugging you looks like. What does the person smell like? What clothing is he wearing?" Sometimes I will ask her to go to a monologue and do it just from the way she is feeling now, not a previous interpretation—whatever helps the actor to find a catharsis. All of these things help the actor to finish the exercise in a safe place.

Afterward—Move Around

After the actor has returned to "the present," I have her get up out of the chair and take big, big strides around the room. She'll need to loosen up and release the tension from her body, so I'll have her swing her arms clockwise as she's walking. As she swings her arms, I'll direct her to make an "AAAHHHH," releasing sound from deep within the torso and opening up the chest.

✣　✳　✣

BLOWOUT ON THE SOCCER FIELD

When I was trying to decide on a moment for my Emotional Recall, Terry suggested that I work on an emotion that I have difficulty express-ing. For me, that would be anger. I had some trouble remembering a good anger episode, and the only one that came to mind was when I was in sixth grade and thrown out of a soccer game after being fouled. I laugh now when I think of it because it seemed so trivial, and I wasn't sure if it would work.

When Terry took me through the recall, I was so relaxed that I was able to picture the most detailed things surrounding the event. Eventually the anger exploded, and after the anger, there were other emotions I hadn't connected to the event in my memory—compassion, disappointment, humiliation, and guilt.

It was difficult at first to take this experience into scene work. Every time I was supposed to get angry in a scene, I launched into this sixth-grader angry. It felt so free—I loved it! But then I had to use the intensity of that anger with adult characters with social morays that forced them to repress their anger. At first I didn't understand how to have it apply, since the mannerisms couldn't be the same as they were with the wild child out on a soccer field. But after applying an obstacle—that a lady has to behave according to societal rules or she won't get what she wants—the frustration mixed with the anger led to a characterization that I never would have gotten on my own.

—Felicia Pensario

* * *

This movement usually brings up and releases any residue of emotion from the exercise. Remember, the actor has been sitting for at least thirty and sometimes as much as forty-five minutes. It's also a nice psychological and physical release. I let the actor continue taking the strides until she gets tired and wants to stop. Then she sits back in her chair in front of the class so she can discuss the exercise.

What We've Learned
- Choose a childhood event, or one that happened at least seven years prior
- Use E.R. for emotions difficult to express on stage
- Acting is not therapy—chose an emotionally *resolved* event
- Do a relaxation before starting
- Use chair "drop-overs" for quick tension release
- Describe details, but make no comments (ugly, pretty, etc.)
- Use sensory details (sight, touch, hearing, scent, taste)
- Smell is the most important memory sense

- Live the moment in the present
- Have the emotion—"Let it happen."
- Leave the event in a safe place
- Release the body afterward

EMOTIONAL RECALL, PART TWO

Now that the actor has her Emotional Recall well grounded in her imagination, it's time to prepare for the second part of the Emotional Recall exercise. In this portion, the actor adds an activity to the Emotional Recall and has both the E.R. and the activity happen simultaneously.

The purpose of this portion of the exercise is to explore how the *life* of the E.R. (now done as an "inner," or unspoken, monologue) affects the behavioral action on stage (or "stage business"), and how the *behavior* (the tasks and various obstacles encountered in doing the tasks) affect the inner life of the E.R. The goal is to keep the E.R., Part One, alive as an inner monologue while being physically involved in four or five tasks. The result will be a realistic and interesting scene with few or no words.

At Home

There is a significant amount of preparation work necessary for Part Two of the Emotional Recall. The first steps are to choose an overall event, and then an activity with a series of tasks to complete.

Choosing the Situation

The actor must choose an event with these guidelines: She is at home alone, she has a very important personal event she is preparing for, and she's fifteen minutes behind schedule to pull everything together. The event is something she cannot be late for.

Examples of important personal events include, but are not limited to: an audition; a first date; a family holiday dinner; a theater show or concert; an airplane, train, or bus trip; an important exam; or an important day at work. An alternative for the actor is that she is fifteen minutes behind schedule in preparing for a very special dinner guest or surprise party.

It doesn't matter which one she chooses, as long as she's clear about the choice and her overall objective, and as long as the stakes are high—she'll miss her audition, her date will see her house in shambles, dinner won't be ready for the family. Most importantly, she's only got fifteen minutes to be prepared to leave or receive guests.

Choosing the Activity (Tasks)

The next step is to choose the tasks that will comprise the overall activity. For example, if the actor's overall activity is to prepare for an important date, she might have to put on makeup, prepare her clothing, get dressed, find her purse and keys, brush her teeth, and perform other preparation activities. The tasks must be something that the student can do currently in a simulated stage home, since she'll actually do them during the rehearsal preparation at home.

I tell my students that I don't want six similar tasks. For example, she shouldn't do three different grooming things in the bathroom and consider it three different tasks. Those things would encompass one task (grooming preparation), not three. I want at least six different tasks that have to be done. It will take some imagination and planning from the actor, but there's plenty to choose from. Dressing can become another task, especially if the necessary clothing isn't readily available. Is she bringing a gift, like flowers or wine? Wrapping or preparing can be another task. "Use your imagination!" I tell my students.

Since the actor has only fifteen minutes, she may not need to complete all the tasks when finally doing the exercise in class, but she should have them planned for the exercise. Also important to remember is that the tasks must actually be able to be done in the confines of the actor's home and then at the staged home at the acting class. For example, if the tasks involve food, actual cooking wouldn't work, while choosing a non-cooking food preparation like chopping vegetables or frosting a cake would work just fine.

Create Obstacles

Some tasks should have an obstacle that interferes with the easy completion of that task. For example, watching someone calmly cook a meal is like . . . well, like watching and waiting for water to boil, literally. Watching someone try to cook a meal when she can't find the right ingredients, the bowl she's using topples over, there's a bug in the middle of her best dish—now that's interesting!

The obstacles shouldn't be so huge that they become the focus of this exercise—we're exploring an Emotional Recall as an inner monologue, not outrageous physical comedy. But they shouldn't be too easy to complete either. "And remember, you've got a time limit here—you're fifteen minutes late!"

First Rehearsal

Once the actor has decided on the event, the tasks, and the obstacles, she finds some time alone at home to rehearse it. She performs the tasks in her home while saying the Emotional Recall out loud, all the while remembering that she's running fifteen minutes late.

"Choosing a time when you're alone to rehearse is vitally important," I remind my students. "An outside observer can throw off the actor's concentration during the rehearsal, and you must say your Emotional Recall aloud while performing the tasks." Having a roommate around while reliving a childhood experience can be an embarrassing situation! But even more importantly, it will compromise concentration and the quality of the rehearsal.

While doing the tasks, the actor must start from the beginning of the recall. "The recall will jump around on you," I explain to the students. Often the key part or "the moment" of the recall will sneak forward during the first one or two tasks, before the actor is grounded in the full emotional state and impact of the recall. "It is important to not let the recall happen too fast."

During this rehearsal period, the actor should explore which tasks parallel or fit with the different parts of the Emotional Recall. "Use the first couple of tasks to set up the Emotional Recall, and the last tasks to bring you to the compelling moment." That's why a selection of at least six tasks is necessary for this process—the actor can't run out of things to do before getting to the big moment in the recall.

"Don't just cut to the event. Go back to the beginning sensory work of the recall," I emphasize to my students. "Keep pulling it back until you're ready to will yourself forward." Speaking the recall out loud will keep the actor on track. For this first rehearsal, the primary focus is on the Emotional Recall, not the tasks or the time limitation.

Second Rehearsal

Several days after the first rehearsal for E.R., Part Two, the actor repeats the steps outlined in the first rehearsal, including speaking the recall out loud if necessary. For this rehearsal, she should put the primary focus on the tasks, obstacles, and time constraints, and less on the recall itself.

Some students will have the emotional life of their recall so alive at this point that they won't need to speak it aloud. But if the primary focus of the actor is mainly on the tasks and the recall is lost or happens too quickly, the student should continue to speak the recall aloud for the second rehearsal, as she did for the first.

Third Rehearsal

The third rehearsal should come several days after the second. This is the final rehearsal before doing it in class, and the Emotional Recall is not spoken out loud but is instead an inner monologue. If the Emotional Recall and rehearsals have gone well, the student's concentration will flow back and forth between the recall and the tasks during this rehearsal.

Rehearsal Note: Don't be surprised if the emotional part of the E.R. doesn't happen in the home rehearsals. Trust the process. It will happen with the heightened reality of being in front of the class.

In Class

If the student has prepared this exercise properly with the three rehearsals, doing it in class shouldn't be much different from doing the third rehearsal—only this time, it's in front of other actors and not in the actor's home.

The "Set"

Since the "setting" for this exercise is her home, it's vitally important that the actor brings in materials and props to create the ambiance of her apartment or house. I encourage students to bring in pictures, photos, pillows, knickknacks, kitchenware—whatever props they need to remind themselves of their homes. Also bring in all necessary props for the tasks—brushing teeth requires a toothbrush, gifts require real wrapping paper, cakes need real frosting.

The Exercise

Once the stage is set and the actor has relaxed and prepared backstage, she begins E.R., Part Two. Some students have started this exercise by entering the stage at the top after coming from the outside world. Others have started in the apartment, doing things like watching TV, sleeping, or working on the computer. Either type works, as long as the "I'm fifteen minutes late" realization starts near the beginning of the exercise.

The actor will then start her overall activity and the various tasks it involves. As she's completing her tasks, the inner monologue of the Emotional Recall will be part of her concentration. *Nothing about the recall is ever said aloud.* Remember, the Emotional Recall is the *inner monologue.* "As the actor, you will see how the inner life influences the tasks and how the tasks influence the inner life," I'll say to my students when explaining the exercise. "You've now got life and behavior driving each other!"

Once the tasks are complete and the actor has relived the Emotional Recall as a full inner monologue, the exercise closes with her either leaving the stage to go to her event, or her greeting the guests at the door.

What We've Learned

I've found this exercise to be vital for actors. In a script, many times a character is given a page or more of stage business (activities with tasks) and no dialogue. The character is not just doing the "business," but has an accompanying "inner monologue" at the same time. These wordless scenes are forwarding the character development and story of the play, and it's vitally important that an actor knows how to do them well and realistically. In essence, this is what the second part of the E.R. is demonstrating for the actor.

This exercise explores how to bring the same reality that was explored during E.R., Part One, onto the stage. When we are sufficiently relaxed in our offstage, "real-life" environment, I feel we function on these two different levels of concentration at the same time, all the time. Developing this Emotional Recall exercise is an attempt to find the same reality for stage life. This exercise, when done well, gives the actor an in-depth concentration as well as privacy on stage. It allows the imagination to form a heightened reality and creates a fascinating stage life.

In doing a play or a film, we work with a combination of life, behavior, and words. In Part Two we put together:

- **Life**—unspoken emotional life. Also called "inner monologue," "inner life," and "life behind the eyes"

- **Behavior**—activity, tasks, and obstacles. Also called "business" or "stage business."

To recap, accomplishing Part Two requires:
  - Choosing an event
  - Choosing an activity comprised of tasks
  - Creating obstacles with tasks
  - Increasing importance with timelines ("I'm fifteen minutes late!")
  - Paralleling Emotional Recall to tasks
  - Rehearsing undisturbed
  - Several days between rehearsals for gestation of the exercise
  - Various rehearsals (at least three) with different objectives—first to relive the E.R., second to focus on activity with tasks, third to blend the two and do without speaking aloud
  - Building up to the recall—don't cut to the event
  - Creating a set with personal items
  - Creating a character-developing scene without words

EMOTIONAL RECALL, PART THREE

Now that we've incorporated Life and Behavior into a mini-scene on stage, the next step is to add Words. We do that in the E.R., Part Three.

Choose a Monologue

Now that the actor is familiar with the Emotional Recall, it's time to use all that homework and apply it to a playwright's words. I have my students memorize a monologue from a play that has an emotional moment coinciding with the emotional moment of the actor's recall. Like the monologue that is memorized for the Fallout exercise, no acting choices are required while memorizing. I want the actor to only memorize the words until we're ready to use them in the rehearsal process with the exercise.

Choosing the right monologue is a key to this exercise. The most important part is that "the moment" of the monologue must parallel "the moment" of the recall in both Parts One and Two. For example, if the E.R., Part One, dealt with a moment of fear, then the monologue must deal with fear as well. The moment of the monologue must parallel the moment of the Emotional Recall or the exercise won't work.

The Jumping-Off Point

In the preparatory rehearsal at home, the actor decides where in the Emotional Recall, Part Two, would be the best jumping-off place in her recall for the author's words to begin. "What is the springboard or motivation from my recall that gets me into the first line?" The actor could be a quarter of the way, halfway, or near the end of her E.R. (as inner monologue) before starting the words of the speech.

Home rehearsal is essential. The actor needs to know where she wants to be in her own recall to start the author's words. She must connect the moment of her recall to the moment in the monologue. In Part Three, this inner life will be augmented by words. We now have Life, Behavior, and Words!

Rehearsing at Home

Rehearsing Part Three of the E.R. is basically the same as rehearsing Part Two, except that the actor adds the words. This is why it's so important that the monologue is memorized before trying to rehearse.

So let's see what's happening at this point: The actor's mind is actively involved in her Emotional Recall (Life), she is doing a number of tasks (Activity/Behavior), and at least through a large part of this exercise, she is speaking a monologue (Words) motivated by the Life and the Behavior. All the work from Parts One and Two still apply—she's still running late, she's only got fifteen minutes. The addition for Part Three is the monologue. That's a lot of stuff going on!

"You're repeating Part Two exactly, only now your mouth is speaking words," I'll explain. "But you're still trusting Parts One and Two. The words could be treated as gibberish—what you're really saying is your Emotional Recall, even if the words being spoken are that of the monologue."

The rehearsal may not make logical sense at this point. There are going to be moments when the words may not jive with the activity or the E.R. The actor could be polishing a shoe and speaking as if she's talking to a human being. That's okay—the purpose of the exercise is to ground the life behind the words so intently in the subconscious that they have a life of their own.

Keeping the tasks for the preparation is vitally important. The tasks keep the actor grounded and allow her to explore the Emotional Recall. Typically most if not all of those tasks would be edited out for a real performance, but they are vital for the preparation process.

In Class

The beginning of Part Three of the E.R. doesn't look much different from the beginning of Part Two. The stage is set to be the actor's apartment or house, and she comes in or starts her Emotional Recall and tasks while preparing for the very important event. She is running late, which means she has to complete the exercise in fifteen minutes. Somewhere in the exercise, while doing the tasks, the actor begins to talk. She continues to do the tasks and to relive the recall while speaking the monologue, the *Words* fully motivated by the *Life* and *Behavior*. The purpose of the exercise is to connect the actor's E.R. moment with the monologue moment.

"Treat the writer's words as if you were speaking gibberish," I'll remind her. "You should be reliving the Emotional Recall. You are not performing the monologue. You are creating and exploring the inner life and behavior behind the words."

If she becomes distracted from the inner life by the recall, I'll have her go back to the tasks. "There is no obligation to make sense or perform for the rest of the class—this is a process." It's a process for accomplishing the major moment of a monologue.

EMOTIONAL RECALL, PART FOUR

Part Three of the E.R. typically takes the same amount of time as Part Two—fifteen minutes, give or take. Then, when the actor is done, I'll take her immediately to the fourth part—speaking the monologue without all the stage business.

I'll help the actor to set up the monologue at this point. She can either sit or stand, and I'll select one prop from her tasks. I then have her put an imagined person on the back wall of the theater, the same way she did with the Spoon River exercise. As she did then, the actor should choose an emotionally significant person to either "give" or "get" something from.

Once the actor is settled, she'll drop back into where she wants to be in the E.R. and do her monologue. At this point, she is still feeding off her Emotional Recall, but hopefully the author's words are also taking over. The images from the recall that the actor has for those words have solidified her feelings and ultimately her emotional response.

I find this exercise extremely effective, especially for audition monologues. Many actors have subsequently taken a monologue prepared this way to an actual audition, with excellent results.

Monologues—Give and Get

So far there have been three exercises with speeches that could be audition monologues: the Spoon River poem, the monologue at the end of the Fallout, and the E.R. monologue. I tell my students to remember to always have an imaginary person to talk to when auditioning, preferably a person whom they're conflicted with—maybe someone who is opinionated, judgmental, or not particularly supportive. The point is to increase the conflict and up the stakes. The actor must be very specific about what she wants to "give" or to "get from" this person. It really helps to center the actor and get her to be specific with the intention of the piece. It's like bringing in another actor to do a scene.

A NOTE FOR LEADERS

These exercises take a great deal of energy on the part of the teacher. Someone who chooses to lead an Emotional Recall must stay extremely focused and aware of the actor every second. The teacher has to guide and lead, and often be one step ahead of the student, especially for Part One, as the student is reliving an experience from the past.

As in the Fallout and Song Exercise, the leader must watch for telltale signs from the actor—signs that indicate what the actor will do next, that show the exercise is working, that the student is stressed and shouldn't proceed forward, or sometimes that a different recall should be used. The decision of which event to use should have been resolved in a prior discussion with the student regarding the Emotional Recall.

One reason why I insist on knowing what the recall is before proceeding with Part One is what I can learn during that discussion. A leader can really tell in the initial discussion what's resolved and what isn't, and a decision should be made then. If the event isn't appropriate, I'll suggest that the actor choose another.

Sometimes, what may seem like an appropriate recall turns out not to be one. Should things go off track, don't keep pushing the exercise. The leader must be one step ahead of the actor and anticipate the next moment. This is especially important for Part One, but also with the second and third parts. It's hard, highly concentrated work—for both parties—and should never be attempted carelessly. Some actors may have to repeat parts of this process, and that's okay—it's a learning tool, not a performance. I tell them to have patience and to come back to this exercise again if necessary. Sometimes it takes time to understand and to unearth the blocks.

WHAT WE'VE LEARNED

The Emotional Recall is one of the most important tools for difficult acting situations. I have found it essential.

Let's say our actor is cast in a play and has to speak a long monologue— one that extends a page or more. The director wants the character to be in a chair for the whole scene. Confined to that staging, the panicked actor might think, "Oh my God, not only am I confined to sitting down in a chair, but I've got all this dialogue to sustain. And I've never had an experience like what this character is talking about—I don't have the vaguest idea how to reach the required emotion. I'm going to bore the audience to tears!"

Using all the parts of the Emotional Recall in a homework rehearsal for this scene may help our befuddled actor turn this situation into something wonderful. Exploring and applying the desired emotion from a personal Emotional Recall may solve the problem of finding the life in the monologue, and possibly in the character throughout the play. It will give an actor the freedom to "get off the words," to find life from staging restrictions, and to fully explore the text and the meaning behind the words—perhaps finding a prop and a bit of business as well. Most importantly, the actor can bring choices to rehearsal from the homework.

The E.R. isn't limited to monologues or solutions for static blocking. Another use of the exercise is as an offstage preparation for a scene where the character has just come from an emotional event. Some actors use it if there are emotional aspects of a character they have difficulty expressing. This exercise can be effective for countless moments on stage or screen.

The more I work with this exercise, the more amazed I am with what the subconscious has retained and, if properly "tricked" with the sensory detail, what it can produce. As an actor develops the process of creating an

Emotional Recall, it will happen faster and faster. "You can become like Pavlov's dog with a sense memory. A smell, a sound, a touch, a sight, or a taste can recall the entire event for you."

That's why I find the Emotional Recall so helpful. Once an actor has understood and executed this exercise, there are countless events from her past that she can use for an E.R. She will have a tool for life.

Sometimes, when an actor is using a tool like this night after night in performance, it needs a little brush-up. If an actor finds that her performance is getting stale and is consequently not as effective, I encourage her to explore other sensory aspects around the Emotional Recall. "Keep working with it and keep your performance fresh."

These are the steps you will need to take to access the full potential of the E.R.

- Choose a monologue with an emotional moment that coincides with the emotional moment of E.R., Part One
- Choose the "jumping-off point" in the E.R., Part Two, to motivate the first line of the monologue
- Practice at home at least three times and fully memorize monologue
- The author's words can be treated as gibberish—what the actor is really saying is the Emotional Recall
- Use the moment of the Emotional Recall to "make the moment" of the monologue
- Speak the monologue without stage business
- The actor selects a person she must say the monologue to—a person of the actor's choosing, not the script's
- The actor decides whether she wants to get something from or give something to this person (an action verb); Usually "get" is stronger
- You can use the Emotional Recall to work on performance materials— to solve problems with monologues, and find freedom in static blocking
- Keep it fresh—go back to the Emotional Recall if your performance becomes stale
- Stick to a resolved Emotional Recall as your selection

12 VALIDATING THE SELF— THE PRIVATE MOMENT

The last individual exercise in my class is the Private Moment. Typically it's the most difficult in the series, yet perhaps the most profitable of all the exercises. The Private Moment is the epitome of what good acting is about— giving the illusion of being private in public. In order to do so, the actor must feel comfortable putting his most vulnerable self on display—hence the reason why I consider this exercise the key to "validating the self."

PRACTICAL PURPOSE

This illusion of privacy is very difficult for an actor to create, whether he is in a rehearsal space, on a stage, or on a television or movie set. Rehearsals can be awkward because there may be a room full of other cast members, stage managers, tech people, and the director. Rehearsals are additionally awkward because they typically take place in a raw, brightly lit space—all things contriving to make being private very difficult. Ultimately, there are audience members and critics present during a stage performance, challenging an actor's ability to attain privacy.

Being private in public can be even more difficult when working on film or television. A studio shoot can have twenty-five to fifty technicians running around. Location shoots may have as many as a thousand bystanders looking on. Even on the most intimate sets there will still be the director, staff, and technical crew watching and doing their own thing—sound, camera, etc.— while the actor works. It's a challenge for even the most advanced actor.

It is the actor's job to give the illusion of being very private in public, regardless of the distractions. In most acting situations, whether on stage or screen, the audience members should feel as if they are watching the actor through a keyhole in a door. An individual audience member should be the proverbial fly on the wall. This is why I feel that before an actor does a *character's* private moment on stage or on film, he should experience what it feels like to do his own in class.

This is an extremely advanced piece of work and should definitely not be done by someone in early stages of training. By the time the actor has done all the previous work in my class, he is ready to tackle this one—the Mt. Everest of all the exercises. The purpose of the Private Moment is for the actor to experience and validate, for himself, what it is like to do three very different, private kinds of personal behavior in front of other people.

BEFORE CLASS—CHOOSING PRIVATE MOMENTS—THE STORYBOARD

For this exercise, the key acting questions of "who" and "where" are answered simply: The actor is in his apartment, alone. The "when" is a Saturday night, and no one else is around. For the "what," one of two premises can be used to structure the exercise:

1. "I am alone and the walls are closing in. How do I make it through the night?"

2. "I am alone, and I am really looking forward to having the place all to myself."

The exercise is the exploration of doing the "what" and "how."

WHAT IS A PRIVATE MOMENT?

In essence, a Private Moment is an activity done by the actor in the privacy of his own living space. In some ways, the Private Moment is similar to the A.C.T. or the second part of the Emotional Recall, especially in the preparation and rehearsal of the activities. But the Private Moment is more than simply a series of tasks—it's an intensely personal activity that would normally not be done in front of relative strangers such as the acting class, or in performance in front of an audience. The actor might have the freedom to do his activities in front of a close companion—*maybe*—but it would be difficult to show this side to strangers such as the class. It's this sense of privacy that makes the Private Moment more difficult and often requires more courage then the other exercises.

The Private Moment is separated into three different parts of various levels of difficulty. Part One is something the actor might do privately that would be difficult (embarrassing or awkward) to do in front of others. For Part Two, a second Private Moment is added, one that is a level harder than Part One. Part Three is a choice that is *intensely* private. If someone came into the room while he was doing whatever he was doing, the actor would be completely and profoundly mortified and probably feel like jumping out the window.

Just as in the A.C.T. or the second part of the Emotional Recall, it's an overall activity that makes up the storyboard of the Private Moment. For example, an actor might choose to sing and dance along with his favorite musician as Private Moment One. Private Moment Two can't simply be another song as a different rock star—the actor should choose a completely different activity for Private Moment Two. But choosing to go from a swaggering Mick Jagger to performing a striptease to "Hello Dolly" would be appropriate choices for the exercise, since the tone, purpose, and mood of the Private Moments are significantly different.

PARTS ONE AND TWO

In class, the actor does these Private Moments in succession—first, Parts One and Two; and then, a few weeks later, he repeats Parts One and Two and adds Part Three. In real life, the actor might not do all these activities on the same night, but the choices are compacted for the sake of the exercise. As with the other exercises, the actor meets with me privately before doing any of the Private Moments in class and reviews his three choices. Before the meeting, I ask the actor to start by choosing, in his own mind, his third and most difficult choice, and then work backward in terms of difficulty for the other two.

Never Violate

I want to stress the following: The actors in my class make their own selections. I will never ask an actor to do something in class that he would never consider doing on stage or film. The point of the exercise is for the actor to select three very different sides of himself and to explore what he can will himself to show publicly. "Don't pick something you would never consider doing or saying in a script." I do not ever want the actor to do something that would violate him.

As I said before, each one of the choices the actor makes should be harder than the previous one and should have been discussed with me ahead of time. The actor, when executing these three choices, must leave himself open to expressing his feelings. As with the general sensory exercise where the actor can choose to "sunbathe" nude, I tell them, "Don't just grit your teeth and do it. You are a thinking and feeling human being, and we want to see your responses."

By being honest about what is really happening within the execution of the exercise, the actor will open any blocked energy pockets of feeling. The overall purpose of this exercise is to find relaxation, concentration, and commitment to choices in creating the appearance of being private in public.

Validate the Self

The Private Moment is also an exercise of self-validation where the actor honors his feelings and does not block them. It's an exercise of enormous risk-taking, of showing the most private side, and honoring all feelings associated with the choices.

Any actor who's serious about his craft has a need for this sort of awareness, practice, and self-validation. Actors are asked to do and to play some very difficult and private scenes on stage and on screen. It takes courage and will to do these scenes. It is more important than ever for the actor to stay open to his feelings and bring depth and meaning to intensely personal character moments. In thirty-six years of teaching, I have never known an actor who did not grow from doing this exercise.

PRIVATE MOMENT—PREPARATION

The first step is for the actor and me to sit down and discuss the exercise. I want to hear about his choices. When the actor discusses these three choices with me, I want to make sure that:

1. He picks three choices that bring out different private sides of him

2. The choices are challenging and not too "safe"

3. One of the choices has a sexual[1] undertone or component

4. None of the choices would violate the actor

Sometimes the choices are rudimentary things, like extensive teeth-brushing and bedtime preparation that the actor might find awkward to do in front of people. Others might be explosive and risky. I once had a football player choose to strip down to his birthday suit and dance a ballet for his third choice. Both extremes are equally valid and important—the actor who popped a zit and obsessively scraped his tongue while brushing his teeth had to have the same quality of privacy as the naked, dancing football player.

Sometimes students try to push for extremes or are concerned that the class might get bored with their private, home-on-a-Saturday-night lives. To this I say, "So what?" Entertaining is not the point of the exercise. "You shouldn't care what we think! The point is privacy."

---

[1] Clarification: "Sexual" does not mean masturbatory.

The Private Moment exercise is not about performing, and certainly *not* about exhibitionism. Rather, it is an opportunity to explore some core components of acting:

① Relaxation—does the actor appear to be "real" in his environment (in this case, at home on a Saturday night?)

② Concentration—is there a full commitment to choices?

③ Imagination—how much openness is there in the Private Moment, and what kind of risks has the actor taken?

The ultimate critique after this exercise is this: Was the actor private? Was he private the whole time? When was or wasn't he private—and at what point did he become private?

What is "Sexual"?

Many of my students will initially be concerned about the sexual component of the Private Moment. As I noted before, "sexual" does not mean "masturbatory" and does not mean that an actor must take off his clothes. *No.* Someone could read erotic literature or a love letter she wrote or received. Physical exercise that includes movements and sounds can be sexual. Putting on clothes that make an actor feel sensual and sexy has a sexual component.

If someone does choose to remove clothing in a Private Moment, nakedness does not necessarily make the Private Moment sexual. The football player who stripped down to nothing and danced a ballet was sexual, but not because of his nudity. The sexual nature came from *what he was doing*—the dance. The nudity simply bumped the risk level up a notch.

How different individuals interpret this part varies widely. I've seen one actor dress a pillow as a woman and dance with her. Another female actor dolled herself up as Ann-Margaret. Many of my students get into dancing in the privacy of their living rooms. One student simply recreated the making of an intimate phone call to his wife who was away on a business trip. That particular Private Moment was intensely loving and sexual, and it didn't require a stitch of clothing to be removed.

Private Moment—Application in Class

I used to have the actors do the Private Moment in three steps—Part One the first time in class, Parts One and Two another time, and finally an abbreviation of One and Two followed by the biggie, Private Moment Three. I found that breaking it up is necessary rather than doing all three parts on the same day. Students who dive in and do all three at once, without doing Part One and Two first, will often blow it because they are so nervous about Part Three.

❖ ❖ ❖

OPENING UP A SENSUAL SIDE

I am an extremely shy individual, and had unintentionally limited myself for years. The Private Moment exercise allowed me to feel empowered in my work and in my body. For Part Three—the most difficult part—I dressed up and did a striptease to a pillow, using my imagination to endow it with someone who is no longer in my life. It was a turning point in my work, and was so liberating as an actor.

Someone in the business once expressed to me that I was sitting on this simmering pot of sexuality and should be using it in my work to pursue these types of roles, but I never could before doing that exercise. Without the safety net of Terry's class, I wouldn't have been able to audition for a stripper with ease and comfort, or play a sexually charged character like Maggie from *Cat on a Hot Tin Roof*, or express sexuality without feeling judged or self-conscious. I carry the freedom from the Private Moment into all character work that I do.

—Diane Reilly

❖ ❖ ❖

I have been able to condense the exercise a bit with my advanced actors. I've found that after completing all the other work in my class, the actor is advanced enough to do Parts One and Two together, and then wait a few weeks to do all three. It all depends upon the actor. Some will feel confident jumping in and doing two parts together immediately. Others will need to ease into the exercise a bit more gradually. Both methods are valid. The Private Moment isn't about showing how brave an actor is, but rather getting him accustomed to being *private in public*. Sometimes it takes practice.

Before the Private Moment

It's important that the actor know and plan what he's been doing prior his entrance. He must ask and answer the questions of where he's been and what he's coming from. If he chooses to start onstage, he needs to know what he's been doing before the start of the exercise. These decisions need to be made and explored during the preparation rehearsal.

There are a few questions that must be answered during the planning stage:

Where are you before the Private Moment starts? Have you come from somewhere? Are you already in your apartment? What were you doing immediately prior, and how has that affected your mood or emotions?

It's Saturday night and you're either returning to or are already in your apartment. Are you happy to be alone on a Saturday night? Frustrated?

Do you know you're going to be alone before the exercise starts, or do you discover this? Remember, it does not necessarily have to be unpleasant to find yourself all alone, even though it is Saturday. This could be time just for you!

The actor must make sure all the choices lead somewhere and do not just end the moment the choice is executed. For instance, physical exercise is over with the first grunt or stretch, unless it really builds to something revealing/private. The same holds true for a personal vocal warm-up. Once the actor has contorted his face and produced a sound, he's pretty much done. The actor must be able to add different exercises or sound to either of these choices, or better yet, a different reason why the moment is private. I've seen physical exercise extend into a dance, or vocal warm-ups turn into a full song routine.

Rehearse Rehearse Rehearse

Like most of the other exercises, the Private Moment must be rehearsed. The ideal space is, obviously, the actor's own home—if he has the proper amount of time and privacy. "Rehearse this at home the same way you're going to do it in class. You must go as full out in class with it as you do when home alone. And make sure you're alone when you rehearse it."

No exercise should be done without the proper preparation, but it's especially important with the Private Moment. "Don't ever come in and do this exercise without rehearsing it first!" Being private in public is an intimidating, difficult task and should not be approached lightly. "Slate time to be at home and rehearse doing the Private Moments as real-life private moments. If privacy is an issue in your household (roommates, family, etc.), then try to schedule time without them so you can be alone." Some students end up renting rehearsal space and do their Private Moments there before coming into class.

Mirrors

If the actor with a choice uses a mirror, he should make it an imaginary mirror, preferably on the fourth wall. It gives him much more to create, especially when shaving, applying makeup, or performing other activities people do privately in front of a mirror. This means that the actor should use a real mirror during the preliminary rehearsals, and then cut the mirror during the last rehearsal so that he is ready to imagine it in front of others.

A Home Away from Home

Just as in other exercises, such as the A.C.T. or Parts Two and Three of the Emotional Recall, the actor must create the ambiance of the set and scene with props—in this case, the actor's home. Items commonly include photographs, books, blankets, pillows, bedspreads, kitchenware, personal bath and grooming items . . . the list is endless. Actors frequently trudge in with what seems to be half of their apartment!

While I don't think that bringing in large pieces of furniture is necessary, small items from home are essential to this exercise. The value of these personal props gives the space the personal ambiance needed for this exercise to create privacy, as opposed to items selected at random off a prop shelf that have no personal meaning. "What you are trying to achieve is a feeling that brings you as close as possible to being in you own environment. Surround yourself with your 'friends,' the props—as many as necessary to stimulate your imagination."

Time the Rehearsal

Because Parts One and Two together should take twenty minutes, it is important to track the amount of time the rehearsals take. Don't look at a watch during the rehearsal, but if a certain activity takes a significant amount of time, explore a way to shorten it during the next rehearsal.

PERFORMING THE PRIVATE MOMENT, PARTS ONE AND TWO

The actor (after setting up his "apartment" and doing a proper warm-up) can begin the exercise by making an entrance or already being on the set. I don't guide the actor into the exercise as I do with others, like the Fallout or the first part of the Emotional Recall—he's all on his own. That's why the relaxation is so important. It's impossible to be private when an actor is tense. Very few people are tense when they're at home, in their own space.

Private Moment, Part One, shouldn't start the minute the actor enters the stage. There should be some time taken setting up the moment: entering the space, realizing he's alone, and then deciding what to do with the situation or opportunity. Taking this time not only sets up the scenario of being alone in a private space, but also allows the actor to adjust to the space and the exercise.

An actor who appears private is relaxed but energized at the same time. For this reason, I don't encourage my students to start this exercise from a static position, like laying on the floor, bed, or sofa. Being in motion makes for better energy at the beginning of this exercise. Many actors will therefore start the exercise by entering the room as if they've come from the outside world, but this isn't absolutely necessary. The overall goal is to start the exercise energized.

Twenty Minutes Total—Including "Adjusting" Time

It's very important that the exercise starts with the actor "being there" mentally. Parts One and Two combined should take twenty minutes total. That doesn't necessarily mean ten minutes for each choice, however. Remember, the actor needs to take some time at the beginning to drop into the space before beginning the choice for Part One. "Adjust to being in the space. Maybe do a little business leading up to the Private Moment, Part One." As the actor drops into his space, he then wills himself steadily forward to his first choice.

Personalize the Moment

Choices in any one of the parts can be real or fantasy, but they must be personal. The actor must will himself to go as far with the activity in class as he goes in private at home. At the same time, he must remain open to what he's feeling by doing the activities in front of the class.

"Do not shut us out when you're doing the exercise. Let us see what you're doing and feeling. You know with a sixth sense that the audience is out there or that the camera is recording. Open up the work to the fourth wall."

Acknowledge All Feelings

It is most important that the actor stays open and available to his feelings when executing the choices in this exercise. If the actor feels embarrassed by what he is doing in front of the class, then he should allow himself to get embarrassed before moving on. Embarrassment is a feeling too—perhaps one of the hardest ones to show publicly. Allowing and exploring this feeling, while not necessarily intended for the exercise, has great value in itself. And unless the actor allows the honest emotion to happen, he won't be able to move past it.

"Don't just grit your teeth and do it. Nothing comes out of a moment like that except resistance."

PRIVATE MOMENT, PART THREE

The actor comes back a few weeks after doing Parts One and Two to add on the granddaddy of them all—Private Moment, Part Three. Parts One and Two are repeated but shortened slightly for Part Three. Each separate Private Moment must flow easily into the next. What the actor ends up with is a fairly tight scenario, or "storyboard," that should take a *maximum* of thirty minutes to complete.

One of the reasons I feel so strongly about no auditing in an acting class is because of this process. The actor, in doing an exercise like this or many of the other exercises I've described, needs the protection of a classroom. It's important that the actor feels comfortable and safe to do the work. Auditors create a "performance" atmosphere. When an actor sees or senses strangers in an audience, there's the tendency to start auditioning for their approval. I think "strangers in our midst" violates a trust and negatively affects the person working.

*　*　*

THE PRIVATE MOMENT, YEARS LATER, ON STAGE

When I was cast as the mother in Sam Shepard's *A Lie of the Mind*, my character had to go from a state of servile passivity to rebelliousness and confrontation, and then back to the original state. It was quite an emotional roller coaster, and I struggled with it for a while.

Then I remembered my Private Moment exercise from Terry's class. I read a love letter at one point, and the emotional pattern from that experience was somewhat similar to what I needed in the play. I was able to bring this experience to bear on my performance and achieve the emotional base the play needed.

—Joanne Bayless

*　*　*

The class atmosphere should be ideal for the work process. There must always be a "permission to fail" attitude, because out of failing and falling on your butt comes growth. We must have permission to fail in the privacy of class. Such failure can't be risked once the actor is out in the professional world. The classroom is the place to explore and, possibly, fail. It's interesting and terribly important to work with our pants down and to know that we are not going to die if we fail.

When this exercise is done well, the growth in freedom, risk-taking, knowing oneself, and taking that brave step with executing choices is phenomenal. Over the years, I have seen many actors take giant strides in their scene work after completing the Private Moment exercise.

Class Work Stays in the Classes

It is also important for me to reinforce to my students the necessity of keeping the classroom work in the classes. I think it is a violation for a class member to discuss with others what he or another actor did during a Private Moment or during any of the exercises.

Non-actors especially may not understand the acting process. And other actors come from different kinds of training and are not necessarily going to understand a lot of this exercise work. Comments can be very judgmental, disapproving, and inhibiting. An actor may be struggling to find his own freedom, and the wrong remark from someone can squelch his "personal permission" and confidence. This is why it's best that what is done in the classroom be kept in the classroom.

Keeping class work between fellow actors at the studio is also a courtesy to the actors who did the exercises. Outsiders do not know the actor or where that actor is in his process, nor is it appropriate for them to know that actor's personal history or private moments. The purpose of the Private Moment is to gain access to the confidence needed for an actor to share a *character's* private moments, not to share his personal background with the world.

* * *

TIPPING POINT OF A CAREER

I had an epiphany in Terry's class when I first applied the Private Moment exercise to a character—one that helped me believe I was a ready-for-employment actor.

Three days before my scene partner and I were to do a scene from *A Day in the Death of Joe Egg* by Peter Nichols, he had to cancel. Not wanting to give up my spot, I signed on to present a Private Moment for my character, Sheila [the mother of a severely mentally handicapped girl]. I had never seen someone do the exercise as a character and not as themselves in class before, but why not?

I thrummed with ideas easily and quickly. I could hardly sleep that first night because there was such energy in the imaging, constructing, and deepening of the playwright's world. I began with the overstuffed living room my partner and I had planned: sofa, lots of pillows, and plants.

I gave a title to each part of the Private Moment, each one significantly different from the others. Part One: "Mother and Feeding Ritual."

Armed with Easter gifts, I discovered husband Bri and daughter Jo not home. Safely alone, I pretended to be a pregnant Fertility Goddess as I fed the cat, the plants, and the ant farm. But the ants were dead! In Part Two: "Death, Funeral, and Faith," I created a formal Anglican funeral for the ants, complete with candles and prayer book, and committed them to a garbage sack. Grief turned to shame and anger over the imperfect birth and life of Jo. In Part Three: "Jo and Faith," I imagined healthy Jo and I wrapping Easter gifts, jumping rope, and tapping the time-step. Then I saw her in her wedding gown! The balm of hope versus daily reality made me keen for a miracle. The ending: Bri wheeling Jo in! Hurry, clear away, tamp down my feelings.

It had been a concrete exploration—not just a written or imagined character bio. Ever since then, I have always worked up my character's Private Moments, Emotional Recalls, and key events by enlarging upon the text or creating while informed by the text.

Three years later, I relocated to New Orleans, and got my first acting job at Southern Repertory Theatre as Annie Sullivan in *The Miracle Worker*. Secret character homework prepped me for a rewarding collaboration with director Joe Warfield. For example, near the play's end, I dared to banish my beloved brother's ghost—an unusual choice, informed by homework on Annie's Emotional Recall of a key event.

Joe encouraged me to build on that, and it became a series of powerful Private Moments. At one rehearsal, Joe said, "Maria, this song you'll sing as this scene ends is to be about pain." Okay . . . I sat in the rocker, my dark glasses still on, clasping Helen's beautiful doll, and sang three verses, each imbued with specific events from my life in the orphanage (which I'd already fleshed out in my preparation). Tangible, actable "stuff."

When I think of a pinnacle moment of understanding that turned the tide on my acting career, it's that first Character Private Moment for *Joe Egg* that comes back to me.

—Maria Mason

✢ ✢ ✢

CHARACTER PRIVATE MOMENTS

Over the years, I've realized how to use this particular individual exercise to deepen the actor's understanding of a character for scene work. I especially like to use this for the characters in complex plays like those by Anton Chekhov, Tennessee Williams, Eugene O'Neil, and others. I ask the actors to do a Character Private Moment based on one of the roles they are playing in their assigned scenes. Rather than being themselves alone on a Saturday night, the actors are the characters instead, and in the similarly solitary situation.

The homework preparation for a Character Private Moment requires a close look at the text for "givens" about the character that can help the actors find clues to their character's behavior. The actor then continues with the homework in much the same way as a personal Private Moment by creating the atmosphere of the character's home with props and rehearsing them, just as he did with his real Private Moment and his own life.

I have found it especially helpful for actors to come to the class fully prepared as their characters on the days they do the Character Private Moments. This preparation can consist of coming to the studio dressed as the character. Often this means the actor must be in public as the character. In New York, for example, the students typically take public transportation (subway, bus, or train). It could be a real learning experience to be seen on public transportation dressed as the character. In other areas, they might be seen in a vehicle while dressed as the character.

*　*　*

A GUT-WRENCHING MOMENT

The first Character Private Moment I did in class was as Frank in the play *Educating Rita* by Willy Russell. I wanted to get a sense of Frank's alcoholic condition, and chose three completely private moments—having his pants fall down as he answers a phone call from his lover, passing gas so putrid that it makes even him sick, and then finally losing it and throwing himself on the floor in complete alcoholic abandon.

What I discovered about Frank in doing the Character Private Moment was the depths of his depression. It became clear as I read the play that his life was caving in on him and he loathed himself, but that was a mental reaction. His desperateness really sank in after the exercise on an emotional level.

I also discovered, quite by accident, that Frank's stomach and intestines are completely ravaged by the drink. During the exercise, I (as Frank) gulped down a half glass of liquor, and my instincts immediately took me to convulsions of pain. I, the actor, hadn't planned the reaction and almost didn't realize what I had done until after the exercise was over. But apparently the burning in my gut was an honest reaction. One of my fellow actors told me that as an alcoholic, he could relate to the entire exercise, and that moment specifically.

—Max Norat

*   *   *

Just as in the personal Private Moment, doing the Character Private Moment consists of making three choices that your character would do in private. Determining these choices requires that the actor be a bit of a sleuth and careful reader, since the choices must be based on information given in the text.

And just as in the personal Private Moment, there must be three very different sides of the character, and at least one of these choices should be a sexual side. One of the wonderful results of this exercise is to see how thoroughly the actors have read the scripts and the intense understanding of their characters they've realized from the writer's givens.

As I have said time and time again, I do not mean masturbatory when I refer to the "sexual" side of the character. This choice should have to do with what it means for the character to be attracted to another human being, and what he or she does about these feelings. Juliet's "Wherefore art thou, Romeo?" speech on the balcony in *Romeo and Juliet* is a good example of a Shakespearian Private Moment with words (also known as a monologue) that deals with Juliet's sexual side. She is in love, but rarely does a director have Juliet be a seductress while musing about her young Romeo.

Character Private Moments—Doing Them in Class

Character Private Moments are especially useful if there are a number of actors studying scenes from the same play or the same playwright. Many times, I have three or four actors doing this exercise in succession, one after the other on the same set. They still do the exercise alone, but will be faced with a series of unexpected obstacles by using the same set.

In preparation, all actors agree on a standard set prior to setting the stage, whether it's a bedroom, a living room, or another space. They each individually prop the set with whatever their character will be dealing with for their overall activities ("business"). Once the set is complete and all actors have placed their individual props, they exit the stage and the exercises begin.

The first actor comes onto the set and works about twenty minutes (at the most) with his three Character Private Moments. Once complete, he exists the set, and the second actor enters for her Character Private Moments. The next actor follows, then the next.

The second actor in the Character Private Moment will typically have a few unexpected situations to deal with. She must deal with the props left out by the first actor and how these props fit in with her own Character Private Moments. The third actor does the same during his turn, only now he must contend with props left out by both of the actors. By the time the fourth actor is on stage, the set often looks completely different, and this last actor has a field day—he's got to deal with all the props from the others and the incongruity of it all!

All of the actors must stay in character even if they might be doing a play during a different time period from the others and have unexpected props on the set. The exercise really explores discovery, overcoming obstacles, and how to react in character to the truly unexpected.

WHAT WE'VE LEARNED

I do not feel that anyone can get up on a set or in front of a camera and be able to easily do many of the moments that are now being asked for in the professional acting world. The actor is hopefully a feeling and sensitive person, working with his heart and soul. He is not a robot or an emotional machine. He needs to ask for (and demand, if need be) respect for himself as a person and as an artist.

This doesn't mean that an actor should be resistant or defensive. Rather, it means being open with a director and saying, "This is hard for me to do," or, "I'd like some rehearsal with no one present but you (the director) and my acting partner if my Private Moment is shared."

There's nothing wrong with admitting, "I'm scared of this, I'm inhibited by it and feel uncomfortable." I as a director would never disrespect an actor for taking an appropriate time to say, "I know this was in the script, I'm willing to attempt it, but I need a safety net." Other things I've heard actors explain include, "I may have to work through my blocks before freeing the creative energy to do what you and the script are asking for."

It is important for all actors to keep in mind that when first taking the job, the dialogue or Character Private Moment demands were in the script from the start. An actor must thoroughly read and digest what happens, and be honest about the difficulty when it comes time to rehearse, play, or shoot.

It is because of this difficulty and discomfort that the actor needs to fully prepare—mentally, physically, and emotionally—before working. This preparation goes beyond the words in the script. Often, a character that an actor's playing will be completely free with doing things that the actor, personally, is not. A tranquil man who would never yell at a child might be called upon to scream in the face of a nine-year-old in a script, for example. Another actor who's careful with vulgarity in her personal life may have filthy scripted dialogue. And often an actor is called upon to improvise an event, especially in film.

In the play, movie, or television show, the character is comfortable with the actions, but if the actor is not comfortable in his personal life, he must take the time to get comfortable. Sometimes a director will be in tune with the difficulty and create an atmosphere to explore and become comfortable with these situations. But more often, the director, whose mind may be on other production problems, may not be aware that a situation will be difficult for the actor. The actor must share his fear and ask for the privacy of working it out without all the others who may be on the set.

"You've got to get comfortable, because the character is comfortable," I remind my students. "You might have to dig into an area of yourself that could say or do what your character does." That's why an actor exploring these aspects of a script on his own is so important. Many times, there's a block or resistance to exposure of this side of himself, and that block must be removed before working in a professional setting. The actor must find his own permission and freedom to go for it with 100 percent commitment.

Importance of Validating Feelings

I always find it incredible how often actors will try to bury their own personal feelings about doing difficult scenes rather than discussing their fears with the director. In the end, "keeping a good face" can backfire with disastrous results. I was an actor in a movie some years back where two fellow actors had to do an intimate nude love scene. Just as the scene was about to start, the male actor got a whopper of a nosebleed, one that wouldn't cease. We eventually had to take him to a hospital and lost an entire day of shooting.

The actor was not in ill health. He admitted to me later that the nosebleed must have come from tension from blocked feelings. They were able to shoot the scene two days later, but only after the actor admitted a few things to himself—and, in turn, to me. He hadn't thought about or planned on the emotional consequence of doing a difficult love scene.

"I knew this was in the script," he said to me. "I just never thought the day would come when we would shoot it. Obviously, all the pressure of my blocked feelings caused that horrible nosebleed to happen."

This is a prime example of exactly why it is so important for all actors to validate their feelings about the work they do. It doesn't only apply to things like love scenes. Often actors are asked to speak language that is difficult to say. Maybe it's cursing and foul language that's just plain ugly. Sometimes it's cruel words and actions that go against our own personal beliefs so strongly that it initially hurts to say the words. Other times, it might be a scene with a sense of intimacy or privacy that is hard to do knowing others are watching, whether it's a set crew or an audience.

Whatever the circumstances, the underlying fact that *acting is difficult* holds true. "Always validate your personal feelings about the work. Doing so will expand your freedom as an actor, and the quality of your art."

This exercise takes a lot of courage, which is parallel to the courage you will need to perform on stage and screen. Stand up for your feelings about this. The steps enumerated here will help prepare you for similar, difficult moments in your professional life.

• Actors must validate their feelings while making these risky choices

• It is important to create a "storyboard" that includes where the actor is coming from before the Private Moments start, how he feels about being alone on a Saturday night (loving the privacy or dreading the solitude), and other factors that influence the emotional quality of the Private Moments

• Relaxation and in-depth concentration helps free the imagination to be as spontaneous in public as it is in private

• Actors, by doing their own Private Moments and conquering inhibitions, can give themselves the freedom to create a character's Private Moment by connecting more deeply to the feelings that are underneath whatever the character is doing or saying

• Character Private Moments, based on the givens of the play, can be useful tools for character development, as well as for practicing with obstacles and objectives

• The director should respect the actor's preparation for difficult moments or scenes, possibly including clearing the set of nonessential personnel during rehearsal or film work, and generally giving the actor freedom to explore taking on something that is difficult

PART IV SCENE STUDY

Exercises alone cannot teach students how to act. They must learn by doing—and that involves interaction with other actors as characters, with real words from real plays. Any class of mine combines the exercise work with scene study in order for the actor to constantly apply the value of an exercise to solve scene problems. Areas that we can break open with the exercises are reference points. They are tools to use when an actor is blocked from the organic understanding of a character, or if she finds herself in a role that does not deal with her natural qualities or personality characteristics. She must explore and apply the tools she's learning when in the role of a character whose behavior is quite opposite her own.

Based on the amount of time I have spent explaining the exercises, it may seem that the vast majority of the time in my class is spent on what I've explained in Part II and Part III. In actuality, the majority of my class emphasizes scene study. The exercises give my students tools, but rigorous scene study prepares them for the professional acting world. I try to help actors break down and prepare different scenes, as well as teach them how to layer rehearsals—both on their own and with other actors. Most of this scene analysis and preparation can be applied to breaking down an entire script for stage or screen.

Everything I do in my class is concerned with learning how to prepare for a role. But I can't take my students through an entire production—there just isn't the time, not if they're expected to go out and work. But I can work on the next best thing to an entire role—carefully picked scenes that require homework, analysis, and rehearsal.

In many acting classes, there are exercises and there are scenes, and never the twain shall meet. This is not the case for my teachings. The individual exercises directly parlay into the preparation needed for scene work. They require immense amounts of homework and can serve as a guide to the preparation needed for scenes. For example, the Spoon River exercise demonstrates how to research the time period and character biography, as well as how to find the givens in a text, how to create parallel dialogue, and how to create the physical life of the character through the psychological center. In the A.C.T., the actor has tasks and obstacles in an overall activity and an objective with the phone call.

The other exercises also serve to demonstrate to an actor how to prepare. The actor "lets herself happen" in the Fallout or Song Exercise. It an essential element, since the actor must do the same thing in a scene. She creates an inner monologue in the Emotional Recall that can put "life behind the eyes"—a useful tool for roles the actor has difficulty connecting to personally. And she validates her feelings in her own Private Moment—all quality acting requires courage—and can find important details and qualities for a character through a Character Private Moment.

No actor should look for the "definitive interpretation" of a role or a scene. Rather, she should be concerned with how she understands the rehearsal process of scene development and character delineation. All of the class work—from the group warm-up to the scene work—is about exploration, discovery, and learning. As I've said many times in the previous sections, what I teach my class is about *process*, and not *performance*.

13 ASSIGNING SCENES

Some instructors like students to pick out their own scenes, and to choose their own acting partners. But I don't do that, at least not with my advanced acting students. The real world is full of situations where actors don't get to choose whom they play opposite. Often they are encouraged to play roles they're unfamiliar with, or wouldn't instinctually gravitate to. The real-world practice alone is enough reason to have an instructor decide the roles and scenes.

But typically, I have more reasons than just situational experience for choosing the work. The scenes that I assign typically vary each time for each actor. I match up individuals who wouldn't necessarily socialize together, but who work together beautifully. When I assign a scene it could be for one of the following reasons:

- The actors should work on that particular type of scene

- The actors can expand their abilities with material that is different from what they normally work with

- The actors can work with a scene that presents an acting problem they typically find difficult

- The scene presents a certain rhythm or regional accent that would be challenging to the actor

In a student's early scenes, I'll often do a little typecasting. It's important the actor is comfortable with roles that connect with obvious casting qualities of the actor. After the actors have gotten used to these "typecast" roles, I'll put them into something different. They are never completely inappropriate characters, but rather ones that are within the actor's reach but not blatantly obvious.

Giving an actor a variety of roles in class does more than simply stretch his acting talents. It may uncover character gems that were hidden under the knee-jerk typecasting, both by others and by the actors themselves. Actors often end up playing the same roles over and over—roles that may not always show the fullness of their talent. If they end up being typed with the scene work in my class, they further limit themselves and their knowledge of their own range and certainly of other styles of writing.

It's important for actors to build a healthy ego and confidence in immediate qualities. They may not have any idea how they are being seen and how they read to others. Once this confidence is established, there is no point in them repeating what they are comfortable with. I encourage them to stretch into different roles—different from previous work, as well as different from their immediate qualities. I'm sure the actor has absolute confidence that she can do certain kinds of role better than anyone else, but I want her to also explore the roles she wouldn't normally be seen as, but would like to play.

I also encourage and assign material that challenges the actors—scenes by Anton Chekhov, Eugene O'Neil, Oscar Wilde, George Bernard Shaw, Shakespeare, Noel Coward, Sam Shepard, Harold Pinter, Clifford Odets, Caryl Churchill, Christopher Durang, John Guare, Tina Howe, Tennessee Williams, Arthur Miller, Wendy Wasserstein, Edward Albee, and others. Some assigned scenes will present problems that are going to be tough for actors to solve, whether it's because the scene calls for feelings, emotions, language, or countless other elements that the actor has problems showing, connecting with, or opening up to.

As the problems occur, I attempt to help the actor break through the block with an outside-of-acting-class exercise such as vocal work, Body Dynamics™, working with a dialect coach, or using any of the exercises in Parts II and III. Solving the problem gives the actor confidence, strength, and courage. This is why I assign scenes that stretch the actor until she has confidence in a new range for herself. Many times, it is worth doing a ten-minute scene just to help the actor solve two minutes of something that has always been an acting problem.

RULES FOR REHEARSAL

Once a scene has been assigned, there is a bit of work that must be done by each individual actor before starting rehearsals. The first and most obvious is the reading of the text—not only of the scene itself, but of the entire play. Before sitting down for a rehearsal, each actor should have a good idea of her character as well as of the other characters in the play. Meeting a scene partner with no prior knowledge of the script is unfair and can rightfully cause resentment from the scene partner. This kind of lack of discipline is a path to disaster.

At Least Three Rehearsals and One Meeting

Prior to putting the scene up for the first time, the actors should have had at least three good-quality, on-their-feet rehearsals. Ideally I would suggest four or five, but one has to be realistic when actors are holding down full-time jobs and looking for work in the business.

This does not mean that an initial meeting at a coffeehouse or elsewhere to read through the scene, agree about beats, discuss the parts, and do some preliminary interpretation of the scene counts as a rehearsal. I encourage actors to meet like this when diving into a scene and do some read-throughs together. They can discuss the entire play and the characters, find the beats in the text, discuss difficult or physical sections of the scene, and generally get comfortable with the other actor prior to starting the first rehearsal. This first meeting is a necessary part of the process that can be done outside a regular rehearsal room. But there still must be three real rehearsals after this first meeting.

Interpretation and Analysis

In most scenes, each character comes on stage either to "give" or to "get" something from the other character. Most of my classroom scene work consists of two character scenes—typically crisis, climax, or resolution scenes. Occasionally I find it useful to assign exposition scenes because they are the hardest to drive and make interesting.

I never direct a scene after assigning roles, but leave that up to the preparation and rehearsal between the actors. They rehearse on their own and then do the scene in class. While most scenes will go up two times, often I'll ask the actors to come back for a third time if there's something vital to be gained by another try. I give my critique after this first viewing of a scene. I also suggest areas to work on and discuss the play and the writing in general. The second time the scene is up, I will nudge the actors along as a director to get them deeper into their choices. However, before I do this, I want to see what choices the actors are making in their rehearsal process. And rarely will I fully "direct" my students. As a result, the actors must always have done their own preparation for my class.

The actor's sense of how to prepare and make choices on her own is needed in the real world as well, not just in my classroom. In an ideal "real-world" acting situation, both the writer and the director are completely available to help the actor in the creation of the role. But these situations rarely exist, and even when they do, the actor is still responsible for achieving the distinct character results desired by the director through what I'd call her acting Road Map. (I'll give more details on how to build a Road Map later in this chapter.) "Never depend on a director to create a character for you," I remind my students.

Memorization—Word for Word

Scenes are never done with scripts in hand in my class. They must be memorized, preferably prior to the final rehearsal, but definitely before bringing the scene into the classroom. There is also a great deal of analysis and breaking down of the scene that needs to be done, which is detailed later in this chapter. But memorization is a must for scene study in my class, as it is in the real world.

Memorization Rules

I included these rules earlier in the book, in Part I, but I want to reinforce how important memorization is to good acting.

1. **Do not paraphrase**. You are the actor, not the author. As most of you will be working on finished scripts, I want the author's lines word for word. By doing the author's lines, you learn the writer's rhythms, which may not be your own.

2. **Study the punctuation, and do it**! If the writer puts a pause, a silence, a dash, or dots, it means something. It was not an arbitrary decision. Playing the punctuation can take you to the right rhythm.

3. **Learn the line *precisely* as it's written**. It's tough to correct once you've locked in the wrong words.

4. **Do not add verbal pauses**. Almost all of us add little words and sounds to our speech when we talk—"uhs" and "you knows" and "likes." It's natural. But when an actor does it for a role, it sounds sloppy. The writer will often insert the little words that are necessary for the role. Extra ones are not only unnecessary, they will interfere with the acting.

Be Punctual

All actors should be on time—*exactly* on time—for rehearsal with their scene partners. The "be punctual" rule obviously goes for all aspects of the acting world, including auditions, professional rehearsals, classes (especially my class!), and call times. But no student should think that allowances should be made because "it's just rehearsal for class." No, no, no! Time is money, especially when renting a rehearsal space. And if someone is going to be late for an unavoidable reason, she should have the courtesy to call her partner. Almost everyone has a cellphone these days.

Actors Are Not Directors

There are always pitfalls when actors work alone, but the most dangerous part of actors working without a director is the relationship that can get established.

Actors should never try to direct each other in a learning atmosphere. One actor choosing to be the leader and treating the other as a subordinate can cause a great deal of resentment.

If a director-leader/actor-subordinate relationship starts in rehearsal, I always tell the actor being directed to say, "Stop—please don't direct me or tell me where to move, how to say my line, or what I should be thinking." Each actor must do her own work and process her character for herself. The instructor will see what's happening (or not happening) when the actor brings the scene in, and will critique, adjust, and direct as the problems present themselves.

An actor may remain silent while the other takes on a directing role, and may do so to avoid a confrontation with the other actor. She may be thinking she doesn't want to offend. But keeping silent will only lead to more problems of resentment down the road. The subordinate will either have to follow the direction given by the other actor (often a bad idea), or completely ignore it—and potentially offend and frustrate the other actor. The longer this kind of passive-aggressive relationship between actors goes on in rehearsal, the more the frustration and resentment will build. But if the actors deal with it early on, the rehearsal process can proceed and the scene can grow.

Find a Space
While the preliminary "homework" session can take place almost anywhere, I suggest renting a space for the actual rehearsals. Apartments or houses are not always conducive for a good rehearsal, especially when doing a bombastic scene or a scene requiring physical intimacy. Any place that is used as a living space will typically limit the ability of an actor to get into a role, and is always subject to interruption—by a roommate, family members, telephone call, knock on the door, or household pet.

Nor does a personal home allow for "safety"—these are places where an actor's real life takes place, and if the scene requires intimacy, either one or both of the actors may feel more awkward than necessary. A neutral site such as a rehearsal room is ideal. It may cost a small fee, but when paying by the hour, the tendency will be to focus more on rehearsal and less on having a "coffee klatch."

14 ROAD MAP

Before the first meeting with a partner, or certainly before the first "on your feet" rehearsal, each actor must be responsible for the following:

- Two or more full readings of the script
- Many readings of the scene being worked on
- As much memorization as possible
- A preliminary "Road Map"

While there certainly is spontaneity in acting, there is also a great deal of planning necessary. Each actor should create a "Road Map" for herself, most of which is not shared with her partner. The spontaneity comes from each actor working from her character and then reacting to the other. But to react spontaneously, the actor must be very clear and grounded in certain elements of the characterization and action in the scene. It is this clarity and grounding—as well as intense memorization of lines—that gives the actor freedom to pay attention to her scene partner and react. These elements do not come during rehearsals, but prior to beginning them.

There may be changes or alterations necessary later, either because the actor realizes that something isn't working, or because the director takes her in a different direction. But without this kind of preliminary homework, rehearsals will often be nothing more than a muddle of recited lines. The actor must create a Road Map before beginning rehearsals. This includes:

- A "Working Title" for the character in the scene
- An Objective for the character[1]
- Beats outlined (to discuss with scene partner)
- Actions (intention), often for each beat
- Givens (background) from the entire text

---

[1] Once in rehearsal, the actor may find a different title and objective from the ones she originally chose.

WORKING TITLE

The Working Title answers the question, "From the beginning, what kind of scene is this for your character?" In other words, the actor is looking for an action word that stimulates her imagination and sums up what the event of the scene is, from the start, for her character. Examples include:

- A Drowning scene
- A Manipulation scene
- A Seduction scene
- A Love scene
- A Rescue scene
- A Face-Off scene
- A Revenge scene
- A Set-Up scene
- An Atonement scene
- A Get-Even scene
- A Domination scene
- An Escape scene

It's important to remember that the Title does not apply to the overall play, just what the character is trying to do in the overall scene. It applies to the emotional and mental mindset of the character from the top of the scene.

Choosing a Title can be a little tricky, but there are more guidelines to assist the actor. She must remember that the Title only applies to her character, not to her scene partner's character. She selects a word that epitomizes what her character is actually doing in the scene.

For example, for her character in the scene, it's a "Drowning scene." For her partner, it's a "Manipulation scene." The Title always applies to the overall action of the character in the scene. What is going on for the character from the top of the scene? The more in opposition the two characters' Titles are for the scene, the more conflict in the outcome. But the Titles should never be shared between the actors ahead of time.

Sometimes my students will choose a Title that describes what happens during the scene, rather than the mental and emotional state from the top. This doesn't work. Making the mistake of choosing a Title out of something that happens in the scene is going to eliminate discovery and possible conflict. The actor should decide what one or two words are most stimulating when used to describe the situation that her character is in from the very beginning of the scene to the end. Let the partner find her own Title.

For example, if the character has gone out onto a porch during a party and ends up kissing another character who follows her out, the actor might mistakenly choose "A Love scene" for the Title. But remember, it's what the character is doing at the *top* of the scene, not what happens during it. "An Escape scene" may be more appropriate, since what she was attempting at the beginning was to escape from the party.[2] "Remember, the action word must be operative from the moment the character is introduced in the scene." A Title doesn't shift once another character is introduced, but is the subtext of the scene for the actor.

Another example: A character suffering from a terminal disease might be "dying." But dying is something that happens to a person and is typically out of her control. But what is the character *doing* about dying? Better Titles might be "Denial," "Vengeance," "Atonement," or "Retribution"—whatever word works best to describe exactly what the character is doing in the overall scene—not, in this case, the condition of dying.

The most important part is to find a Title that works to inspire the imagination. I've had some students use catchphrases or even song titles that capture the emotional and psychological mood of the character at the top of the scene. Others will follow my example and use simple action words as I've described. If the right word is used, both are equally effective.

OBJECTIVE

Finding an "Objective" is a concept that should be introduced in beginning acting scene study classes. It is the center of all acting, and comes back to answering the question, "What did the character come on stage to do?" To my knowledge, Stanislavski is the first person to use the concept of the "super objective" as pertaining to a character's overall driving force throughout an entire play—the character's "through line." I narrow this down to the character's Objective in the particular scene. The actor is to find a one-sentence Objective for the character, beginning with the words, "I must . . . "

The actor should always use the words "I must." The Objective is that important. It isn't "I might" or "I may" or "I probably could." It is, "I MUST." I am constantly reminding my students of the importance of the Objective to their characters. "If you really go after your Objective, you will get out of your head, give up control, and be 100 percent involved in obtaining your goal," I'll say. "It is not enough just to define an Objective. You must pursue it with mind, heart, and will." It is this importance that motivates the character to do,

---

[2] This scene description may seem familiar—it's exactly what happens in *Proof* by David Auburn.

and do it now. And *doing* is essentially what acting is about. Some examples of Objectives include:

- Romeo in *Romeo and Juliet*—"I must have Juliet or I'll die."
- Nora in *A Doll's House*—"I must take responsibility for myself."
- Hedda in *Hedda Gabler*—"I must control my fate."
- Hamlet in *Hamlet*—"I must avenge my father."
- Stanley in *A Streetcar Named Desire*—"I must rule the roost."
- Lenny in *The Homecoming*—"I must punish my mother."

These are working examples for the characters in certain scenes, and perhaps could even serve as the "spine" of the character for the entire play—Stanislavski's "super objective."

But once again, the Objective must serve the character's event from the top of the scene. There are times when an actor might not fulfill her Objective in the scene because the other character's Objective overwhelms hers, but that's okay—unfulfilled Objectives are equally valid, and often more interesting.

Having established a Title (imaginative action word or phrase) and an Objective (an "I must"), the actor now has the beginning of the Road Map that she will pursue in each rehearsal. "But remember—be flexible. Do not be so dogmatic as to resist change. You may encounter a stronger Title or Objective in the rehearsal process. Then change it!"

These are the parts of the Road Map that the actor keeps to herself. "Do not discuss either the Title or the Objective with your partner. It does not concern him. He will have his own, and if you both are working well and making the right choices, you will find the conflict in the scene."

BEATS

The next step is to break the scene into Beats and score the scene like a piece of music. *A new beat occurs when the previous subject matter or a physical activity changes the previous action.* A new Beat can be created from an entrance, exit, kiss, slap, or shout, or simply from a change of direction in conversation. Each one of these Beats should be given an action/intention verb, and the verbs should be what the actor is playing/doing in an attempt to fulfill her overall Objective.

While I emphasize the importance of the actors keeping their Title and Objective from their scene partners, I emphasize equally that the Beat breakdown must be discussed with both partners. Both should agree where the Beats change. Knowing exactly where they change can assist greatly in rehearsal, so the actors can rehearse the scene in parts rather than running through the scene.

Some Beats may require more work or choreography, and being on the same page with a scene partner simplifies and defines the rehearsal process.

* * *

RELEARNING

I had plenty of eclectic and experimental educational experience in theater in college before I met Terry, but didn't realize how much I was missing until I was embroiled in his class. Aside from some general ideas from Stanislavski, I really didn't know how to approach a scene or a role strategically, and felt like I completely relearned everything in Terry's class.

My approach to a role is much different than before. I thoroughly research the time period and setting for the play, I analyze the script for givens, and I assign Titles to my scenes. While I did Beat breakdowns and defined overall or "über" Objectives before, I now enhance this analysis with specific Objectives in each scene and prefer to rehearse beat by beat rather than immediately run through the script in the early rehearsals.

Terry's training also helped me solve a habit of thinking too far ahead and focusing on what I needed to do later rather than what I was doing in that moment. Having an Objective from when I first walked into the room rather than at the bottom of the scene helped me to not anticipate.

I've found assigning Titles to scenes to be extremely important. My favorite choices are song titles, and I know when I've gotten something right during the rehearsal process when I feel that little jump in my heart and my mind screams, "That's it!" After that, the scenes come together quickly, magically, and easily.

I was able to put all the training into action recently. I was cast in an emotionally complex play and the director didn't believe in holding the actors' hands and leading them through each and every detail of the play. In the past, I would have been frightened, lost, and confused from the freedom, and my performance would have probably reflected that. But I was armed with the ability to do what I needed on my own, and I brought much more to the role than if I had been fed everything from someone else.

—Donna Abraham

* * *

Beat scoring is more than a guide for rehearsal. Understanding the Beats helps the actors to see the transitions in the scene and see how the individual characters move from A to B to C to D. Without Beat scoring, these transitions can be muddied and choices become general. But if an actor knows the Beats of a scene, these transitions will be clear and the characters will spring to life.

All Beats should be played out as the author intended. For my classes, I insist that no internal cuts are made within a scene. While some of the scenes I assign can be rather long, I'd rather have the actors decide to do only a consecutive portion of the text rather than remove chunks from the middle. Cutting to the middle of a scene creates transition problems. "Stick to the script," I tell them.

ACTIONS (ALSO CALLED "INTENTION")

The Actions are the verbs the actor is playing to fulfill the Objective. Some directors or teachers speak of "intention," and I mean exactly the same thing by using the word "Action." For example, Romeo's overall Objective is "to obtain Juliet." He may first try the Action of "to cajole." If that doesn't work, he may try "to plead." If that further fails him, he may try "to seduce"—anything he can do to obtain his Objective as Juliet presents obstacles.

There could be dozens of actions in a scene, depending on how long the scene lasts and how many Beats are in the scene. I believe that each Beat will only have one Action. Some Beats and Actions may seem short, but often, the same Action continues after a short interruption or interjection.

I will typically present my students with a list of about two hundred action verbs to help them with their scene preparation. The actor is welcome to add two hundred more to this list, but she should pick nitty-gritty verbs, not fifty-dollar, scholarly ones. "To obfuscate" is fine in a director's book, but is far too removed for an actor. She would be much better off using "to confuse," "to muddle," "to swamp," "to trick," or "to control." Gritty verbs appeal to an actor's imagination, not just her intellect.

Some Action verb examples from my sheet include: to abandon, accuse, annihilate, appeal, assert, attack, beg, berate, blast, bolster, break loose, discover, disown, dominate, enjoy, escape, fight back, flirt, fool, forbid, forgive, get their attention, get them off my back, love, lure, make them feel guilty, make a stand, menace, mock, oppose, order, overthrow, patronize, pester, please, prohibit, promise, provide, provoke, punish, question, reach out, reason, rebel, recognize, seduce, take over, taunt, teach, tempt, trap, unburden, undress, vent, violate, warn, welcome, win, worship, yield.

These are the ones I see often, but the options are limitless.

Each Beat Gets a Verb

Verb selection for each beat is very important. Not only will it help the actor in going after her Objective, but it also helps her to play different colors and choices. We've all seen inexperienced actors make an interesting choice and then play that same choice for the next ten minutes. The actor becomes static and dull, and our audience ear and eye fade quickly. But if the actor switches her Actions in order to further fulfill her Objective, the scene becomes rich and full of life. Ideally, the scene partner will be playing his Action, Objective, and Beat choices as well—and as this happens, conflicts arise and an interesting scene is created.

THE GIVENS

There is always information that the playwright gives about his characters, even in the most obtuse piece of work. This is where careful examination of the entire text and not just the scene will delineate character behavior from the playwright's point of view. The text will tell the actor what she needs to know about the character and what the character is doing about these facts, or "Givens."

Knowing the Givens of a text is essential, which is why it's so important to thoroughly read the full play, even when playing a short scene. When working with deeply psychological writers like Henrik Ibsen or Arthur Miller, the actor will find that if she brings the Givens from previous scenes, the scene will play itself.

Most plays I use in class are from writers who fuel the actor with their Givens. But when dealing with a nonlinear writer, much has to be brought by the actor because the playwright may give little or no background. Some of the questions of "who, what, when, where, why" have to be filled by the actor and an imagined biography.

For example: Harold Pinter's characters exist as they appear. Little or no background is given, so the actor must imagine it. This is where an exercise like the Spoon River comes in handy. Remember the biography and parallel dialogue work? It can be used for this kind of nonlinear writer. By taking notes of the Givens while reading the entire play, the actor will find a path of clarity as to what character and scene issues she must solve.

Givens Are Clues to Actions and Responses

Givens will often let the actor know why a character behaves in a certain way. For example, a character's response to a situation in a scene may be entirely different from the way the actor playing the character would respond. The differences will be apparent in the Givens in the text. During her immersion process, the actor must work to accomplish the character's response as the author has written them, rather than giving her own personal response. The life, behavior, and words must be authentic and truthful, not indicated or played at generally.

Here are some examples of extracting Givens from a drama in order to play the role.

Brick in *Cat on Hot Tin Roof* by Tennessee Williams

Tennessee Williams is a writer who thoroughly knew how to write for the actor. There are many Givens in the text that let the actor—and the audience— know about Brick's motivations and life. The actor playing Brick, before starting rehearsals, should note:

- There are some explosive relationships in Brick's life that the other characters discuss, especially his gossipy family members. The actor should know who all the other characters are in the play and how he relates to them: Maggie (his wife), Big Daddy (his father), each member of his family, and especially his best friend, Skipper. Skipper's not in the play, but he greatly influences Brick's life.

- Williams sets the atmosphere very clearly. It's a hot summer day in the South. He also sets other physical-condition and sensory work the actor should pay attention to: Brick has a broken ankle and has been drinking constantly for hours. The actor can do sensory work on heat, a broken ankle, and an alcoholic stupor.

- There is a great deal of information about the psychological life of Brick. He's a romantic and an idealist, he rich and spoiled, he's a frat boy and a football hero, and he's in sexual denial. He also has masochistic side, a tendency toward self-destruction and punishment.

Annie Sullivan in *The Miracle Worker* by William Gibson

This character was a real person and a great deal was written about her life. There are plenty of biographies about her and the other main character in the play, Helen Keller, the blind and deaf woman who was able to communicate with Anne through a special kind of sign language.

Since she really existed, the biographical details on Annie are Givens:
- Upbringing. She was dirt-poor and Irish.
- Profession. Life in a charity workhouse.
- Sign language.
- Failing eyesight.
- The Keller family and work with Helen.

- The lifelong friendship between Anne and Helen.
- Tenacity and patience. Incredible will to succeed at making contact with Helen.

These Givens are only a fraction of what is known, both from the play and from the biographies of this incredible character. But the actress who plays her shouldn't solely focus on her. Remember, there's a whole world out there that's different from the one we live in today. Science was at a different phase, as was care for the indigent and the roles of women in society. All of this information is fodder for the actor.

Stanley in *The Birthday Party* by Harold Pinter

Very little is ever directly expressed in plays by Harold Pinter. The actor has to hang on to every little thread that is mentioned. The same problems exist with works by Samuel Beckett, Eugene Ionesco, and every experimental writer. But discovering Givens is not impossible. In fact, the lack of exposition is what often makes these playwrights so interesting. For a Pinter work, the actor must pore over the text and dig out any possible little piece of character information. Some of the information discovered could include things that take a careful eye and keen insight:

- Stanley is an artist—he plays the piano—and is hiding out in a cheap seaside resort, apparently running from something.

- Meg is his landlady, but also his "mother/mistress." He dominates her.

- Stanley has tremendous fear of being dominated.

- Stanley is accused of social betrayal for having left "the organization" (no explanation of what the organization is—up to the actor to decide).

- Stanley knows "the organization" is out to get him.

- Stanley is shabby, unshaven, and unpresentable.

- There is a feeling of invasion of Stanley's space and property—he feels he is the victim of psychological inner terror that is menacing and intrusive.

- Stanley projects his own feelings by terrorizing Meg.

- Stanley is not articulate.

- Stanley reverts to childhood and childish malice when provoked.

From Shakespeare's ornate iambic pentameter to contemporary abstract plays, Givens can be found through exploration and reading. As Anton Chekhov said, "It's all there in the text." The actor must dig it out and then use the actor's tools to fulfill the totality of the character.

ESSENTIAL SCENE PREPARATION

Preparation and blocking are absolutely needed if the scene requires physical control and contact, such as a slap, pushing, shoving, or any kind of roughhousing. Very violent scenes that involve weapons require especially intense preparation. Rehearsal is particularly important when doing class scene work because of the probable absence of a fight choreographer. It's up to the actors to fully prepare in the absence of a trained professional directing the violence.

The actors should stop in rehearsal and do the moves slowly, step by step, until the physical blocking is set. "Do not step up the pace until you have established trust with one another and you know the precise moves," I tell them. "And *never* lose eye contact during the skirmish, either during the rehearsal time or in class. It's that connection that will keep you both safe."

Remember, presenting the scene will cause tension and heightened energy. Therefore, any physicality must be well prepared and be safe. There is no excuse for an actor getting hurt, either during rehearsal, in a scene in class, on stage, or on a film set. A slap across the ear, a smacked nose, a chipped tooth, or any other body injury . . . that kind of stage realism has nothing to do with acting and is the worst kind of self-indulgence on the guilty actor's part. Actors should talk to me if there are questions about blocking or how to be generally safe during this type of scene, and I'll either assist or send them to a stage combat expert.

Sensual Scenes

If the scene is a love scene, the partners should discuss what they are each comfortable with before beginning rehearsal. If the two actors are going to open up their sexual sides to each other, there must be communication. The more relaxation and trust they can have, the better it is for the work.

Intimacy between acting partners should always be confined to the scene work. "Do not use class to enhance your romantic life. Use it for the work. A partner is not going to feel comfortable if he or she feels they're going to be 'hit on' after (or during) rehearsal." As a general rule, the less actual outside-of-class involvement with one another, the better it is for objectifying the work in class—or in the real acting world. An affair can make the work very complicated and seldom productive. I never put husbands and wives, or lovers, together in the same class for this very reason.

If the scene requires disrobing, the actors should work to become comfortable with this in rehearsal. "It's hard enough to do in front of the class, so give yourself a break by not waiting until you're actually presenting the scene."

15 SCENE WORK
REHEARSAL PROCESS

I've already explained a lot about this first meeting in the previous section. As I said, it can be done informally in an apartment, in a quiet restaurant, at a local coffeehouse, or even on a bench in a park—anywhere where the actors can congregate for a couple of hours, undisturbed.

PRELIMINARY MEETING

The first meeting should be confined to a get-acquainted session, especially if the partners do not know each other very well. But it should not be turned into a coffee klatch, gossip session, or personal discussion. Getting acquainted and becoming friends is laudable, but when there's work to do, the actors should focus on the work.

After getting acquainted, the actors should begin by reading the scene. Each should have read the entire play at least once (preferably more than once), and read the scene many times prior to this first meeting. Certain parts of the Road Map will have already been filled in, such as the Title, Objective, and many of the Givens. (But not the Beats—I'll explain in a moment.)

The preliminary meeting may prompt some changes, or maybe during the discussion, an actress decides to change her Title on her own accord (*not* because her partner suggests it). Perhaps during the conversation, one actor discovers more Givens than she had initially found. There will be a lot of sharing of ideas at this point, but the actors will not reveal their individual Title, Objectives, and Actions.

Before coming to this pre-rehearsal, the actor should make a list of Givens or other aspects of the piece coming from the playwright that may require additional work and attention. Sometimes it might be a fight scene or an intimate moment. Other times, the actor might need to do an exercise to propel the right emotional quality. This might require personal sensory or physical-condition work. Or maybe there's a prop or action that will take extra attention. If the scene requires the character to demonstrate the ability to play the guitar, the actor who has never played in her life might want to learn how to strum a few chords.

This preliminary meeting is essentially the first read-through, and the actors each read their parts out loud. "I strongly suggest you push away from all the preconceived homework and just make yourself available to your partner. Be open in reading out loud for the first time to what other new images, thoughts, and ideas may occur."

The actors should position two chairs facing each other for eye contact and read very slowly, as if they are encountering the words for the first time—just as in the Spoon River exercise. "Taste and savoring their meaning. Do not push for feelings or emotions. If something of a feeling or emotional response does come up, great—if it's real. But don't work for it at this stage."

The actors should read for sense, logic, arc, and flow of the scene. "Listen and hear your partner. Adjust off of what you are getting from her. Take in what you are being given. Maintain eye contact as much as possible. Do not begin to 'act' the scene, but read for understanding, new ideas, and fresh inspiration."

After reading the scene together first, the actors then decide the Beat breakdown together. While the Actions that each actor chooses for the Beats only apply to each individual actor, the Beats must be agreed upon by both scene partners. (I typically suggest marking these Beats in pencil, in case the actors decide they made an error and change them as they work.)

I encourage my students to read the scene like this two or three times during the preliminary meeting, but to not put the scene on its feet. "Don't act! Wait until the rehearsal, when you're in a real rehearsal space."

This is also the time for the actors to establish boundaries with each other, or at least acknowledge any aspects of the scene that require discussion, such as violence or intimacy. "Don't wait until the rehearsal to discuss these aspects. It will serve you well to acknowledge them early." Finish the meeting by setting the next rehearsal time, date, and space.

FIRST REHEARSAL

The actors should try to find a good rehearsal space that is convenient for both. If the actors must rehearse at an apartment because of economic or other reasons, they should be sure there is privacy. There should be no husband, wife, lover, child, or roommate lurking in the next room, and the actors should have enough space to work comfortably.

At the rehearsal, the actors should discuss the set to be used in class. Sometimes it helps to initially use a set of some sort for the rehearsal. Rental spaces will often have extra chairs to use. Others will allow actors access to furniture and props. Some furniture can be suggested or replaced at the rehearsal, but essential props should be brought in.

I encourage my students to be creative. "Be imaginative with your set. Ambiance—creating your space—is very important. Bring in items from home, anything that will help you to feel 'in' the space. I want props! Your surroundings are important. Do not just settle for a couple of pieces of furniture, unless that is the abstract and spare world the play calls for."

This first rehearsal should be done with scripts, and the actors should stay away from acting or playing at feelings and emotion. Instead, their focus should be on getting comfortable in the space. They should not block the scene, nor stage each other. In a two-character scene, once they find the life, the actors will find the correct organic movement. Armed with their Road Maps (Title, Objective, etc.), they are now ready to work.

This rehearsal should last between two and three hours. The actors should stop and work beats, not just plow through the script. "You and your partner are in a joint venture. Feel free to stop and say, 'Can we go back on these two beats?' It's a working process, a rehearsal, and it must not be result- or performance-oriented." They should work a couple of beats, especially the opening beat, for thirty minutes. Then they should add two more beats for the next half-hour. After an hour and a half of working like this, they should run the first six to eight beats. "You may not get through the whole scene in the first rehearsal."

Relaxing and letting the scene happen is the most important aspect of the first rehearsal. "Leave yourself open to new ideas and to exploration of yourself in this event. Explore how you begin to immerse yourself into your character's way of functioning. Find organic reasons to do what you do, not just intellectual thoughts. Pursue instincts. Try your ideas. Don't intellectualize and dismiss them. Your need room to breathe."

The actors may also want to experiment with different kinds of exercise work from Parts II and III. However, if one of the actors needs a lengthy preparation prior to starting, she should not take up her partner's rehearsal time. Instead, the actor who needs the preparation time should get to rehearsal early or do some of the work prior to meeting with her partner.

In concluding the first rehearsal, the actors should run the Beats they worked on. Then they can see what works and what doesn't from their stop-and-start Beat work and can leave rehearsal evaluating which choices work and which don't work.

Ideally the scene should be ten minutes maximum. As I've said before, the actors should not make internal cuts simply because they want to get to a certain section. Instead, they should only focus on part of the scene rather than the whole scene. Making internal cuts can create beat and motivation problems that would not exist if they had stayed in context.

I suggest ten minutes for a scene because that's a good "learning" time. Quality, not quantity, is always more important in scene work. Growth in the acting process is the ultimate goal. "I assume you can learn lines. But it's the work process, the solving of character problems, and knowing how to do layered work that I want to see."

Words Words Words

A short reminder for the actor: Learn the lines exactly as they are written. *Do not paraphrase.* Be aware of the writer's punctuation. It's of paramount importance to the rhythm of the scene, to the playwright's music.

That doesn't mean the actors can't eliminate the rest of the "suggestions" in a script, such as emotional indications, stage business directions, and blocking. I definitely support the use of a black felt-tipped pen to take out all stage directions that indicate what the actor is supposed to be feeling or states how to say the line. Playwrights like O'Neill and Shaw will drive an actor crazy with these kinds of directions. The actor will forever have an image in her mind of what the writer put in parentheses. She must instead trust her own exploration and homework to find out what the character feels.

Depending on who wrote the play (or sometimes who directed it), the actors should, in certain cases, peruse the stage business suggested. If they can't top the business with their own choices, they should go with what is suggested until they've got the freedom to explore more or different activities or different "business" choices of their own.

My point: While I am not a stickler for removing all blocking, the actors should not be glued to it. Certain moves were made by a different actor on a specific, completely different set. The students doing the scene are not those actors, and rarely will anyone—professional or amateur—have all the accommodations of the original set. I tell my students to be aware of what is suggested, but to see what they might find that works better for them.

This first rehearsal is of great importance. The actor and her partner are establishing a rapport and a way of working with each other—without directing each other. "You both must be open to having the other say, 'If this is how you're going to play that moment, then this is my response.' Do not correct your partner if she is playing something opposite of the way you feel it should be played. Just play your response from what he or she is doing."

Each actor should work on what she thinks in rehearsal are the most important choices in getting inside her role. "Let the teacher decide what's not working or what's being misinterpreted when the scene is done in class." When one of the actors expresses concern that the scene won't work, I reassure her that it's the leader's job to interject, not the actor's. "I'll see what's misinterpreted when you put up the scene."

Upon finishing this rehearsal, the actor's Title, Objective, and overall journey in the scene should be clear. She will discover these much more quickly if she does not try to "act" anything at this stage of rehearsal.

"Remain objective rather than subjective. See the signposts, and it will be much clearer as to what homework you have to do and what character problems you have to solve." This rehearsal, like others, is akin to being on an archeology dig. The actors must stay open and accessible to what they might find. "You have your map, you know what you're looking for. You know the inner connection you want. Trust the exploration as a route to the result."

SECOND REHEARSAL

The actors should drop the books for this one. They can't do the work if their noses are buried in the script. They should know the lines cold, because they can't do the work if they do not know what they are going to say next.

The actors should also be sure they know what they have come in to work on or to solve. The Objective should be very clear to the actor by now, as well as what tools she has to use and apply to fulfill her Objective. The arc or flow of the scene should also be clear at this point. The actor should ask herself, "What are the most important things to work on for me to solve in the scene? What's major and what's minor? What's solved and what still needs work?" She should tackle one thing at a time. An actor cannot solve everything in a scene in one rehearsal.

As the actors work the scene over this two- or three-hour rehearsal period, I expect them to layer each work-through with other choices. One actor may alert her scene partner that she will try different things. For example, she might say, "I won't be giving you the same thing this time because I want to add another layer. I'll focus on that other thing again once I add this color." The other partner should exercise the same request. It makes for an exciting and discovery-filled rehearsal.

Finally, the actors should remember to not look for the definitive interpretation—that is subjective to a director and a production concept. In class, I am looking to see what sense and logic the actor is making out of the work process. The interpretation might be changed after it's presented in class, just as a director might change it in a real acting situation. The work won't be in vain. This kind of homework creates a structure and foundation that can be easily altered at the suggestion of a teacher or director. Without the structure and foundation, there's nothing to work with.

THIRD REHEARSAL

This rehearsal is about honing in on the final choices the actors have made. After this rehearsal, they should be prepared to bring the scene into the classroom. Everything the actors are going to do and wear should be at this rehearsal. The proper costumes and props should be used; activities such as eating or drinking should be done with actual silverware and glassware, not mimed.

This is also the last chance to bring in anything new and work it through with your acting partner. "Do not spring surprises on your partner when doing the scene in class. Stay with what you've worked on and want me to see. Trust your homework and do not suddenly panic and throw it all out."

If the rehearsal process has been thorough, the scene should be fully ready to put up in class. Actors who follow the steps of preparing a scene thoroughly can avoid eleventh-hour panic. They will also know what to say in the critique following the scene, when I ask, "So, what are you working on?"

I always ask that an actor does not try to wing it on class day. Everyone will see right through the actor's lack of preparation, and the instructor should have every right to stop the scene. Students who try to put up an unprepared work waste everyone's time, but mainly their own. Classes are expensive and time-consuming, and actors should use every moment of rehearsal to get their money's worth and to grow in the craft.

16 SCENES IN CLASS

No actor should ever just jump up and do a scene. As with the group and individual exercises, preparation is needed. Before the scene starts, the actors should go to a dressing room and prepare—preferably alone, and preferably fifteen or twenty minutes before the scene. Some actors need more time, and should take it. "Use the time off stage to first get relaxed, centered, and ready to work. Once that's set, work on your preparation—where you want to be psychologically and emotionally to start the scene. Use this time to create your subtext." Do not use the time to run lines.

In my class, when one scene is complete and these actors are receiving notes from the class and me, the actors in the next scene are setting up their stage. But just because they're lugging around furniture and setting props doesn't mean their preparation work wanes. "Bring your preparation into the set-up. Be the characters as you set the stage, and stay in the emotional state that you have prepared for the top of the scene." The actors might be vaguely aware of the discussion going on, but their job is to ignore it, concentrate, drop into their space, and be ready for the opening beat.

Actors should take the scene work in class seriously. Time and time again, I have seen actors barely make any effort, using the excuse that "It's only class." No! The point of this scene work is to be as prepared as possible for real acting situations, and the only way to prepare is to practice. Advanced scene work is so actors can learn how to work *before* rehearsal, as well as during.

This goes for all aspects of the process—memorization, Road Map, and general attitude. I can't work with an actor who's carrying a book in her hand. Nor can an actor learn anything by doing a scene without proper preparation and analysis. And the attitude from an advanced actor in a scene work class should be just that: advanced and professional. Beginning classes have all the work explained and explored in class. Advanced actors who want that kind of coddling should go back and work at that level.

* * *

PUTTING IT ALL TOGETHER

The character of John Merrick in *The Elephant Man* was one of the more challenging parts Terry gave me in class. James Carey Merrick lived in the 1800s and suffered from severe multiple neurofibromatosis, which made portions of his body grow freakishly.

I started my research by looking at photos of Merrick, but realized as I read and reread the play that another character has a speech and describes in poetic detail what Merrick looked like, how he talked, and the manifestations on the deformity on his body. The givens gave me a huge head start. And being from the Philippines and spending years trying to lose my accent, I also related to Merrick's inability to get what he wants in the "normal" world.

The rest took some imagination. For example, his spine was curved, so I explored walking and eating as if I suffered from the same problem. At first I practiced privately, but once I had it set, I rode the subway with the deformities, and used them in rehearsal.

I had thought the physicality would be the hardest part, but I was wrong. It was actually one of the easier elements, since once I had it set, it became part of me. It was the emotional vulnerability of the romantic scene Terry assigned that was tough.

Merrick had consistent contact with only one female in his life—Mrs. Kendal, his tutor. He had fallen in love with her, and confessed his attraction. The physical condition helped to enhance the barrier between Mrs. Kendal and me (as Merrick). But I wanted more, so I used an Emotional Recall from my childhood to explore his inexperience with intimacy.

Mrs. Kendal responds to Merrick's curiosity about the female form by disrobing and displaying her nude upper body. A beat after she does this, another character enters the room and catches them. Terry told me to go back to that Emotional Recall from my youth and pretend my father had entered the room and caught me doing something I wasn't supposed to.

It worked, but my instinct was to put my head down. "No," said Terry. "Keep your head up. Look at your father."

I did, and the effect was like lightning. I realized after a few seconds that tears had been falling down my face, unconsciously and quietly. The emotion was real and unforced—it was rather like a small explosion. I'm so glad that I got that note from Terry. As hard as it was to do and as hard as it may continue to be for future roles, I want to keep my eyes up.

—Eric Bondoc

✳ ✳ ✳

Sometimes in class, a student will forget a line or two, especially if I generate additional exploration. That's okay! In my class, I insist that a student observing a scene hold the book so the actors can call for lines. "Stay in character, don't break the momentum and the moment." Obviously, if an actor is calling for a line every other line, there's a memorization problem. In those cases, I don't bother to waste any more time and will stop the scene. The actor can come back and do it another day, once the lines are memorized.

This doesn't mean that a scene has to be perfect when it's up in class. We're not looking for the definitive interpretation of a scene, but rather that the actors are fulfilling their Titles and Objectives, and have fully explored their Givens to create full characters. Each rehearsal prior to putting up the scene should be about discovering more and more of what the individual actor needs to make the scene work, with the class time as the culmination of this work. Through this process, the actor learns how to layer the rehearsal process.

FIRST TIME

The first time two actors are up with a scene, I generally wait to see what they are doing, and I do not interrupt unless the scene is incredibly misinterpreted—so far off the mark that it would be a waste of time to play through.

The completion of the scene will typically come with one or both actors on stage, and one of them will simply say "Scene" to mark the end. If one partner makes an exit, the other actor on stage plays through until she or the leader says "Okay" and stops. The scene is never over simply when the last word is spoken, but rather when the emotional quality of the last beat is full and complete. Most of the time, there are final moments and emotions that must be played through to the end. The actor must give herself a closure.

Right after the actors have their first time up in class with their scene, I have them sit in chairs to discuss the scene the rest of the class and with me. I want to hear what both actors have chosen as their Title, Objective, and Givens for their character. They can also talk about what problems the character is presenting to them. I feel very strongly that if the actor will use and trust the basic outline I've described, a solid and reliable beginning can be made in finding the moment-to-moment life of a scene.

The first thing I do is ask each actor for her Title and Objective. If the actors are not clear as to their Titles or Objectives, the work they've done will be equally muddled. I will discuss the Title and Objective with them until each actor's eyes light up and I know we've found it.

After that, I ask what choices they specifically want to talk about. "What Givens are you working on? What do you want us to see?"

I find that when the actor has picked the right operative word for her Title, and when her "I must" Objective stimulates the imagination, the scene has been equally as clear and works to allow the actor to give up control and be driven by her Objective.

"Remember, the Title must serve the actor for the entire scene, not just when the other actor enters." As I outlined before, the Title must be a strong word that stimulates the actor's imagination. It should also help her find an Objective that she must fulfill.

Many actors become bogged down in finding the perfect word or words for their Titles. Others become entangled in trying to articulate their Objective. Often they'll pick an Objective that is really more of a Beat than an overall Objective for the scene. I can usually tell this by how long the actor talks when explaining her Objective. Whenever an actor takes two or three sentences to explain what should take one or two words, the scene has been just as unspecific.

I've also seen actors make the mistake of picking an Objective that is too altruistic. "Don't be nice! The best Objectives are the ones that are self-centered and self-serving. In life, these kinds of Objectives are the ones that drive us, so why shouldn't that apply on stage?"

Once the Title and Objective have been reviewed, the Givens are then discussed—especially ones that may have been overlooked by the actor. Analysis of this kind will often solve many problems that the actor has with a scene.

As-If, or Personal Life?

If I see that an actor is having a problem, I will work with her during the critique to stimulate a connection. By this time, I should have gotten to know the actor's work well enough to sense whether she works better from an as-if standpoint (like using only the biography in the Spoon River exercise), or from her own personal reality (using an Emotional Recall, for example). I may try to appeal to the imagination by having the actor explore the as-if, or to parallel the character profile with a similar event in the actor's life. As I said, it doesn't matter to me how we get to "the life," as long as we get to it.

Many times, this discussion takes a good deal of prodding, pulling, and clarifying, even within the limited time period that I typically set. Patience is of the utmost importance, on all our parts. Ultimately, it's the actor's job to ask herself the same questions. Hopefully this kind of discussion will generate just that.

SECOND TIME

A good actor will take notes during the first critique so she can go back to rehearsal and know what to work on. Actors shouldn't simply trust their memory to remember the details. "Grab your acting journals."

The actors should refer to these notes from the critique during the subsequent rehearsals. They should have a minimum of two more good working rehearsals before remounting the scene. This is when they each go to work from their specific notes and dig much deeper into the character.

When they bring the scene in again—typically a week or two weeks later—I watch to see what they've done with the notes. If I see some progress but not enough to completely fulfill the scene, I generally jump in and start to work with the scene as an actual director. I'll never "act" the scene for them, but I want to encourage them to dig deeper with choices that are starting to work.

Typical work includes encouraging a deepening of the feelings and emotional values, as well as an adherence to the language and the writer's patterns, or what I like to call the "writer's music." I sometimes work on body or vocal problems. But the bulk of my time is spent attempting to help the actors get to the event of the scene, and determine how their characters are going about fulfilling their Givens and Objectives.

Once their second time up is complete, we pull up chairs again and discuss the work and what the actors were after and what they felt happened. While I want other actors in class to comment as one actor to another, I monitor the comments very carefully. I discourage typical "audience" comments that have little to do with the acting process. If actors say, "That was really good," or "I liked that," that's great and supportive, but I want to know why they liked it or found it good in acting terms.

The actors' feedback to the work at this second stage is important for me to hear. It tells me how they are observing and articulating the work. But this is also when I monitor the comments closely and never allow hostile, personal, or destructive comments. I want the actors to support each other, not attack one another. Nor am I interested in a comment such as, "Well, I would have . . ." That kind of egoism is useless in the class. I will often point out to such a commentator, "But you're not the person who is playing it."

That doesn't mean a comment can't be a criticism. I have no objection to someone saying, "I've heard Terry give you the same comment for two or three months, but you don't seem to be working on it." That's healthy feedback from a peer and can sometimes light a fire that I am not lighting. The open dialogue can be very helpful to an actor's further understanding of the work process and its application. The interaction is helpful for clarification and stimulating an exciting and healthy discussion about what we're all gathered for—acting.

17 APPLICATION OF EXERCISE WORK

With the help and support of the actor's Road Map, the next step is solving the active problems the scene presents. It's at this point that the lessons learned from the individual exercises or other acting instruction can be applied.

I encourage my students to use the tools that work for them, whether they're ones I've introduced them to or ones they've learned elsewhere. The actor should create and organically fulfill an interesting character life that fleshes out and fulfills the writing. I don't care if she stands on her head and whistles "Dixie" to get there. The one unforgivable sin for me when it comes to performance is to be "dull." In scene work in my class, we devote time to the process and the discovery, much like an ideal rehearsal for a play.

RELAX AND PREPARE

I think I've said it a hundred times in this book . . . and I'm going to say it again: An actor should never start working without relaxing first. This means getting rid of tension and centering the energy. Some people like to jump or run to eliminate excess energy, but often these methods won't be available if the actor is backstage before a show or in a cramped dressing room before doing a scene in class. In these cramped conditions, she might try portions of the warm-up that I led before the group exercises.

Other actors might need to simply sit in a quiet place and take a little time in addition to the warm-up, especially if the stress of the day is overwhelming. Whatever the method, the actor must ensure that she is into her body and on her breath. Once relaxed, the actor then goes into her preparation.

The actor always has to know the character's psychological and emotional state for the beginning of the scene. Even in the first scene of the play, the character comes from *somewhere* and feels *something*. This is when the Emotional Recall exercise or a sensory task can be very effective. This kind of work can take an actor to the given state they desire from the character's entrance. The actor may prepare by working from her own reality of a similar event or use the as-if to imagine the event.

I've often had my students do their preparation on stage before doing their scenes, while they're setting their stage and after, in full view of the rest of the class. Sometimes the work is quiet and small, while in other instances, it resembles Character Private Moments. Preparing in front of a group may seem awkward, but it makes sense for actors to practice getting into their characters in front of others. It helps them learn to deepen their concentration, as well as heighten their confidence in front of others. Actors are often required to prepare in front of others, especially in film and TV. The time to practice this skill is in class, not when the actor's got a paying gig. If she can't deal with the real-world circumstances, she won't have the job for long.

* * *

PREPARATION AT 6th AND 9th

When Terry first had us do our scene work preparations on stage, I found it quite unsettling. I didn't like being watched while I prepared. I liked the privacy of the dressing room.

But my opinion changed after I shot an episode of the emergency-crew-and-police television show *Third Watch*. I played a pregnant woman who got into a car accident. Bandages around my head, laying on a stretcher while the paramedic examined my belly, expressing fear of losing the baby, expressing remorse for hitting those people . . . heavy stuff! The accident scene was shot outdoors in Greenwich Village at a busy intersection at rush hour, and the actors and crew had to be ready on a moment's notice. I was very grateful to Terry for teaching me that I had to be able to prepare anywhere, anytime, in front of anyone, and was able to put it to the test in a paying acting situation.

—Irene Glezos

* * *

DON'T PREDICT

While the actor may be preparing an overall psychological and emotional state for a scene in an offstage prep, that emotion may not appear until midway through a scene. For example, think of young Juliet waking up next to her Romeo. At first she thinks she's escaped with him and will live a happy life. But then the realization that he has killed himself hits her, and her mood takes a 180-degree turn.

The actor playing Juliet must from her own reality or as-if be able to create the horror of seeing her lover die for her second discovery, but she must start the scene with her first discovery, an abundance of joy. Otherwise, she's playing the wrong emotional life from the start. She must play the joy. Obviously the second discovery of horror and sorrow must also be worked on, but it will be more accessible by going from wild joy. Having spent rehearsal time finding the loss, her offstage preparation immediately before the scene starts must take her to the joy of being reunited with Romeo. It's a difficult and demanding task. If the as-if of the scene doesn't put the actor into the right emotional state, the ideal tool is an Emotional Recall that parallels this pattern—joy followed by anguish.

FIGHT AGAINST EMOTIONS

One of the great dichotomies in acting is that fully realized characters will often feel an emotion, but be doing everything to work against it. Think of a woman whose mother just died but must smile through her pain, or the love-struck young man who lost his virginity the night before and tries to keep a straight face at his parents' breakfast table. Or two family members who, while furious with each other, work with all their might to control their tempers until they finally explode. In all three examples, the actors must prepare for one emotion and then fight against expressing it until they have to get it out during the scene.

The "verbal fight" scene is particularly tricky. Sometimes an actor's instinct is to display that anger and get into a fight from the get-go. But with so much fury right from the start, there's no place for the scene to go. My first rule in a verbal fight scene is, "Try not to have a fight." The actors, as the characters, should attempt actions to avoid the confrontation—that is, until they run out of options and the fight is on.

SCENE PROBLEMS—PERSONAL PROBLEMS

No actor alive can solve and play any kind of role, but the exercises and scene work can help an actor to open up a large range of possibilities with her instrument. But sometimes the block preventing the life of a character is the same block the actor has in her own personal life. If an actor going through a painful divorce in his own personal life is playing a character going through a similar situation, there is a tendency to block those emotions, even if they are fabricated ones for a scene. It's the natural instinct of emotional self-protection—exactly what keeps emergency-room doctors and first-response social workers from going insane. But in the acting world, I've observed that until the actor resolves that block, she will only play an idea of the character's responses rather than express the true emotion.

That doesn't mean that an actor can't play a character whose emotional life parallels her own. Quite the contrary, since there is an understanding of the character that other actors might not tap into. But the actor must have a sense of resolution about the emotional situation. This is exactly why acting instructors should tap into the psyche of their students. If an actor is blocking an emotion, there is probably a good reason why, even if she's not fully aware of it. This is also why these overwhelming emotions shouldn't be "pushed" in an acting class, but rather taken into a suggested therapeutic setting, where they can get the attention they deserve.

HANDLING DANGEROUS EMOTIONAL ACTING SITUATIONS

Does this mean that an actor who hasn't quite resolved something from her past can't work on a scene that triggers the problem? I'd be against giving her a scene in my class in this situation—it would probably be unhealthy and create fear of the work. But often this situation will arise in the professional acting world, and the actor simply can't avoid the issue. For this kind of situation, I'd suggest that the actor look for another tool to achieve the appropriate result.

* * *

USING THE E.R. TO GO TO PIECES

I've used an Emotional Recall—just one—time and time again in my professional work. It's all I've needed.

I was playing Mark Antony in Shakespeare's *Julius Caesar* and was having difficulty expressing the horror of seeing Caesar's murdered body in Act III. I chose to explore a great tragedy I lived through in my own life—a car accident that killed a young child. The act of re-experiencing the sensory elements of the accident worked perfectly to catapult me into the play, and I received accolades for my performance.

That E.R. stayed with me in my psyche. I never had to review the car accident, because the feeling had seeped deep into my subconscious. Years later, I was playing Horatio in *Hamlet*, and went to pieces every night as Hamlet died in my arms. I used it again in *Night Must Fall* by Emlyn Williams, where I played a murderous nutcase who has a breakdown in the second act, seemingly out of nowhere. And again on a film set, where the character completely breaks down. I told the cameraman to give me some space, count to five, and then move the camera to me.

That I don't have to go too deep any longer is just fine with me. Even though I'm emotionally resolved about the event (I was not at the wheel and the accident wasn't my fault), I wouldn't want to dwell on it. I don't have to. All I have to do is actively remember sensory elements—like the fact that the mushroom soup from lunch had lumps that day—and I'm immediately catapulted to where I need to go.

—Dennis Lipscomb

* * *

For example, many characters deal with the psychological aftermath of combat during a war. Any actor who was anywhere near the World Trade Center on September 11 obviously has a real-world example of this kind of horror and death. But if she's still suffering from shock, I'd never suggest that she—or anyone else, for that matter—use September 11 as an acting tool.

Instead, I'd encourage something else, most likely an Emotional Recall from childhood. I had one actor recall a situation from her adolescent years when she discovered the evidence that her sister was bulimic. She used the emotions from that situation to enhance a speech her character gave about watching her husband being torn apart by a mob.[1] It worked beautifully, and preserved her own personal emotional integrity.

Blocked emotions aren't the only problems an actor is faced with when doing a scene. There are many other situations that can cause difficulties. But there are also typically a number of tools from the group and individual exercises that can be utilized. Some examples:

"My character has an intense relationship with his brother. I don't have a brother." (*Substitute a very close friend—Face exercise*)

[1] Tennessee Williams, *Suddenly Last Summer.*

"I have a real problem letting people see my anger, and my character goes off like a skyrocket." (*Fallout*)

"I have a problem showing my vulnerability, and my character is ultra-sensitive." (*Song Exercise or Fallout*)

"I have trouble constructing the arc of this scene. I see where the character is going, but I am not connecting." (*The A.C.T. or Private Moment*)

"My character is really in touch with her sexuality, and I'm uncomfortable being public with that side of myself." (*Song, Fallout, or Private Moment*)

"My character seems bitchy, but I can't tell why or where it comes from." (*Physical Condition, especially Pain*)

"I have trouble finding business and behavior in a scene. I just sit and do the words." (*All the exercises are designed to help the actor deepen her concentration and find the stage life that the words often come from*)

"I want to fulfill my character life when I am alone on stage." (*Private Moment or Emotional Recall, Part Two*)

"I want to solve my character's physical condition of having a fever and being slightly drunk." (*Sensory exercises*)

IT ALL COMES DOWN TO TEXT

Certain writers may present problems to an actor because the character's rhythm and vocabulary is different from or totally foreign to the actor's. Regional accents formulate sentences in a particular manner, as do individual characters. The playwright has done a great deal of work creating the characters, and it's up to the actor to play them realistically. This is not possible if the actor changes the words or sentence structure to fit her own sense of language. One complaint that I have about today's actors is that so many of them are poorly read in the field. Few have read the great playwrights that I've mentioned in this book and listed in the back.

Knowledge and study alone isn't enough, however. I have previously noted in this book how important body and voice training are. "Your body is the instrument you play on. Good movement capability and a richly developed vocal range are of paramount importance to fulfilling the text."

Actors must deal with this rhythm and not paraphrase lines for comfort or laziness. A stage play is about the written word. It is a great asset to read many different playwrights and to analyze and understand their plays. Attempting to gain knowledge of playwrights who have a large canon of work and understanding their themes and mythologies only widens an actor's range of what she might play or train to play. And this literary practice and knowledge will translate to even the simplest of films and television shows, adding layers of insight that I rarely see in Hollywood today.

As she continues her work in scene study and in her career, the actor will start to become aware of not only the playwright's themes, settings, rhythms, and kinds of characters, but the milieu, period, and setting as well. The awareness and appreciation of words is vitally important. Our art form is ultimately one of making language come alive, and presenting—to the fullest extent we are capable of—the life of the play. We are vessels in interpreting the words, harmonizing them, and playing them with depth, feeling, voice, and heart.

CONCLUSION

Posted at the T. Schreiber Studio is a sign that reads, "Acting is a terrible way to make a living, but a wonderful way to live a life." This motto has been a guiding principle in my life. But being dedicated to the craft can be difficult. Acting is an art form that can be as ephemeral as sculpting in snow. Just when an actor thinks he knows it, he starts a new play, movie, or television show, and the process starts all over. So does the insecurity, doubt, and trial and error.

I hope that what I've done with this book is at least hone the sculptor's tools. Though each new play or scene takes actors to new lands and tests their skills, the actor who takes the time to practice what I've described here will, I think, have a better chance of striving for that "perfect moment."

Every actor who's been bitten by the bug knows what I'm talking about. It's the moment when he stands at one with the life, behavior, and activity of a character, so much so that he is living as that person. It's the moment when the mind, heart, and will are centered and alive. It's a moment of magic. If an actor can have one of those during each performance, he is working at the top of his craft and skills—and is the envy of the rest of the acting world.

Exactly how to best create rich characters has been a matter debated in the acting world for over a century. Who has the correct theory—Strasberg, with his use of an actor's personal life reflected in characters? Or the other instructors of the as-if technique, who encourage the use of the imagination?

We could spend hours discussing which comes first—the inner life or the external life—but I think it would be a moot point. If the actor is working with relaxation and concentration, the imagination kicks in and the inner and external lives are happening together. Proper preparation cements this all together, giving the actor immense freedom. The ultimate acting goal is to put the *life*, *behavior*, and *words* together so that all three are flowing spontaneously to serve the characterization and the text, and it doesn't matter if the actor has a hyperactive imagination that can use the as-if, or if he relies on personal experience to jump-start the process. But he has to know which process serves him better, and that is only achieved through practice.

Let me stress again that most of these exercises are not appropriate for a beginning student. No beginning actor who picks up this book should think he now knows how to act. It's just not going to happen. Basic and intermediate classes deal much more with improvisation, theater games, sound and movement, risk exercises, sensory and physical-condition work, repetition exercises, and various and other exercises that are appropriate at these levels of acting training. As the actor moves from class to class, the exercises become more demanding and difficult, and no actor should jump into an advanced exercise without training in the basics first.

Nor should any actor quickly drive through the material here. He needs to be on his feet, practicing and working. The series of individual exercises from the program I've developed, along with the group exercises I lead once a month and the scene work that the students do constantly in my classes, takes a minimum of two years to properly finish. Many of my students take longer to complete this work. Some take time off for acting jobs for financial concerns or personal reasons. Others stay longer so that they can take their time to get the full bene-fit of each exercise and more scene work. Each student is different. It takes some actors longer to have the "light bulb go on" when they finally understand how to make the organic connection through mind, heart, and will.

While some actors, leaders, and directors may choose to pick out certain exercises from this book, I strongly recommend they adhere to the order of the individual exercises. The organization of the exercises in my class has been based on gut instinct and experience. After many years of teaching, I have learned that it's best to start students with the Spoon River exercise, and to make the Private Moment be the grand finale for the program.

Working as an actor—actually landing real parts and making money—is not an easy task. Fully preparing for roles in the professional atmosphere is extremely difficult, especially in the lucrative areas of film and television. In today's world, actors must be able to prepare roles without the assistance of a director or acting coach. Memorization and analysis is often expected within twenty-four hours, and rehearsal time can be reduced to a thirty-second intro-duction to the scene partner before beginning to roll camera. Setting out an actor's Road Map as I demonstrated in the scene study section can help hone the process so the actor can be prepared at the spur of the moment.

Being able to work alone is the key to success in the acting world. An actor will rarely find an "actors' director" these days, especially in television and film. Sometimes I think actors forget that there's more to directing than working with the players. Many directors' talents lie with the other elements of the projects, such as the rewriting of a film or play. Others are special-effects experts. Many have brilliant visions for the overall concept and, with compe-tent and independently working actors, can deliver breathtaking final results.

There are other elements of a production to consider as well. Television and film directors have impossible deadlines, as well as literally hundreds of elements and responsibilities. Theater directors have to split their focus between the acting and other elements of the project, and a large cast or heavy technical demands can be overwhelming to even the most actor-friendly director. Occasionally directors find themselves in the uncomfortable and overextended position of having to be producer, stage manager, or rewriter as well. And, truth be told, some directors have no idea what they're doing, but are in a position of authority and prestige anyway.

The actor must be prepared for these real-world situations. All actors should get used to working on their own and knowing how to do so. The Road Map work of breaking down scenes and doing script analysis is vitally impor-tant, as are the exercises to create the emotional life.

I can't emphasize enough how important independent work is for actors. Over my thirty years of teaching, I have heard hundreds of actors complain that the director was of little or no help to them. I am not speaking of the actors who bring nothing to rehearsal and expect the director to fully analyze and prepare the role for them, but rather of conscientious and talented actors who have been told, "Just do it." No guidance, no discussion of character, and sometimes no rehearsal, especially for film or television. If the actor can't prepare alone, he is going to have a hard time getting work.

Even the "actors' director" needs actors who can work outside of the rehearsal process. While I believe that all performances—whether it's stage, film, or television—require rehearsal, I also feel strongly that it is the actor's job and responsibility to know how to work and how to deliver the results desired without being dependent on the director. No actor should limit himself by only wanting to work with an "actors' director." He'll have trouble finding that ideal. The actor who can develop full characters and roles independently of the director has a much better chance at success.

I feel that the journey can be a "sane obsession," filled with solid and healthy work habits, demanding of commitment and dedication and a continual striving for "that moment of truth" when the center is all one, and we experience the feeling that comes from truly and honestly working well. It's what makes acting a wonderful way to live a life. Sharing what I have learned with others who are as dedicated as I am has been a large part of my life. It is the point of this book, and the reason why I've been teaching for over thirty-six years.

APPENDIX A

RECOMMENDED READING

ACTING TECHNIQUE

Adler, Stella. *The Art of Acting*. New York: Applause Theatre & Cinema Book Publishers, 2000.

Adler, Stella. *The Technique of Acting*. New York: Bantam, 1990.

Boleslavski, Richard. *Acting: The First Six Lessons*. London: Routledge, 1970.

Chekhov, Michael. *To the Actor: On the Technique of Acting*. London and New York: Routledge, 2002.

Chekhov, Michael. *To the Actor*. New York: Harper Resource, 1991.

Easty, Edward Dwight. *On Method Acting*. New York: Ivy Books, 1989.

Gordon, Mel. *Stanislavsky Technique: Russia*. New York: Applause Theatre & Cinema Book Publishers, 1998.

Hagan, Uta. *Respect for Acting*. New York: Wiley, 1973.

Lewis, Robert. *Advice to the Players*. New York: Harper Collins, 1980.

Lewis, Robert. *Method—Or Madness?* Portsmouth, NH: Heinemann, 1960.

Meisner, Sanford and Dennis Longwell. *Sanford Meisner on Acting*. New York: Vintage, 1987.

Moore, Sonia. *The Stanislavski System: The Professional Training of an Actor*. New York: Viking, 1960.

Rockwood, Jerome. *The Craftsmen of Dionysus*, Rev. Ed. New York: Applause Books, 1992.

Stanislavski, Constantin. *An Actor Prepares*. New York: Theatre Arts Books, 1989.

Stanislavski, Constantin. *Building a Character*. New York: Theatre Arts Books, 1989.

Stanislavski, Constantin. *Creating a Role*. New York: Theatre Arts Books, 1989.

Strasberg, Lee. *A Dream of Passion: The Development of Method*, reissue Ed. New York: Plume Books, 1990.

SCRIPT/TEXT ANALYSIS

Adler, Stella, and Barry Parris (ed.) *Stella Adler on Ibsen, Strindberg, and Chekhov*. New York: Vintage, 2000.

Tucker, Patrick. *Secrets of Acting Shakespeare: The Original Approach*. New York: Routledge/Taylor & Francis, 2001.

FILM TECHNIQUE

Barr, Tony. *Acting for the Camera*, Rev. Ed. New York: Perennial Currents, 1997.

Caine, Michael. *Acting in Film: An Actor's Take on Movie Making*, Rev. Ed. New York: Applause Books, 1997.

Carlson, Steve. *Hitting Your Mark: What Every Actor Really Needs to Know on a Hollywood Set*. Studio City (CA): Michael Wiener Productions, 1999.

Guskin, Harold. *How to Stop Acting*. London: Faber & Faber, 2003.

Tucker, Patrick. *Secrets of Screen Acting*. New York: Routledge, 2003.

BODY AND VOICE WORK

Lowen, Alexander. *Bioenergetics*, Rev. Ed. New York: Compass Books, 1994.

APPENDIX B

PLAYWRIGHTS SUGGESTED FOR STUDY

This is not a definitive list, but a suggested one for serious students to review a body of work, especially for script analysis purposes. Many more names belong here, but it's a good place to start.

Edward Albee	David Mamet
Alan Ayckbourn	Terrence McNally
Samuel Beckett	Arthur Miller
Caryl Churchill	Eugene O'Neill
Noel Coward	Clifford Odets
Anton Chekhov	Harold Pinter
Christopher Durang	Neil Simon
Horton Foote	William Shakespeare
Brian Friel	John Patrick Shanley
Athol Fugard	George Bernard Shaw
John Guare	Sam Shepard
A. R. Gurney	Tom Stoppard
Lillian Hellman	Wendy Wasserstein
Israel Horovitz	Oscar Wilde
Tina Howe	August Wilson
Henrik Ibsen	Tennessee Williams
William Inge	Lanford Wilson

GLOSSARY

A.C.T.: Action, Condition, Telephone Call, individual exercise. Fantastic tool to introduce a student to some of the basic elements of doing a scene by using overall actions (with tasks) and physical-condition work.

acting a negative: Making an acting choice that supports inaction. Should be avoided at all costs. See the Spoon River exercise.

Actions: The verbs the actor is playing to fulfill the Objective. Some directors or teachers also use the term "intentions."

Activity: A specified pursuit an actor partakes in, which is comprised of a series of tasks. Also called "overall activity."

actor's notebook: Series of notes taken by actors as they work through the training and acting process. Used both to assist the actor with immediate projects and to serve as a reference for future ones.

actor's secret: Sensory, physical-condition, or other exercise work that is not obvious to someone watching the actor. Leads to meaningful and interesting acting. Actor's secrets should be shared sparingly, if at all.

animal work: Sensory and body work based on the observation of animals, birds, and reptiles. See the sensory exercises in Part II and the Spoon River exercise, Part Two, in Part III.

as-if: The process of creating an emotional reality for an actor by imagining oneself into the role, versus using personal emotional experiences.

auditing: The act of observing an acting class. I strongly discourage auditing and never allow it in my classes.

Beats: Parts of a scene. A new Beat occurs when the previous subject matter or a physical activity changes the previous action.

Bioenergetics: A series of exercises and movements used to minimize body tension. Initially developed by Alexander Lowen, M.D., and used extensively in my suggested warm-up.

biography: Important background information on a character.

block: To set the movements of actors on a stage or set.

business: An activity or task done on stage to provide depth to a characterization or scene. Sometimes called "stage business."

call "line": To request the words of a line while running a scene. The actor who can't remember the line pauses and says "Line" in a strong and forceful voice, and the individual reading the text states it with as little emotion as possible. The actor then picks up and continues the scene.

center of movement: The area of the body (human or otherwise) from which movement gravitates. Used to define character. See the animal exercise in the sensory exercises section and the Spoon River exercise, Part Two.

character: A person portrayed in a play, in a movie, or on television.

Character Private Moment: An individual acting exercise where the actor does an intensely personal activity or series of activities as a character (versus as himself), giving the illusion of being "private in public." Character Private Moments are built around Givens in the text and give the actor a deeper insight into the character, as well as some potential business on stage.

concentration: A directing of the attention or the mental faculties toward a single object, action, or idea.

Detchire: A relaxation exercise that involves minor body movements and patterned breathing, first introduced to me in Japan.

director: A person who supervises the creative aspects of a dramatic production or film and instructs the actors and crew.

E.R.: See **Emotional Recall**

Effective Memory: See **Emotional Recall**.

emotion: A mental state that arises spontaneously, not through conscious effort. In my opinion, there are five prime emotions to choose from in an acting context: anger, sadness, fear, love, joy. Refer to the Spoon River exercise.

Emotional Recall: An individual exercise that explores the sense memory surrounding a past personal experience to use for an emotional effect on stage. Also called "effective memory" (a Stanislavski and Strasberg term). The E.R. incorporates three elements of acting—life, behavior, and words—and is the best individual exercise to explore the subconscious.

emotionally resolved: The state of having negative emotions surrounding an experience worked through to an eventual closure. All recollections used for the Emotional Recall exercise should be emotionally resolved (refer to the E.R. exercise). Hopefully, most experiences become resolved over time; others are too intense and should not be used as a tool.

energy: Usable power that can be translated into action and is transmitted throughout the body. Energy flows easily and can be utilized when the body is relaxed. By giving up the mind as the actor works to free the upper- and lower-body tension, he may be able to take energy from the floor.

event: A significant occurrence. In the Emotional Recall exercise, the event refers to building to the pinnacle moment that defines the emotion of the overall experience.

Fallout: An exercise where the actor, as led by the instructor, repeats words or short phrases and allows spontaneous emotional color and honesty. Combined with the Song Exercise, an incredibly useful tool to explore emotional blocks, trust emotional instincts, and free the acting instrument.

fourth wall: The space separating the audience from a theatrical performance, traditionally conceived of as an imaginary wall facing the audience.

give or get: To hand something over or take something away. The actor, when speaking a monologue or doing a scene, should either give or get something for the other actor or person he is speaking to. Refer to the Spoon River exercise.

Givens: The information that is known or assumed based on the text of a script or the historical and biographical context of a story.

Group Theatre: The renowned American theatrical company of the 1930s that based its acting on the teachings of Constantin Stanislavski. Its members included Lee Strasberg, Stella Adler, Bobby Lewis, Sanford Meisner, Harold Clurman, and other acting instructors. These actors/teachers are credited with reforming American acting technique.

heightened language: Complex prose or poetry; language with color. Heightened language often uses alliteration, metaphor, and other poetic devices to create a life with words.

indicating: When an actor is playing at a feeling, rather than connecting with it. Playing an idea.

inner life: Description of the apparent working of the imaginative mind while an actor is playing a role. Inner life is what the actor makes seem "real."

instinct: A powerful impulse. Actors strive for instinctual responses grounded in emotion to create a sense of reality.

instrument: For an actor, the collective working of the body, voice, mind, and imagination.

intentions: See **Actions**

internal-to-external: Using personal emotional experiences to catapult an actor into an emotional quality, as first championed by Stanislavski and taught to members of the Group Theatre.

intuition: The act of sensing without the use of rational processes.

leader: Generic term for a teacher or director who instructs others in *Acting*'s exercises.

Meisner Technique: A generic term to describe an acting program that uses (among other things) repetitive exercises first devised by Sanford Meisner of the Group Theatre. Meisner also emphasized using the actor's imagination to create emotional reality—the creative as-if—over the personal, emotional experience philosophy championed by fellow Group Theatre member Lee Strasberg.

Method, the: A generic term used to describe the acting philosophy of using personal emotional experiences in acting, as first introduced to the Western world by Stanislavski and furthered by members of America's Group Theatre in the 1930s. When used today, "the Method" most often refers to the deeply personal emotional work taught by followers of Lee Strasberg, one of the Group Theatre members, and can be summed up as "training the subconscious to behave spontaneously."

mind-to-heart-to-will: The three ingredients of an actor's work. The *mind* understands the text and director's comments, the *heart* adds the feeling and emotional life, and the *will* confronts the actor's personal protections to allow vulnerability and emotion to be viewed in public.

moment-to-moment: Experiencing the acting process as a chain of small periods of time and concentrating on the present, not what's going to happen or what needs to happen in the future. Living in and through the exact moment the actor is in.

monologue: A long speech from one character.

Objective: Something striven for—the driving force behind a character's actions.

obstacle: Something that stands in the way of the completion of an activity or Objective.

parallel dialogue: A tool that uses replacement words for the written text to give the actor a deeper understanding and identification with the speech. Parallel dialogue can keep the body of text intact but replace the names and places with those that have more personal meaning for the actor; or the text can be entirely rewritten in such a way that the overall meaning is completely clear to the actor. Refer to the Spoon

River exercise. WARNING: This does not mean replacing the author's words in performance.

physical condition: State or status of the human body or parts of the human body. Some physical conditions are temporary (pain, cold, drunkenness) or permanent (blindness, impairment). Physical-condition work can either be obvious to observers, or hidden as an actor's secret.

predicting: Acting with a specific emotional quality before the character has a reason to have that emotional quality.

Private Moment: An individual acting exercise in which the actor does an intensely personal activity while alone and gives the illusion of being "private in public." The best exercise to gain freedom and confidence as an actor and validate the self.

process, not performance: To present exercises and scenes in a learning environment in order to understand how to act, not how to entertain others. The guiding principle in my classes.

props: Objects on a theatrical or film set, often utilized by the actors.

psychological center: The imaginary center of movement that significantly affects the personality of a character. First explored by Russian acting instructor Michael Chekhov.

Road Map: A preparatory outline the actor creates before rehearsing a scene. Includes a Working Title, Objective, Beat breakdown, Actions, and Givens. Refer to the Road Map in Part IV.

script analysis: Study of a play or screenplay. For the actor, it should include very similar information to the Road Map, but also explore the questions of theme, spine, and overall event of the play.

sensory: Relating to the five senses—smell, taste, sound, sight, and touch. Sensory details can catapult an actor into a spontaneous emotion and memory.

Song Exercise: Like the Fallout, an individual exercise that is an incredibly useful tool to explore emotional blocks and exercise emotional instincts, thereby freeing the acting instrument. The actor repeats a song's refrain in a variety of ways and inspired by spontaneous emotional color and honesty. Also contains a great deal of movement for body freedom results.

Spoon River: An individual exercise (in two parts) that uses the characters from Edgar Lee Masters' *Spoon River Anthology* as a basis. Introduces students to the tools needed to create a character.

storyboard: An outline of activity or activities of an individual exercise or scene.

T.S.S.: The T. Schreiber Studio.

tasks: Piece of work or functions that need to be done, the total of which comprises an overall activity.

Title: A word or phrase that stimulates an actor's imagination and sums up what a particular scene is about for the character in the scene.

Working Title: see **Title**.

ABOUT THE AUTHOR

As the founder of T. Schreiber Studio in New York City, Terry Schreiber has taught thousands of actors since 1969. He has directed Broadway and Off-Broadway productions, including the Tony Award–nominated *K2*.

Terry has also taken his love and talent for the craft beyond T.S.S. and the bright lights of Broadway by producing and directing numerous Off-Off-Broadway shows; contributing as director at regional theaters throughout the United States; mounting six productions in Tokyo, Japan; and conducting acting workshops around the world.

Recently, he concluded *The Pinter Project* to rave reviews. He received special permission from Harold Pinter to present two of the renowned playwright's most famous plays, *The Birthday Party* and *The Homecoming*, in a rotating repertory. Terry lives in New York City.

This book was completed with the help of Mary Beth Barber, who started her writing career as a political journalist, working for magazines, newspapers, and e-zines such as the *California Journal* and *OffOffOff*, among others.

As an actress and playwright, she has been on stages in Sacramento, San Francisco, and New York; her play *Minha Rosa* was produced at the New York International Fringe Festival in 1999; and her shorter plays have been read and shown in New York and California. Mary Beth is also the recipient of the prestigious Hopwood Award for short story and the Dennis MacIntyre Award for playwriting from the University of Michigan, her alma mater.

Most recently, Mary Beth worked for California Governor Arnold Schwarzenegger on his event-planning team, and is currently the Director of Communications for the California Arts Council.

INDEX

Books from Allworth Press

Allworth Press is an imprint of Allworth Communications, Inc. Selected titles are listed below.

Improv for Actors
by Dan Diggles (paperback, 6 × 9, 246 pages, $19.95)

Movement for Actors
edited by Nicole Potter (paperback, 6 × 9, 288 pages, $19.95)

Acting for Film
by Cathy Haase (paperback, 6 × 9, 224 pages, $19.95)

Acting That Matters
by Barry Pineo (paperback, 6 × 9, 240 pages, $16.95)

Mastering Shakespeare: An Acting Class in Seven Scenes
by Scott Kaiser (paperback, 6 × 9, 246 pages, $19.95)

The Art of Auditioning
by Rob Decina (paperback, 6 × 9, 224 pages, $19.95)

An Actor's Guide—Making It in New York City
by Glenn Alterman (paperback, 6 × 9, 288 pages, $19.95)

Creating Your Own Monologue, Second Edition
by Glenn Alterman (paperback, 6 × 9, 256 pages, $19.95)

Promoting Your Acting Career
by Glenn Alterman (paperback, 6 × 9, 224 pages, $18.95)

The Best Things Ever Said in the Dark:
The Wisest, Wittiest, Most Provocative Quotations from the Movies
by Bruce Adamson (7 1/2 × 7 1/2, 144 pages, $14.95)

Technical Film and TV for Nontechnical People
by Drew Campbell (paperback, 6 × 9, 256 pages, $19.95)

The Health and Safety Guide for Film, TV and Theater
by Monona Rossol (paperback, 6 × 9, 256 pages, $19.95)

Please write to request our free catalog. To order by credit card, call 1-800-491-2808 or send a check or money order to Allworth Press, 10 East 23rd Street, Suite 510, New York, NY 10010. Include $5 for shipping and handling for the first book ordered and $1 for each additional book. Ten dollars plus $1 for each additional book if ordering from Canada. New York State residents must add sales tax.

To see our complete catalog on the World Wide Web, or to order online, you can find us at ***www.allworth.com.***